G. Bernard Shaw.

PROPHETS
PRIESTS, & KINGS

A. G. Gardiner

LONDON & TORONTO
J. M. DENT & SONS, Ltd.

To W. H. H.

IN TOKEN OF PERFECT
FRIENDSHIP

A

PREFACE TO NEW EDITION

In the six years that have elapsed since these sketches were first published, much has happened affecting the subjects of them. Four have died, and the positions of several have undergone important changes. Mr. Haldane, for example, has succeeded Lord Loreburn as Lord Chancellor, Mr. Rufus Isaacs has passed through several offices to the position of Lord Chief Justice, Mr. Chesterton has vanished from Fleet Street and has become a sort of mediæval recluse at Beaconsfield, Prince Bülow has gone into retirement, Henry Bolingbroke, in the person of Mr. Bonar Law, has supplanted Mr. Balfour in the leadership of the Unionist party, Mr. Harcourt no longer "wheels the perambulator," and Mr. Lloyd George has justified the reference to "the key of the future." Apart from these and similar changes, there have been developments which would modify in some measure the views expressed as to certain of the subjects—notably Mr. Snowden. But to have dealt with these changes would have meant re-writing the sketches and the loss of the angle of vision from which they were originally conceived. They represented a contemporaneous impression of men and conditions at a certain period—the period immediately prior to the remarkable series of events that followed the introduction of the Budget of 1909. It has been thought best to preserve that impression at the expense of some conflict with the recent facts and later impressions. Hence, except for minor alterations and amplifications, the sketches are presented in the shape in which they originally appeared in *The Daily News* and in book form. The portraits in this volume are from drawings by Mr. Clive Gardiner.

HAMPSTEAD, *April* 1914.

CONTENTS

Prophets, Priests, and Kings

LIST OF ILLUSTRATIONS

PROPHETS, PRIESTS, AND KINGS

KING EDWARD VII

CHARLES LAMB, referring to the fact that he had no ear for music, said he had been practising "God Save the King" all his life, humming it to himself in odd corners and secret places, and yet, according to his friends, had still not come within several quavers of it. Lamb did not know his good fortune. King Edward probably regards him as the most enviable man in history. For his Majesty would not be human if he did not tire of that eternal reminder of the gilded cage in which he is doomed to live. Does he go to Church, then "God Save the King" thunders through the aisles; does he appear in public, then enthusiastic bandsmen salute him at every street corner with "God Save the King"; does he go to a dinner, then grave citizens leap to their feet and break out into "God Save the King." He cannot escape the Bœotian strain. He never will escape it. It is the penalty we inflict on him for being King. It is a penalty that should touch any heart to sympathy. If one were offered the choice, "Will you dwell at Windsor and hear 'God Save the King' morning, afternoon, and evening, at work and at play, at home and abroad, or work, a free man, in a coal mine?" can there be any doubt what the answer would be if one were sane?

Prophets, Priests, and Kings

When the Archduke John of Austria disguised himself as a seaman and vanished for ever from the tyranny of Courts, he was regarded as a victim of mental aberration. He was, of course, one of the very sanest of men. No man in his senses would be a King if he could be a cobbler. For a cobbler has the two priceless privileges of freedom and obscurity, and a King has only a prison and publicity—a prison, none the less, because its walls are not of stone, but of circumstance. The cobbler may have friends; but where among the crowd that makes eternal obeisance before him is the man whom the King can call friend? Walled off from his kind, living in an unreal and artificial atmosphere of ceremonial, pursued by the intolerable limelight wherever he goes, cut off from the wholesome criticism of the world, fawned on by flunkeys, without the easy companionship of equals, without the healthful renovation of privacy, what is there in Kingship to make it endurable? The marvel is not that Kings should so often fail to be Kings, but that they should ever succeed in being tolerable men.

Now, King Edward is, above everything else, a very human man. He is not deceived by the pomp and circumstance in the midst of which it has been his lot to live, for he has no illusions. He is eminently sane. He was cast for a part in the piece of life from his cradle, and he plays it industriously and thoroughly; but he has never lost the point of view of the plain man. He has much more in common with the President of a free State than with the King by Divine right. He is simply the chief citizen, *primus inter pares*, and the fact that he is chief by heredity and not by election does not qualify his view of the realities of the position. Unlike his nephew, he never associates the Almighty with his right to rule, though he associates Him with his rule. His common sense and his gift of humour save him from these exalted and antiquated assumptions. Nothing is more characteristic of this sensible attitude than his love of the French people and French institutions. No King by " Divine right " could be on speaking terms with a country which has swept the whole institution of Kingship on to the dust-heap.

And his saving grace of humour enables him to enjoy and poke fun at the folly of the tuft-hunter and the collector of Royal cherry stones. He laughingly inverts the folly. " You see that chair," he said in tones of awe to a guest entering his smoking room at Windsor. " That is the chair John Burns sat in." His Majesty has a genuine liking for " J. B.," who, I have no doubt, delivered from that chair a copious digest of his Raper lecture, coupled with illuminating statistics on infantile mortality, some approving comments on the member for Battersea, and a little wholesome advice on the duties of a King. This liking for Mr. Burns is as characteristic of the King as his liking for France. He prefers plain, breezy men who admit him to the common humanities rather than those who remind him of his splendid isolation. He would have had no emotion of pride when Scott, who, with all his great qualities, was a deplorable tuft-hunter, solemnly put the wine-glass that had touched the Royal lips into the tail pocket of his coat, but he would have immensely enjoyed the moment when he inadvertently sat on it.

It follows that he would disclaim that he is either a seer or a saint, though in his education every effort was employed to make him at once an Archangel and an Admirable Crichton. There has probably never been a personage in history upon whose upbringing there was expended so much thought and such variety of influences as upon that of Albert Edward, Prince of Wales. There have been cases in which equal solicitude has been displayed by fond parents on behalf of their children. In the preface to Montaigne's Essays we are told that the great writer's father resolved that his son should be a perfect Latinist, so arranged matters that the boy heard no language but Latin till he was seven or eight years of age. In his presence even the servants had to speak Latin or not at all, the result being that in Montaigne's native village there was for long afterwards a strong element of pure Latin in the local French. Montaigne was never allowed to be awakened suddenly, but was wooed back to consciousness by soft music played near his chamber. And so on. But this was a case of mere paternal affection. The education of the Prince of Wales, on the other hand, was a national, almost an international question. Baron Stockmar, the Coburg adviser of the Queen's family, wrote elaborate treatises on the subject, bishops and peers and educationists were consulted, rival schemes of treatment were considered, and every precaution was taken to make the little Prince a prodigy of scholarship and a miracle of virtue.

But there is no royal road either to saintship or knowledge. The Prince was endowed neither with the attributes of intellectual passion, nor of mystical fervour, nor of artistic emotion, and the attempt to graft these upon the stem of ordinary human instincts was destroyed by the world of levity and flattery into which he was plunged as a young man. It is easy to cast stones at the King; but it would be more rational to ask how many of us would have come through such a career of temptation with a better record. When a distinguished scientist, celebrated for his destructive criticism, was questioning the efficacy of prayer, he chose the Prince of Wales as his test. He was unfair both to the Prince and to prayer. It is true that the world has prayed much for King Edward. It is estimated on a modest calculation that during sixty years a thousand million prayers have been offered on his behalf. But while the world prayed, instead of helping him to fulfil its prayers it encouraged him by its sycophancy to think he was a law unto himself, and left him in the heart of Vanity Fair, without a duty save a desolating ceremonial and the pursuit of idle pleasure. And then, when a sudden flash of publicity has lit up some particular aspect of his private life, it has turned and rent him in a fury of righteous indignation. It is as irrational as King Theebaw, who, when his favourite wife lay sick unto death, prayed fervently to his gods and made extravagant promises of endowment of the temple, and, when she died, massed his artillery in front of the temple and bombarded it without mercy. It engineers a conspiracy to destroy character, and is astonished that the result is not a moral miracle.

It is just, too, to remember that the King's private life is not only subject to a merciless scrutiny that the lives of his people are fortunately spared, and to the prurient gossip of every club idler; but that his position denies him the defence which the law accords to humbler people. He must be mute under all attack. There is only one instance in which he has been heard in his own defence. It is the letter to Archbishop Benson, written after the Tranby Croft scandal, and published in the life of the Archbishop. In it he says:

A recent trial which no one deplores more than I do, and which I was powerless to prevent, gave occasion for the Press to make most bitter and unjust attacks upon me, knowing that I was defenceless, and I am not sure that politics were not mixed up in it! The whole matter has now died out—and I think, therefore, it would be inopportune for me in any public manner to allude again to the painful subject which brought such a torrent of abuse upon me not only by the Press, but by the Low Church, and especially the Nonconformists.

They have a perfect right, I am well aware, in a free country like our own, to express their opinions, but I do not consider that they have a just right to jump at conclusions regarding myself without knowing the facts.

I have a horror of gambling, and should always do my utmost to discourage others who have an inclination for it, as I consider that gambling, like intemperance, is one of the greatest curses which a country could be afflicted with.

Horse-racing may produce gambling or it may not, but I have always looked upon it as a manly sport which is popular with Englishmen of all classes; and there is no reason why it should be looked upon as a gambling transaction. Alas! those who gamble will gamble at anything. I have written quite openly to you, my dear Archbishop, whom I have had the advantage of knowing for so many years.

The sentiment of the letter—which was, of course, published with the King's sanction — is perhaps better than the logic; but it reveals a man keenly sensitive to criticism under which he must be silent, and anxious to avoid collision with public opinion. An expression of horror at gambling was not lacking in courage in such a connection; but the reference to horse-racing suggests that his Majesty does not quite appreciate the view of those who regard it not as evil in itself, but evil in its associations. No one imagines that horse-racing *per se* is immoral. Did not Cromwell own race-horses? He was a sportsman. But is Mr. Robert Sievier a sportsman? It is not the sport, but the parasitic accompaniment of the sport that is immoral, and his Majesty would do a lasting service to the pastime that he loves, as well as to the commonwealth which is so largely his care, if he emphasised his horror of gambling, and gave his countenance to the suppression not of racing news, but of betting news, which brings to ruin multitudes who never see a horse-race, and which is poisoning the blood of the industrial classes.

When Henry V. ascended the throne, and the news was borne to Falstaff, the boon companion of his riotous youth, that splendid vagabond turned to Pistol and said, " Ask what thou wilt: 'tis thine," and, calling for his horse, he hastened back to London to receive the rewards of friendship. But when he shouldered his way through the crowd and saluted the King as he rode from the Coronation, the monarch turned on him and cried:

> I know thee not, old man: Fall to thy prayers;
> How ill white hairs become a fool and jester!
>
> . . . .
>
> Presume not that I am the thing I was;
> For Heaven doth know, so shall the world perceive
> That I have turned away my former self;
> So will I those that kept me company.

King Edward is not built in this heroic mould. He did not " turn away his former self " when he came to the Throne; but he did reveal a seriousness of purpose and a delicate appreciation of his office that we were not entitled to look for from such an apprenticeship. He is, indeed, by far the ablest man and the best King his stock has produced. Contrast him with the Four Georges and he is an angel of light. Judged even by more severe standards, he emerges with credit. For he has that plainness of mind which is the best attribute of a constitutional monarch. Genius is the essential of an autocrat, for exceptional powers alone can justify and sustain exceptional pretensions. But in a constitutional monarch the best we can ask for is common sense and a nice regard for the true limits of the kingly function. And King Edward is in these respects an ideal King.

Prophets, Priests, and Kings

He realises that his function is not active, but passive; not positive, but negative—that his duty is to act on the advice of his ministers and that there is no exception to that principle. He has leaned to no party, cultivated no " King's men," aimed at no personal exaltation, uttered no " blazing indiscretion." Few men in his position would have done so well. No man with strong convictions, a forceful personality and what Meredith calls " an adventurous nose," would have done so well. We want a King whose convictions hang about him easily, " like an old lady's loose gown," who has many sympathies and no antipathies, who can be all things to all men, who, in fact, stands for citizenship, which is common, and not for sect or party, which is particular. We want, that is, a plain, prosaic, simple citizen, and that is King Edward's character. He is the citizen King, and the most popular of his line. If ever we have a man of genius as King, we shall probably end by cutting off his head.

He is the Imperial smoother, and deserves the jolly title of " L'oncle de l'Europe " which France has conferred on him. There is an avuncular benevolence about him which is irresistible. He likes to be happy himself, and he likes to see the world happy. Does Norway want a King? Then he is the man to arrange it. Does the king lack a queen? Who so accomplished to fill the rôle of uncle? Does the King of Spain want, like Dame Marjory, to be " settled in life "? Again he assumes the familiar part. And his activity does not end with marriage bells. He loves to play the part of missionary of peace. He plays it skilfully and constitutionally, and not in any assertive or authoritative spirit. He is far too astute for that, and they are his worst enemies who encourage the fatal theory that the King is his own Foreign Minister—a theory which would make the external relations of a great people dependent on the private feelings of an individual whom it could not control, could not interrogate or depose, and whose mind it could not know. Nor is it only the graver aspects of his office that he takes seriously. He is equally solicitous about that life of etiquette and forms which is the affliction of kings. Should the Queen advance three steps or only two in receiving a particular visitor, should the coat of this or that attendant on him at some ceremony have three buttons or two, should it be buttoned or unbuttoned, these are the kind of problems with which he will wrestle strenuously. They may seem negligible details to the plain man; but the life of courts is made up of these niceties of deportment, which are not wholly idle, but may be the outward and visible sign of far-reaching realities.

Considering the delicate path he has had to tread in public and the fierce light that has beat upon it, he has made singularly few false steps. The exclusion of certain members from a garden party apparently because of a vote given by them in the House of Commons was a startling departure from correctitude that by its singularity emphasised the general propriety of a career which has been a model of public deportment. We can have no more sincere wish than that this country will have always upon the throne one who understands his place in the Constitution as well and does his task as honestly as Edward VII.

I like to think of him as one sees him on those sunny days at Windsor when he holds his garden party, and moves about industriously smiling and gossiping, while the band plays the interminable tune and the fashionable world crowds around him in

Prophets, Priests, and Kings

eager anxiety for notice. It is then that one understands the boredom of Kingship, and the heroism that enables him to play his part so cheerfully and unfailingly. Hard by the brilliant scene you may come suddenly upon solitude and a colony of rooks holding high revel in the immemorial elms. Their cry—the most ironic sound in Nature—seems like a scornful comment on the momentary scene yonder and all it signifies. Perhaps when the shadows fall athwart the greensward and the last guest has gone, King Edward strolls off with a cigar to take counsel of these wise birds, who seem to know so well what is real and what is transitory, and tell it with such refreshing candour.

GEORGE BERNARD SHAW

I ONCE had the duty of presiding at a gathering assembled to hear an address by Mr. Bernard Shaw. " What is the title of your lecture? " I asked. " It hasn't got one," he replied. " Tell them it will be announced at the close." I did so, adding that afterwards he would answer any reasonable questions. " I prefer unreasonable questions," he said in a stage whisper. For forty minutes he poured out a torrent of mingled gibes at his audience, flashes of wit and treasures of good sense. Then he leapt into his coat, seized his umbrella, cut his way through his admirers with good-humoured chaff, suffered the addresses of an old Irish lady who had known him in childhood and was as voluble as himself, and finally fled along Regent Street " like a soul in chase," his tongue flaying all created things, until at a " tube " station he turned on his heel and vanished as if by magic.

It was like the hurry of the wind, keen as a razor, dry and withering as the east. Mind and body alike at the gallop—trained down to the last ounce. He is a hurricane on two legs—a hurricane of wrath flashing through our jerry-built society. He is the lash laid across the back of his generation. He whips us with the scorpions of his bitter pen, and we are grateful. He flings his withering gibes in our faces and we laugh. He lampoons us in plays and we fight at the pay-box. We love him as Bill Sikes' dog loved that hero—because he beats us.

His ascetic nature revolts at our grossness. I once invited him to a dinner to a colleague. He accepted

the invitation and came—when the dinner was over.
He would not sit at meat with men who eat flesh like
savages, fuddle their brains with wine, pollute the air
with filthy smoke. Lady Randolph Churchill has
recorded that when she invited him to dinner he
declined to come and " eat dead animals."

What can we look for, he asks, from a society based
on such loathsome habits except the muddle we are in
— a morass of misery and sweated labour at the
bottom sustaining an edifice of competitive commerce
as greedy as it is merciless; at the top a nauseous mix-
ture of luxury and flunkeyism. Waste and disorder
everywhere: religion an organised hypocrisy; justice
based on revenge which we call punishment; science
based on vivisection ; Empire based on violence. God,
perchance, is in heaven, but all's *wrong* with the world.
What can a reasonable man do but war with it?
" What are you people crowding here for? " he asked
a fashionable audience at an anti-sweating meeting.
" To hear me gibe at you, not because you care a rap
for the wretched victims of your social system. If
you cared for them you would not come here for
amusement. You would go outside and burn the
palaces of fashion and commerce to the ground."

For he has in an unrivalled degree the gift of being
unpleasant. It is a rare gift. Most of us, even the
worst of us—perhaps, especially the worst of us—are
full of tenderness for the susceptibilities of others.
We cultivate the art of polite falsity, because to give
pain to others is so great a pain to ourselves. We are
like the Irish driver in *John Bull's Other Island*—
" Sure he'd say whatever was the least trouble to
himself and the pleasantest to you." We lack the
courage to be unkind. If we stab at all we prefer to
do it in the back. Mr. Shaw enjoys giving pain
because he knows it does you good. He cuts you up

George Bernard Shaw

with the scientific serenity of an expert surgeon who loves the knife. He probably never paid a compliment to anyone save Mr. Bernard Shaw in his life. When a well-known Free Trader, now in Parliament, sat down after reading an elaborate paper before the Fabian Society, Mr. Shaw rose, and observed: "We have come to the end of the intolerable tedium inflicted upon us. It is incredible that anyone should have prepared this crude alphabet of the subject, above all for the Fabian Society." There is something to be said for Mr. Shaw's frankness. It clears the air. It tears away the cloak of shams, and confronts us with the naked realities. It does not make him loved; but, then, he would hate to be loved. He rather loves to be feared.

He has spoken of himself somewhere as being "by temperament economically minded and apprehensive to the point of old-maidishness." It is a happy figure. He is like an elderly spinster, with a fierce passion for order and a waspish tongue, coming into a house turned upside down by a crowd of boisterous, irresponsible children. Of these, by far the worst are the English—the dull, unimaginative English, full of illusions and incompetence and unctuous humbug, with "the cheerful bumptiousness that money, comfort, and good feeding bring to all healthy people." A nation of Tom Broadbents, made great by coal and iron and the genius of quicker and more imaginative peoples. "The successful Englishman to-day," he says, "when he is not a transplanted Scotchman or Irishman, often turns out on investigation to be, if not an American, an Italian, or a Jew, at least to be depending on the brains, the nervous energy, and the freedom from romantic illusions (often called cynicism) of such foreigners for the management of the sources of his income." But he loves the Englishman, and he will tell you frankly why. He loves him because he is fool enough to make a lot of Bernard Shaw.

We have had no more merciless satirist since his fellow-countryman, Swift, was amongst us. But, unlike Swift, he does not hate men. He is only filled with scorn at their follies, their sentimentalities and superstitions. He has no reverence and no respect for the reverences of others. Religion to him is like a fog in the mind, blurring the vision of realities. "*Ecrasez l'Infâme*," he would say with Voltaire, and he looks for the age of pure reason, when intellect shall have straightened out all the tangled skein of life, and men, resting secure in their sciences and utilities, shall laugh at the pathetic superstitions of their fathers, and turn with content to the exquisite syllogism of material things that they have put in their place. It is not a new dream. It is a dream as old as the conflict between intellect and emotion. It is based upon the assumption that the human soul has no yearning that cannot be satisfied by the scientific adjustment of our material relationships to the universe, a theory to which the Aristotelian replies that social wrong is only the symbol of spiritual wrong, and that spiritual remedies will alone heal what is ultimately a spiritual malady. Mr. Shaw sees everything sharp and clear, and without atmosphere. He is all daylight; but it is a daylight that does not warm. It is radiant, but chilling. He affects you like those March days when the east wind cuts through the sunshine like a knife.

And there is another difference between him and Swift. He has none of the great Dean's morbidness. It was said of Swift that he had " the terrible smile." It was the smile that foreshadowed insanity. Mr. Shaw has a smile of sardonic sanity. Max Beerbohm's caricature of him as Mephistopheles, holding his forked tail with one hand, nursing his red beard with the other, is astonishingly true in spirit. As he leaps to his feet, straight and lithe, with that bleak smile upon his lips, you feel that here is a man who sees through all your cherished hypocrisies, and can freeze up all your emotions. He sprays you with acid as if you were an insect, and you curl up.

Like the Fat Boy, he " wants to make your flesh creep, mum." Mrs. Grundy is always present to his mind—the symbol of smug self-satisfaction, of ignorant content, of blind superstition, the symbol, in fact, of English society. He had a double motive in shocking her. It appeals to his Puck-like instinct for mischief. He loves to see the look of horror overspread her features as he smashes her idols. But there is a more serious purpose behind his iconoclasm. He breaks the image in order to restore the reality. Shakespeare is a fetish, and he tells you he is a greater than Shakespeare. The English home is the Englishman's boast, and he tells you that it is the source of our selfish exclusiveness, and that no good will be done till it is destroyed. " Pull down the walls," he would say with Plato: " they shelter at best a restricted family feeling; they harbour at the worst avarice, selfishness, and greed. Pull down the walls and let the free air of a common life blow over the place where they have been." Or, as Whitman expresses it:

Unscrew the locks from the doors!
Unscrew the doors themselves from their jambs!
By God! I will accept nothing which all cannot have their
    counterpart of on the same terms.

He is careless about having a beautiful home: he wants a beautiful city. He is indifferent about his wife's diamonds: he wants to see the charwoman and the sempstress well dressed. If they are not he would send them to prison. For his philosophy comes from " Erewhon," where poverty and illness were the only punishable crimes. " If poor people were given penal servitude instead of sympathy, there would soon be an alteration for the better," he says, with his characteristic extravagance. " The love of money is the root of all evil," we say unctuously as we snatch for more. " Money is the most important thing in the world," he says, and he insists that every one of us shall have £500 a year. " Money represents health, strength, honour, generosity, and beauty, as undeniably as the want of it represents illness, weakness, disgrace, meanness, and ugliness." " Flee from sin," says the preacher. " Flee from poverty, which is the root of sin," says Mr. Shaw.

He is a preacher in cap and bells. He calls the crowd together with the jingle of jest, and then preaches his sermon in extravagant satire. He is so terribly in earnest that he cannot be serious. Least of all is he serious about himself. He is himself his own gayest comedy. " I have been hurt to find myself described as a middle-class man," he says. " I am a member of the upper classes. My father was a second cousin to a baronet. That is what gives me self-respect and solidity of standing." His father was an ex-Civil servant in Dublin, who invested his money in flour-milling—" and a most surprising failure he made of it." His mother kept the pot boiling by teaching music, and young Shaw earned £18 a year as a clerk. At twenty he came to London and passed several years in an atrociously seedy condition. " I haven't a penny in the world," said a beggar to him one night. " Neither have I," said the delightful Shaw, with cheerful comradeship. He lived on his parents, who found it difficult to live on themselves. He is not ashamed: he boasts of it. " I did not throw myself into the struggle for life: I

George Bernard Shaw

threw my mother into it." He wrote novels which nobody read, scintillated in the *Star* as a musical critic, helped to found the Fabian Society, wrote plays on the tops of omnibuses, married—" for money," he will tell you with engaging raillery, while his charming wife smiles at his rogueries—and became the idol of the intellectuals and the most piquant figure in the English-speaking world.

Riches have poured into his lap from the pay-boxes of every civilised land, and his fame is a part of the common stock of the world, but he is unchanged with it all. He is still the gentleman of fortune, living upon his wits, his sword ever in his hand. He comes into your midst with the tail of his coat trailing on the floor. What, sir, you will not tread upon the tail of my coat? You will not fight? You have no quarrel, sir? A fig for a quarrel! I will tweak your nose, sir! And what a duellist the fellow is! What irony, what jest, what diabolical self-composure! His wit is as swift as the lightning, as happy as the song of birds. "Boo!" roared a voice from the gallery when he came forward, amid thunders of applause, at the close of one of his plays, —"Boo." "I agree with you, sir," he said; "but what are we two against so many?" "Mr. Shaw," said a friend who had beguiled him to hear a string quartette from Italy, and, finding him bored, sought to wring a word of praise from him—"Mr. Shaw, these men have been playing together for twelve years." "Twelve years?" yawned G. B. S. "Surely we've been here longer than that."

Few men have rendered more conspicuous service to their time. The English stage had become a by-word—a thing of no more intellectual significance than a skittle-alley. Mr. Shaw has worked a revolution. He has done it with the smallest of dramatic equipment, for he has little imagination, slight instinct for character, and none of the symbolic sense and suggestiveness that make the dramas of Ibsen so vast and cosmic. But he has made the contemporary English drama the vehicle of ideas and has rescued it from contempt. He has brought it into relation with realities and turned it into a medium for permeating society with the philosophy of Mr. Sidney Webb. In a word, he has become a playwright in order to preach his extremely unorthodox sermon, and if he uses extravagances — well, so did Dr. Parker, so does Father Vaughan. He exaggerates in order that you may see the truth to which familiarity and convention have blinded you. He shocks you in order that you may be shocked at yourself. He denounces love because his asceticism revolts from the sensuality that is the desecration of love. He denounces conventional morality because he is so fierce a moralist. He denounces the law because of his passion for justice. He has such an enthusiasm for humanity that he would put the poor in gaol because of their poverty and misery. He would punish the people who have the wickedness to be ill; but he would treat the criminal as we treat invalids. For the sickness of the body is our own wrong, the outrage of natural laws; the sickness of the mind is the wrong imposed on us by a false and vicious social system. In all this topsy-turveyism he is astonishingly sane. I know of no political writing which goes more ruthlessly to the heart of realities than his prefaces to his plays. Take, for example, his treatment of the Irish question. "Home Rule means Rome rule" cry the Protestant Nonconformists. He turns the aphorism inside out. "England in Ireland is the Pope's policeman," he says, and proves it. "Shaw has stated the Irish case once and for all," said John Dillon to me.

George Bernard Shaw

He is the tonic of his time, very bitter to the taste, but stimulating. He clears the mind of cant. He clears the atmosphere of fog. He is admirable in small doses; but as a sustained diet—I say it with the comfortable knowledge that he is not by—he is inferior to Shakespeare. "The professional moralist," it has been said, "is moral by the strength of his antipathies; Shakespeare is moral by the strength of his sympathies." Mr. Shaw is all antipathies. He is "agin" everything, from the government of the universe to the starch in your collars and the blacking on your boots. He has never agreed with anybody or anything. He rests on himself, secure and self-assertive—his intellect against the world. You turn from his cold lucidity and magnificent cocksureness to the men who speak not to the intellect alone, but to the heart, who are not merely humanitarians, but human beings, who say with Lowell that they believe more than they can give a reason for, and with Carlyle that all our sciences are nothing beside that great deep sea of nescience on which we float like exhalations that are and then are not. Realities are much; but the mystery that invests being is more. The mind is wonderful, but no less real are the intimations of the soul. Let us have a clear intellect; but it is an arid world that shuts out the intuitions of the heart.

I see the curl on Mr. Bernard Shaw's lips. "Cant," he says. "The cant of these dull-witted English, with their ridiculous illusions and sloppy emotions." Perhaps so. And yet I believe that behind that scornful smile there is a heart as sensitive as any; but a heart which he is ashamed to reveal. He has, perhaps, come nearest to revealing it in that fine saying of his with which one may well close:

" I am of the opinion that my life belongs to the

Prophets, Priests, and Kings

whole community, and as long as I live it is my privilege to do for it whatsoever I can. I want to be thoroughly used up when I die, for the harder I work, the more I live. I rejoice in life for its own sake. Life is no brief candle to me. It is a sort of splendid torch which I have got hold of for the moment, and I want to make it burn as brightly as possible before handing it on to future generations."

ARTHUR JAMES BALFOUR

MR. A. J. BALFOUR has probably done the greatest service to his country of any man of his time. He has saved it from Protection.

When Mr. Chamberlain came back from South Africa with the full knowledge of his failure, he resolved on one last desperate throw. He would blot out the past. He would set up a new fever in the blood. Philip sober should be Philip drunk again. "You can burn all your political leaflets and literature," he said to Mr. Herbert Gladstone, the Liberal Whip, in the lobby one day. "We are going to talk about something else." And so he gathered up all the forces of wealth and interest into one frenzied assault on the economic fabric of the State. All his hopes hung upon instancy. There must be no time for the country to recover its equilibrium. It must give its decision while it was reeling under the impact of the blow. It must be carried by storm.

And it was nearly carried by storm. Looking back on the tornado that began at Glasgow and collapsed at the Guildhall with the most memorable interruption to a political speech on record, it is difficult to resist the conclusion that, had Mr. Chamberlain got an appeal to the country forthwith, he would have won. His calculations were sound. Philip was momentarily drunk with the new wine. He forgot the past; he lost his reason; he was at the mercy of the adventurer. But the debauch was brief, and every day of returning sobriety was a new defence flung up against the attack. Mr. Chamberlain was destroyed by delay. And it was Mr. Balfour who wrought that delay.

To this hour no man can say what his motive was in carrying on that amazing duel with his impetuous rival. Perhaps it was personal, for the triumph of Mr. Chamberlain meant Mr. Balfour's definite deposition. Perhaps it was for the sake of the party, for the adoption of Protection involved an organic change in its character and aim. Perhaps it was the love of a situation which called out all the resources of his astonishing intellectual agility. Certainly it was not devotion to Free Trade nor antagonism to Protection, for he cares for neither.

He cares for neither because he is essentially a sceptic. He looks out on life with a mingled scorn and pity—scorn for its passionate strivings after the unattainable, pity for its meanness and squalor. He does not know the reading of the riddle, but he knows that all ends in failure and disillusion. Ever the rosy dawn of youth and hope fades away into the sadness of evening and the blackness of night, and out of that blackness comes no flash of revelation, no message of cheer.

> The Worldly Hope men set their hearts upon
> Turns Ashes—or it prospers; and anon
>   Like Snow upon the Desert's dusty Face
> Lighting a little Hour or two—is gone.

Why meddle with the loom and its flying shuttle? We are the warp and weft with which the great Weaver works His infinite design—that design which is beyond the focus of all mortal vision, and in which the glory of Greece, the pomp of Rome, the ambition of Carthage, seven times buried beneath the dust of the desert, are but inscrutable passages of glowing colour. All our schemes are futile, for we do not know the end, and that which seems to us evil may serve some ultimate good, and that which seems right may pave the path to wrong. In this fantastic mockery of all human effort the only attitude is the " wise passiveness " of the poet. Let us accept the irrevocable fate unresistingly.

In a word, Drift. That is the political philosophy of Mr. Balfour.

What, then, brings him into the world of affairs? If all action is idle, if interference with the machine is foolish impertinence, a meddling with what we do not understand and cannot control, why quit the Whittinghame woodlands for the field of battle? The explanation is twofold. He enters Parliament to protect the privileges of his caste and to taste the joys of intellectual mastery.

In defending his caste he is absolutely sincere, even disinterested and patriotic. He believes in the rule of the aristocracy, not in the naïve, bucolic way of Mr. Chaplin, the last of the " squires," but intellectually. He does not regard the democracy with animus, but as uninstructed and sometimes unruly children, whom it is his task to keep out of mischief. Pity for the poor was bred in him in those far-off days of the Lancashire cotton famine, when his mother taught her children to forego their little luxuries in order to contribute to the funds for the starving operatives. But it is pity for an inferior creation with which he has no common fellowship. He dwells in another hemisphere, breathes another atmosphere. There is no vain assumption in this. It is a plain, indisputable fact of existence, about which he would as little think of being vain as he would of the fact that he stands six feet two or so. He is too astute and too delicate in feeling to express his contempt for the people with the brutal candour of his godfather, the Iron Duke; but essentially his view of democracy is Wellingtonian.

Prophets, Priests, and Kings

It is this aloofness which has prevented him being a popular figure, just as it prevented his uncle from ever touching the heart of the rank and file even of his own party. For Toryism, though essentially an aristocratic system, has to wear the disguise of democracy—to affect a virtue even if it have it not. Whenever it has become vital, it has been at the inspiration of some man who has appealed frankly to the democracy, not from the elevation of a superior caste, but as the authentic voice and obedient instrument of its needs and aspirations. It was so that Disraeli, Lord Randolph Churchill, and Mr. Chamberlain in turn breathed upon the dry bones of Toryism and made them live. The Cecil philosophy cannot win the democracy: it can only use it.

This conception of aristocratic rule extends to the realm of race. In all his career Mr. Balfour has never lifted his hand or raised his voice on behalf of an oppressed people. It is not that he is wanting in sympathy. It is simply that he is on the side of the aristocratic authority. If the Russian knouts the Jew and the Turk slays the Armenian, he is sorry for Jew and Armenian. But they are the under-dog: they must suffer. If they rebel they must be punished. It is not that he bears malice against Jew or Armenian. If they were the aristocrats in the racial conflict, he would be on their side. He reverses that saying of Goethe's that " when the people rebel the people are always right." When the people rebel the people are always wrong.

Hence his memorable tenure of the Irish Secretaryship. The Irish were to him a mutinous nursery in revolt against the authority of an aristocratic rule. His uncle called them Hottentots. Mr. Balfour was less picturesque, but no less emphatic. He did not hate the Irish: he only despised them. " They have

great gifts," he was not unfairly represented as say
ing; " they have wit, imagination, eloquence, valour;
in many respects they are our superiors. But in
one respect they are our inferiors, and no amount
of Gladstonian rhetoric can make them otherwise.
They are politically incapable of self-government.
Why not govern them as the Scotch, you ask? Because they are not the Scotch. They cannot be
trusted to govern themselves, for the simple and
sufficient reason that Providence, in giving them
many gifts, omitted to give them the qualities which
ensure stable self-control." And so he whipped
them, put them in prison, turned them naked and
homeless on to the roadside. There was no bitterness
in this. He did it honestly for their good. He did
it in obedience to a considered philosophy. The
Irish were children in rebellion: they must be broken
with the rod. They were the under-dog and must
learn to obey their masters.

It is this aristocratic detachment from realities that
is at the root of all his mistakes. He cannot enter
into the mind of the inferior castes. He cannot
understand that if you prick them, they will bleed.
Their resentment fills him with sincere amazement—
with a certain sadness at their want of gratitude.
His surprise at the passionate indignation of the
Nonconformists in regard to the Education Act was
not affected. He still believes that these good
people—honest, but dull and unenlightened—did
not know their blessings. It is not that he deliberately outrages a sentiment that he does not share:
it is that he is insensible to it.

His vision of society is of a refined company,
dowered with delicate appetites and gracious sentiments and protected from the raging mob without by
a moral police that is crumbling away and by the more

material defence of ancient privilege sustained by the authority of law. Within there is abundance for all— light and air, music and perfumes. The mob at the gate clamours to share these, and he does not blame them. But he would hold them at bay, because he believes that their triumph would mean the desolation of the little oasis of culture that is the one reality worth preserving in this phantasmal world. It is not animus against the mob that governs him, but the passion to hold the one priceless thing. Nor is it, perhaps, the sense of aristocratic exclusiveness. He believes that the ravage of his oasis would bring no joy to the hungry horde. It would only blot out the beauty that is the flower of the ages and leave the land

> A wilderness indeed,
> Peopled with wolves, its old inhabitants.

And the other reason for his presence in politics is to " drink delight of battle with his peers." The House of Commons is the first debating society in the world, and Mr. Balfour is the supreme debater. On the platform he is dull and uninspiring, for he has no message for his time; but on the floor of the House he is the incomparable swordsman. His spirits rise with the combat. The worse the case, the more desperate the attack, the more formidable he becomes. The air of slack nervelessness vanishes. Every faculty awakes to astonishing activity. He twists and turns with diabolical elusiveness. A dozen swords are at his throat, and lo! he is under the enemy's guard and through them, dealing venomous thrusts on every vulnerable point. He clouds the issue with the dust of his dialectics and with a sudden flank movement changes the whole face of the battle. His one weapon of defence is to attack. If he cannot meet the enemy on the ground they have chosen, he

Arthur James Balfour

wheels round to a new position, and before they realise that he has escaped they are defending themselves in the rear. There was truth as well as vanity in his complaint that "the House of Commons did not extend his mind." Parliament has never witnessed so accomplished an intellectual gymnast. There is only one rival to him in these days, and I was not surprised when the Bishop of Southwark one day told me that Mr. Balfour had great admiration for Mr. G. K. Chesterton.

But the country is not governed ultimately by intellectual gymnastics. It is amused by them; it applauds them; and it distrusts them. Mr. Balfour wins his dialectical battles and loses his campaign. He is at once the hope and the despair of his party. They cannot replace his leadership in the House, where intellectual address is necessary; they cannot survive his leadership in the country, where moral purpose alone counts. If Toryism is to rise from its ashes it must make some appeal to the hearts and imaginations of men. It must believe. And Mr. Balfour does not believe. He is a creature of negations and doubts. "You cannot fill your belly on the east wind," said the wise man. The people ask for bread, and Mr. Balfour offers them the east wind of a withering intellectuality.

He breathes no moral oxygen into the air. The murmurs and the agonies of men touch him to no passionate purpose. They cry, and, like those gods of old,

He hears a music centred in a doleful song,
Steaming up a lamentation and an ancient tale of wrong,
Like a tale of little meaning, though the words are strong.

Ireland asks for the deliverance of a dying people, and he says, "Don't hesitate to shoot." Macedonia cries its ancient cry, and he discusses " the balance of criminality." Outraged citizens ask for defence against the madness of a mob, and he talks of " the limits of human endurance."

Temperamentally, he belongs to the æsthetic cult of the eighties—the cult satirised so ruthlessly by Du Maurier and Gilbert, languorous and sensuous, to whom the decorations of life—music, art, literature— are the only realities. He is a man of emotions, without a moral, and would " Die of a rose in aromatic pain." Intellectually, he finds in philosophy that extension of the mind which he complained that the House of Commons did not afford. Public affairs interest him only on their speculative side, and his loose hold on facts and figures is characteristic of one whose adventures are all of the mind, and whose ultimate interest is really engaged only when he is discussing some new guess at the nature of matter or the nature of the soul. In politics he is caged, and beats his wings against the bars of circumstance: it is only when he escapes to the limitless realm of speculative ideas that, free and unencumbered, he is truly happy.

Charm he has in a high degree; but it is an illusive charm. His address is curiously winning and appealing; but politically it has no basis in loyalty or rooted affection. He smiles upon his friends and leaves them to the wolves. No man ever had a more chivalrous follower than he had in George Wyndham, but when the Ulster pack were hot upon the scent he sacrificed him without a word—sacrificed George Wyndham to Sir Edward Carson! Even the ties of blood are no check to this incurable disloyalty. He saw his cousin, Lord Hugh Cecil, the ablest man on his side, hounded from the party by the Protectionists, and never lifted a finger to save him. He

saw honest Sir Edward Clarke hounded from the City and remained darkly silent.

It follows naturally from this that he is acutely jealous of his honour. Nothing moves him to such brilliant frenzy as the least hint of a stain there. Nothing wounds him so much as a word of reproach from those whose loyalty and honour are above challenge. A rebuke from Sir Edward Grey cuts him to the quick, and it was only when the Duke of Devonshire left his Ministry with words of blunt candour that he was stung into shrill and eager defence of his impenetrable policy.

He has a feminine sensitiveness to personality. He takes the criticism of Mr. Asquith cheerfully, but Mr. Churchill fills him with petulant resentment. It is the resentment of the aristocrat against one who, in his view, is disloyal to his caste. It is the resentment, too, of a mind of subtle refinements against one who is broad and popular, and who, he suspects, deliberately appeals to the gallery. He used to flee from the House in ostentatious scorn when Mr. Churchill assailed him. As he was disappearing on one of these occasions, Mr. Churchill, secure in his triumph, cried, " The right hon. gentleman need not leave the House. I am not going to refer to him." Amidst the shout of laughter that followed, Mr. Balfour turned, and a word of withering scorn was seen rather than heard to issue from his lips.

It is the highest testimony to the fascination of his personality, and the honesty of his point of view, that, in spite of his provocative policy and an ingenuity of mind that suggests disingenuousness, he has no enemies. His smile disarms you. It has been called the chief asset of his party, and it is certainly irresistible. Even the Irishmen, when they emerged from prison, were conciliated by its tender sympathy. He inquired after their health. He hoped they had not been inconvenienced. It was all done quite simply and sweetly. He leaves nothing to rankle in the wound he makes.

His future is one of the most interesting speculations of the political world. He retains the titular leadership; but the army has passed him by. It has gone over, horse, foot, and artillery, to a new idea. It openly scoffs at him. It distrusts his lukewarm surrender, and has ceased to find any pleasure in a conundrum which seems to have no solution. Its most powerful voices in the Press have called repeatedly for his deposition. He is without a policy, without a following, without a purpose. He has nothing but a crown. It is the crown of Richard the Second. His party only await the advent of Henry Bolingbroke.

JOHN SINGER SARGENT

It is a perilous thing for contemporary criticism to express itself in ultimate terms.   Jeffrey's " This will never do " stands as an historic reproof to cocksureness.   Who knows anything of Bononcini to-day? Yet Byrom reflected contemporary opinion when he linked him with Handel in that jingle which has passed into the nursery:

> Strange that such difference should be
> 'Twixt Tweedledum and Tweedledee.

These things—and history is strewn with similar examples—should put a salutary restraint alike upon our appreciations and our depreciations.   We should remember posterity, which does the winnowing itself and sets our judgment remorselessly aside.   Who knows but that it may say that Mr. Yeats wore the mantle of Blake and that Mr. Hall Caine had a juster view of himself than you or I had?   When, therefore, we say that we have lost the breed of great men, let us do so with reserve, and when we point to John Singer Sargent as an exception that proves the rule, let us add a rider to placate posterity.   Let us agree with Mrs. Meynell that he is the sole heir of Velasquez; but let us qualify—heir to his technical genius, but not heir to the nobility of his spirit.

There was probably never a painter who held a more undisputed position in the art of his own day than Mr. Sargent holds.   Titian's supremacy was challenged by Veronese and Tintoret.   Rubens and Rembrandt ran their course together, one living among princes and the other and greater dying in a garret.   Velasquez was their contemporary, and in a sense the rival of Rubens. Reynolds and Gainsborough divided the crown. Turner, it is true, towered above his contemporaries in lonely splendour; but his greatness was never undisputed in his own day. Mr. Sargent has the field to himself. The Royal Academy has become a sort of background to his dazzling achievements. We hurry through the quadrangle with one thought in our minds. What has Sargent to show us? A few years ago a second question was just emerging—What has Furse to show us? But that fine, chivalrous spirit vanished in the first pride of the morning, and the only possible challenge to Sargent vanished with him. It was the challenge of a nobler and simpler spirit. It was as though Handel had come to dispute the palm with Strauss, or gallant Gainsborough to bring back the old, happy English feeling into art.

Mr. Sargent does not appeal to us spiritually. He does not belong to us. He has the modern note of cosmopolitanism—a thing almost as unattractive as the word that expresses it. He reflects a world that has lost the sense of nationality and does not know the meaning of home—a world that lives in capitals, and flits from one palatial hotel to another. " D— the fellow, how various he is! " said Reynolds of Gainsborough; but in all his variety he spoke of England—English lanes and English folk and English thought — just as Rembrandt translated even the Gospel story into Dutch terms and Velasquez breathed the spirit of Spain into every stroke of his brush. Mr. Sargent is various too, but it is a variousness that has no root either in himself or in us. He is a nomad. The son of American parents, born in Florence, trained in Paris, living in London, a citizen of the United States, speaking Italian, French, German,

John Singer Sargent

Spanish, almost as fluently as he speaks English, painting Jews for business and hot southern scenes for pleasure, he knows nothing of geographical or racial boundaries. Having all the earth as his artistic inheritance, he has no foot of ground that is peculiarly his own.

Nor is his art anchored in any abiding human purpose. Millet and Watts were technically as unattached to any given soil as he is; but they were each governed by a purpose greater than their art—a purpose of which their art was only the instrument. They were prophets who chose, as it were, by accident, the medium of the brush instead of the pen. So with Velasquez and Rembrandt. Their appeal is primarily to the heart and after that to the æsthetic sense. Velasquez, it is true, tells us little of himself. He has the aloofness of Shakespeare. He reveals as the sun reveals, impartially, unemotionally, veraciously. He does not vitiate the statement of absolute truth by comment of his own. It is true that the essential nobility of his soul pervades all he does—that in the grave, cool world he sees with so serene a vision even the clowns and the dwarfs are gentlemen. There is nothing mean, nothing for scorn. His water-carrier, painted when he was nineteen, has the dignity which is older than Courts, the dignity which belongs to nature and the sorrows of the earth. He sees the cunning that lurks behind the feline gaze of Innocent X. and puts it down with unerring truth; but he adds no note of his own. He does not criticise: he states. He had, as Mr. Clausen has said, " the surest eye and the truest hand of any artist that ever lived." He had also, with the possible exception of Durer, the most truthful mind.

There is truth also in Rembrandt; but it is the truth not so much of objective vision as of subjective emotion. He is the painter of his own soul, the most intense, the most personal of dramatists. We admire Velasquez as we admire Shakespeare for his all-comprehending vision; but we love Rembrandt as we love those who have taken us into the inner sanctuary of themselves, or as Desdemona loved Othello, for the perils he had passed. In short, the enduring hold of Velasquez and Rembrandt upon the world is less through their technical genius than through their human sympathies. In each case the artist was less than the man.

Now Mr. Sargent is the artist *sans phrase*—the most accomplished artist of our time, one of the most accomplished artists of all time. He is an artist like Rubens, rejoicing in his incomparable dexterity. He has a hand light as a cloud, a touch swift as the lightning. His pictures affect you " like a melody that's sweetly played in tune." He is the virtuoso, in love with his instrument, delighting in the effects he can extract from it, careless of everything except his astonishing art. Sometimes, as in the " Mountain of Moab," the more intimate of the portraits and his great decorations at Boston, there are hints of something that goes deeper. But in general he takes his subject as a theme, not as Beethoven took it, to sound the deeps, but as Liszt took it, for rhetorical display. The analogy of music is inevitable in speaking of him, for his art has the mobility and rhythm of the orchestra. He fulfils the injunction of Sir Toby Belch, " Thou shouldst go to church in a galliard and come home in a coranto. Thy very walk should be a jig." Max Beerbohm's caricature of him expresses the essential spirit of his work. He is seen leaping at his canvas with a brush in either hand, while the fiddlers in the foreground scrape a tempestuous accompaniment. Nor is the analogy merely

John Singer Sargent

intellectual. Music is among the many accomplishments of this versatile man, as it was of that other Admirable Crichton, Lord Leighton. His recreation is the piano, and there are few more constant figures at the opera than his.

His facility of execution is astonishing. He has this quality in common with Gainsborough and Hals, that he seems to see the vision as a whole and to transmit it to the canvas with all its instancy and freshness and momentary delight. Take the incomparable portrait of "Lord Ribblesdale," or that audacious rendering of the "Misses Wertheimer." They are seen with the instancy of the camera and rendered with the pulse of life that the camera cannot give. It is as if the vision and the accomplishment were one action. Partly this is due to his enormous capacity for sustained labour. He can paint a portrait at a sitting and he can work on a canvas for six hours without loss of his wonderful vivacity and energy of mind. But this facility is rooted in the capacity for taking infinite pains. I am told that in the case of that dramatic "A Vele Gonfie," he went over most of the canvas twenty separate times, though the swift, untroubled brush strokes left no sense of labour, but rather of a careless improvisation. One remembers the historic reply of Whistler, "And do I understand, Mr. Whistler, that you ask £200 for knocking off this—this little thing?" "No, I ask £200 for the experience of a lifetime." There is the experience of a lifetime in those broad, confident sweeps of Sargent's brush. That is what is overlooked by his imitators, who copy his methods without his knowledge and achieve only that flashy cleverness that is the most desolating thing in art.

Nor is his intellectual insight less remarkable than

his technical dexterity. He seizes his subject in all
its qualities, body, mind and spirit, and communi-
cates the result—pleasant or unpleasant: he is indifferent—in one startling unity, so that it is as if
you knew these people, the tones of their voice, the
quality of their thought, their origin and their career.
It would not, I think, be difficult to write a character
sketch of the Wertheimers simply by studying
Sargent's portraits. Take as an example of this
faculty of reflecting the spirit in externals, the portrait of President Roosevelt, with its sense of power
cunningly realised by such devices as the outstretched
right hand, muscular and exaggerated, that grasps
the support as if it were the great globe itself that he
held in his iron grip. There is a legend that a doctor
puzzled by a certain case found the secret that he
could not diagnose in the patient himself revealed in
a portrait of the patient by Sargent. True or untrue,
it is not difficult to believe, so searching is his vision.
This swift instinct for the individual note in character,
coupled with his rapidity of work, is illustrated by
his portrait of Mr. Pulitzer. The famous New York
journalist had been to his studio several times and
his picture was approaching completion. But one
day, on arriving at Mr. Sargent's door, he found
awaiting him on the pavement a certain peer who had
sought some favour which he was not disposed to give.
" I cannot stay: I am due in the studio," he said.
The other thereupon coolly proposed to accompany
him. Mr. Pulitzer blazed with wrath at the suggested intrusion and when he entered the studio his
face was still transfigured with passion. " That's
what I want," said the painter, as he saw the face of
the real man at last, and turning to the canvas he
obliterated the previous work and with swift energy
and broad strokes put down in one brief sitting that

John Singer Sargent

brilliant impression of Mr. Pulitzer which is now in New York.

He is, more than any great portraitist on record, a satirist. Velasquez painted mean people and made them great. He painted great people and sometimes made them ignoble. But he never expressed his own contempt, for he had none. Mr. Sargent's palette has usually a little acid in it. The note of scorn is subtle but indisputable. Mr. Dooley expressed a truth with his delightful extravagance when he told how Mr. Higbie of Chicago got his portrait painted by Sargent:

Number 108 shows Sargent at his best. There is the same marvellous ticknick that th' great master displayed in his cillybrated take-off on Mrs. —— in last year's gallery. Th' skill an' ease with which th' painter has made a monkey iv his victim are beyond praise. Sargent has torn th' sordid heart out iv th' wicked crather an' exposed it to the wurruld. Th' wicked, ugly little eyes, th' crooked nose, th' huge graspin' hands, tell th' story iv this miscreant's character as completely as if they were written in so many wurruds, while th' artist, with wonderful malice, has painted onto th' face a smile iv sickenin' silf-complacency that is positively disgustin'. No artist iv our day has succeeded so well in showin' up th' maneness iv th' people he has mugged. We ondershtand that th' atrocious Higbie pa'l wan hundherd thousan' dollars f'r this comic valentine. It is worth th' money to ivrybody but him.

It is in his portraits of children, and occasionally in those of old age, that we find the note of human sympathy which is generally wanting. Here sometimes the heart as well as the intellect is engaged. There are few things more fresh and appealing than the Boit children or little Laura Lister. Greuze had no finer instinct for unsullied innocence.

But it is as the artist that Sargent will live. The man will remain obscure behind the achievement that astonishes and delights the mind, but leaves the sympathies cold. His conception of the province of art is the antithesis of that of Burne-Jones, to whom a picture was a spiritual stimulus, a vision and an ideal, lit by a light that never was on sea or land, " the consecration and the poet's dream." It is not a view of life, nor is it a revelation of self. It has nothing to do with morals or emotions. It is art for art's sake, a thing self-contained and apart from the personal life of the artist. It remains to be seen in his case as in Whistler's how far that divorce is consistent with his inclusion by posterity among those whom it calls " great." Two things are certain. One is that if the technical mastery of the medium constitutes greatness, John S. Sargent is among the immortals. The other is that it is through his eyes that the future will see our time in its ornamental aspects, just as to-day we see the eighteenth century through the eyes of Gainsborough and Reynolds. The one person the future will not see will be Mr. Sargent himself. He will be for ever inscrutable—not a man but a technique.

George Meredith

GEORGE MEREDITH

MR. MEREDITH is "the last leaf upon the tree in the spring." Mr. Swinburne and Mr. Hardy belong in some measure to our own generation, both in spirit and in time. But Mr. Meredith gathered in his sheaves in that rich harvest time when Tennyson and Browning, Carlyle and Ruskin, Dickens and Thackeray were his fellow-gleaners; when Darwin was recasting the history of man, as Copernicus had recast the structure of the heavens; and when Thomson was daily adding to the story of man's conquest over matter. He is the last of the giants.

It is nearly sixty years since Tennyson's ear caught a fresh note in the woodland song, a brave, joyous note, thrilling as the lark, pure as the nightingale. For young Meredith burst on the world singing that matchless " Love in the Valley," and Tennyson was haunted by its liquid, full-throated melody. It haunts us still. It will haunt the world for ever. For it is one of the indisputable things of literature. Listen:

> Happy, happy time when the white star hovers
>   Low over dim fields fresh with bloomy dew,
> Near the face of dawn that draws athwart the darkness,
>   Threading it with colour, like yewberries the yew.
> Thicker crowd the shades as the grave East deepens
>   Glowing, and with crimson a long cloud swells.
> Maiden still the morn is; and strange she is, and secret.
>   Strange her eyes; her cheeks are cold as cold sea-shells.

It was the glad song of the dawn. And now the long summer day has drawn to evening—evening serene and joyous as the dawn: the deep, resonant voice clear and thrilling as of old, the light of the dark eye undimmed, the intellect undarkened, the frequent laughter buoyant and infectious as a child's.

He is the spirit of unconquerable youth. He brings into our querulous and near-sighted time the spacious cheerfulness of a more confident day. "People talk about me," he says, "as if I were an old man. I do not feel old in the least. On the contrary, I do not believe in growing old, and I do not see any reason why we should ever die. I take as keen an interest in the movement of life as ever. I enter into the passions of youth, and I watch political affairs with the same keen interest as of old. I have seen the illusion of it all, but it does not dull my zest, and I hold more firmly than ever to my faith in the constant advancement of the race."

Life to him is a gallant adventure of the soul. The victories of the common man are the victories of ponderable things. They are recorded in the banker's ledger. George Meredith's career has been one long victory of the spirit—a buoyant, indomitable spirit, all sunshine and fresh air. He is the captain of his unconquerable soul. Long years of failure and neglect could not sour him; age cannot dull the edge of his blithe spirit. When, far away in the fifties, he was reduced to the last verge of impoverishment, he bought himself a sack of oatmeal, and having no money with which to get fuel, he subsisted on oatmeal and water, and on that Spartan diet wrote *Evan Harrington*, the most joyous comedy in the language, a novel full of the singing of birds and light-hearted laughter, of the gaiety of the incomparable Countess, and of jolly cricket on the village green. And when the world would still have none of him, he cheerfully set himself to other tasks to win his bread, wrote "leaders" for the *Ipswich Gazette*, turned an honest penny as *locum tenens* for his life-long friend, Mr. John

George Meredith

Morley, on *The Fortnightly*, and having failed in his bid for a popular success wrote for himself, growing ever more subtle and oblique, displaying ever more of the Virgilian *obscuris vera involvens*. If he thought of his public at all he must have thought of it as Savage Landor thought—" I shall dine late; but the room will be well lighted, the company few and of the best."

Success in the ordinary material sense has never come to him. The largest sum he has ever received for a novel, I believe, is £400, and even the ripple that *Diana of the Crossways* caused on the surface of the popular mind was due less to its amazing merits than to the fact of the supposed identification of Diana with Mrs. Norton, who was said to have sold the famous secret to the *Times*. But he never asked for success. The joy of living has been all-sufficient. We catch a glimpse of him in middle life in Justin McCarthy's *Reminiscences* :

He loved bodily exercises of all kinds; he delighted to take long brisk walks—" spins " as he called them—along the highways and byways of the neighbourhood; and he loved to wander through the woods and to lie in the grass, and I have no doubt he would have enjoyed climbing the trees. He seemed to have much of the temperament of the fawn; he seemed to have sprung from the very bosom of Nature herself. . . . It amazed me, when I first used to visit him, to see a man, no longer young, indulge in such feats of strength and agility. It delighted him to play with great iron weights, and to throw heavy clubs into the air and catch them as they fell and twirl them round his head as if they had been light bamboo canes.

The long country walks are over, and no longer he indulges in heroic feats with the clubs; but all the rest is as of old. He has still the " temperament of the fawn " and the unquenchable passion for life. As you meet him driving on the country roads near his delightful little home under the shadow of Box Hill, you are arrested by the quick vivacious glance

that roves the landscape and scans the passing faces
with eager interest. And if you have the good
fortune to go with him into his garden with the beautiful yew hedge and the little wooden châlet at the top
of the garden slope, you will find his talk full of the
light and laughter of youth, and you will find his
attitude to the world reflected in his genial comradeship with his gardener, who is not a servant but an
old friend. For he has none of the aloofness of genius
—that haughty pride that made Wordsworth turn
his back on De Quincey, who had dared to praise *his*
mountains. Nothing to him is base or trivial, no one
too slight for his joyous fellowship; and so he enters
into the heart of " Old Martin's Puzzle " as keenly
as into the secret of the " hymning night," and shares
the careless gaiety of the boy as readily as the mystery
of a woman's soul. There are no boys in literature
like Meredith's boys, no cricket matches so full of the
true glamour of the game as his.

He has an intimacy with Nature which has nothing
in common with that of the student who would
" peep and botanise upon his mother's grave." It is
intuition rather than erudition. He has not learned
the secrets of Nature from without, but seems to
come from the heart of Nature bearing those secrets
with him. William Sharp records that he walked
over from Meredith's one day to visit Grant Allen
at Dorking. When he was about to return, Grant
Allen said he would walk with him, as he wanted
to ask Meredith about a disputed point in natural
history. Sharp expressed surprise that a specialist
like Allen should wish to consult an amateur on
a matter of intimate knowledge and observation.
" There are not half a dozen men living," replied
Grant Allen, " to whom I would go in preference to
Meredith on a point of this kind. He knows the

George Meredith

intimate facts of countryside life as very few of us do after the most specific training. I don't know whether he could describe the greenfinch in the wild cherry yonder in the terms of an ornithologist and botanist—in fact, I'm sure he couldn't. But you may rest assured there is no ornithologist living who knows more about the finch of real life than George Meredith does—its appearance, male and female, its song, its habits, its dates of coming and going, the places where it builds, how its nest is made, how many eggs it lays and what like they are, what it feeds on, what its song is like before and after mating, and when and where it may best be heard, and so forth. As for the wild cherry ... perhaps he doesn't know much about it technically; ... but if anyone can say when the first blossoms will appear and how long they will last, how many petals each blossom has, what variations in colour and what kind of smell they have, then it's he, and no other better. And as for *how* he would describe the cherry tree ... well, you've read *Richard Feverel* and ' Love in the Valley,' and that should tell you everything.''

This delight in the visible, tangible phenomena of Nature distinguishes him from the mystics who, like Francis Thompson, '' unsharing in the liberal laugh of earth,'' having no physical rapture, no sensuous joy in things, see Nature only as the strange garment of their dreams—

> How should I gauge what beauty is her dole,
> Who cannot see her countenance for her soul,
> As birds see not the casement for the sky?

That expresses with rare beauty the Uranian passion of Thompson. With all the splendour of his imagery, there is no sensuous joy in the contacts of earth. The pageant of noon and night, the appeal of the universe of sound and vision and touch and all the dear intimacies that bind us to this world of visible and tangible delights leave his translunar spirit unfettered. He cannot see the casement for the sky and has no kinship with our common life. But Meredith shares our " sensible warm motion " and shares it without the fears of the " kneaded clod " that affrighted Claudio's mind. He loves the earth with the warm, homely love of a son for his mother—with a love that has no place for fear.

He is the lyric voice of Nature, as Wordsworth was her reverie. He turns to the East and the morning as instinctively as Wordsworth turned to the West and the glowing embers of the day. Like his own Lucy, Wordsworth " leaned his ear in many a secret place," and the beauty of the earth and the peace of Nature slid into his soul. To him, as to Beethoven, every tree seemed to cry " Holy, holy! " The anthem of incommunicable things came to him out of the sunset and the silence of the starry sky and the quiet of the lonely hills. Nature was a Presence " to be felt and known in darkness and in light," a personal voice uttering its secrets in his reverent ear. It was the voice of God, and he the consecrated vehicle of its message. Meredith's attitude is more Pagan. He does not lean his ear in the secret place. He looks out on the universe with a delighted wonder, and surrenders himself to Nature " more joyfully than a deer lies down among the grass of spring." He, in his own buoyant words,

> . . . seats his soul upon her wings,
> And broadens o'er the windswept world
> With her,

gathering in the flight

> More knowledge of her secret, more
> Delight in her beneficence,
> Than hours of musing, or the love
> That lives with men, could ever give.

. . . .

George Meredith

For every elemental power
Is kindred to our hearts, and once
Acknowledged, wedded, once embraced,
Once claspt into the naked life,
The union is eternal.

And out of that union with Nature comes the victory
—not the victory over things, but the victory over
self. For the self is merged in the whole, the personal
in the impersonal, the mortal in the immortal. We
are made one with Nature, and are

. . . lost in the notes on the lips of the choir
That chants the chant of the whole.

In this joyous surrender of self there is nothing for
tears, nothing to affright or dismay. The dawn is
magical, but night is magical too. Life is a splendid
pageant; but Death has no terrors. He does not,
like Keats, " call it soft names in many a mused
rhyme," for he has nothing of the hectic morbidness
of Keats. He welcomes it rather as Whitman
welcomed it—as the strong deliverer. It is the arch
wherethrough gleams the untravelled world:

Death shall I shrink from, loving thee?
Into the breast that gives the rose
Shall I with shuddering fall?

It is this unquestioning acceptance that fills the
Meredithian world with such a sense of radiant optimism. He has written tragedies; but he has not the
spirit of tragedy. Stevenson called *Richard Feverel*
a brutal assault upon the feelings, and complained
that Meredith had played the reader false in starting
a tragedy in the spirit of comedy. But the truth is
that tragedy to be tragedy must have in it the terror
of death as well as the lust of life. It must ask for
an individual immortality and be denied. It must
have the secret of Hardy's sombre thought. He, too,
sees Nature as a vast, sentient, inscrutable being;

but he sees man, not as a child taken to its bosom, but as a rabbit caught in its ruthless trap, crying, not for a vague absorption in Nature, but for its own personal, tangible existence. And out of that cry of terror comes tragedy.

Meredith has none of this terror, and if he touches the fountain of tears it is only to reveal the image of the rainbow. He is the spirit of high and noble comedy. He looks at life with a certain spacious calm, a serene tranquillity. His vision has something of the impartiality as well as of the veracity of Velasquez, something of the sovereign comprehension of Shakespeare. For with all his psychology and introspection his view is essentially objective. The world of men passes like a pageant before him, and he reads it as if it were a printed page. He sees life sanely and sees it whole, and he sees it with that robust and wholesome humour that keeps the vision true and the mind sweet.

H H Asquith

THE PREMIER

I ASKED Mr. Birrell on one occasion what he thought of the oratory of the present Parliament.

" Oratory! " he replied. " There is none. Parliamentary oratory is dead—dead without hope of resurrection. The House wouldn't listen to it to-day. The speeches it likes best are in the style of Asquith —plain, lucid statements, gathering up all the arguments, the right word, the clean phrase and no frills."

" And sincerity—does that count? " I said.

" Not a straw," he answered with that wholesome cynicism with which he checks all tendency to pretence or preachiness. " I left Rowland Hunt talking in the House just now." (We were dining below.) " He's as sincere as they make 'em, and the whole House is rocking with laughter. No, no—a plain tale without any missionary fervour—that's the thing that counts. Asquith is the model."

I went into the House later in the evening, and there chanced to find Mr. Asquith in the midst of a speech. He stood at the table firm as a rock, hard as adamant, his heavy voice beating out his theme with great hammer strokes, his eye fixed implacably on the front Opposition bench. So had I seen him stand fifteen years ago on the platform of a Northern town, while " Featherstone! Featherstone! Murderer! " echoed round the hall. It was the greeting which always assailed him in those days. Possibly it assails him still. He stood with his arms folded, the massive head thrown back, the strong mouth clenched, the eye lit with a cold indifference and scorn. He made no protest, offered no comment, but allowed the cries to flicker out and then proceeded as though nothing had happened. Here was a man who at least was not afraid. He might be wrong; but he would never run away. A man of granite.

Mr. George Russell, I believe, has been heard to say that he envies the brain of Lord Milner more than that of any man living. Needless to say, he would have had it motived by other enthusiasms. If I were disposed to envy other people's brains and wanted power and not imagination, I should envy Mr. Asquith's. It is of the same class as Lord Milner's, and, I think, better of its class. It is the Balliol brain at its best. It is incomparably the most powerful intellect in the House of Commons to-day—not the finest, nor the subtlest, nor the most attractive, but the most effective. It has none of the nebulous haze that invests Mr. Balfour's mental evolutions, none of the cavalry swiftness of Mr. Churchill or Mr. Lloyd George, none of the spaciousness and moral exhilaration of Lord Morley. It is dry and hard, lacks colour and emotion; but it has weight, force, power. It is a piece of faultless mechanism. It works with the exactness of mathematics, with the massive, unhasting sureness of a natural force. It affects you like the machinery that you see pounding away in the hold—so measured, so true, so irresistible. It is the Nasmyth hammer of politics. " Go and bring the sledge-hammer," said " C. B." to one of his colleagues on the Treasury bench in the midst of an attack by Mr. Balfour. And Mr. Asquith duly appeared.

This mental precision is reflected in his tastes. He is an ingenious mechanic, and I have been told that years ago, when cycling was the sensation of the hour,

The Premier

he constructed and rode a machine with so many original devices that the King, then Prince of Wales, invited him to make him one like it. Perhaps this is only one of those legends that gather about distinguished men; but it is in keeping with the character.

He has the directness of the Yorkshire stock from which he springs. " Asquith will get on," said Jowett, " he is so direct." He does not skirmish or finesse. He does not feint or flourish. He heaves himself on the enemy's centre and caves it in. The sentences of his orderly speech march into action like disciplined units, marshalled and drilled. Every word has its mark. At every sentence you see a man drop. He creates the impression of visible overthrow. It is as though you hear the blow crashing on his opponent's front, as though you see that opponent reeling to the ground. Take any of those speeches with which he pursued Mr. Chamberlain through the country — the Cinderford speech for example. It read like a succession of " bull's eyes " at a shooting range. You could see the flag go up at every sentence. " He talks like an advocate from a brief," said Mr. Chamberlain bitterly. Perhaps it was so. But what a brief! What an advocate!

He has the terseness of phrase that is taught by the pen rather than by the tongue. The art is natural to his clear intellect, but it was perfected in those days when briefs were scarce, and when as a contributor to the *Economist* he acquired that mastery of economics and finance which made him supreme when the Free Trade issue emerged. " I forgot Goschen," said Randolph Churchill. " I forgot Asquith " might be Mr. Chamberlain's summary of that Titanic duel. He understands the value of brevity as no other man does. He can be compact as an essay of Bacon.

His capacious mind brings up all his legions at will
into one massive movement, and discharges them
in a series of shocks. Take that instance when the
House had been engaged in the familiar task of trying
to discover whether Mr. Balfour was a Free Trader
or a Protectionist. The debate had reached its close.
Mr. Balfour was still both and neither. Mr. Asquith
rose, and in a speech of two minutes and half a dozen
sentences left him a wreck, shattered fore and aft.

If the object of controversy is to clear the air and
carry conviction to the mind, he is incomparably the
most powerful debater of his time. As a boy his gift
of lucid statement and breadth of comprehension
was apparent. When he came up from Yorkshire to
the City of London School, Dr. Abbott, the headmaster, was at once struck by his powers of debate.
While the boys' society debated Dr. Abbott corrected
exercises. " But when Asquith entered the society,"
he said, " I began to find this difficult. . . . Finally,
whenever he entered the lists of orators I resigned
myself to a willing attention, and was content to
take my exercises away with me uncorrected." He
has nothing of the tumultuous energy and passion of
Fox as pictured in Hazlitt:

> Everything showed the agitation of his mind: his tongue
> faltered, his voice became almost suffocated, and his face
> was bathed in tears. He was lost in the magnitude of his
> subject. He reeled and staggered under the load of feeling
> which oppressed him. He rolled like the sea beaten by a
> tempest.

Mr. Asquith does not roll like the sea. He stands, as
Pitt stood, like a rock beaten by the sea.

He creates confidence and carries conviction, but he
does not inspire men with great passions. His eloquence keeps to the solid earth: it does not fly with
wings. It assures you victory; but it denies you
adventure. It is a favourite saying of Lord Morley

that "great thoughts spring from the heart." Mr.
Asquith does not utter great thoughts. No Balliol
man of the Jowett tradition does. The Balliol mind
distrusts "great thoughts" even if it thinks them.
It believes they come from weak minds and soft
hearts—from zealous persons with good emotions
but defective intellects. Balliol, in fact, is really
atrophy of the heart. It is exhaustion of the emotions. It has produced the finest mental machines
of this generation, but they are sometimes cold and
cheerless. They lack atmosphere and the humanities.
They have none of our frailties. They are intellectual
sublimities beneath whose huge legs we creep, " peeping about to find ourselves dishonourable graves."
We admire them, we respect them: we do not love
them, for we feel that they would be insulted by the
offer of so irrational a thing as love.

Mr. Asquith is handicapped by this apparent chill
of the spirit. It gives him the sense of remoteness
and hardness which those who know him best declare
is unjust to the real man. Behind that exterior of
adamant there are the shy virtues of geniality and
even tenderness, and in personal contact you are impressed not merely by his masculine grip of affairs,
but by his courtesy and consideration. But a popular
figure he is not, perhaps does not seek to be. He
comes to the front by sheer authority of intellect, and
owes nothing to the magnetism of personality. He
meets the world in the office, not in the parlour of
his thoughts, and no genial stories gather about his
personality.

He has the merits as well as the defects of the
Jowett tradition. It was material and unimaginative. It produced Curzonism and Milnerism. It
lacked sympathy and insight, because sympathy and
insight, like great thoughts, spring from the heart.

It built upon facts and scorned human sentiment, which is the greatest fact of all in the government of men. But it has the high quality of reserve. It cultivates no illusions, raises no false hopes. It understates itself with a certain chill repudiation of popular applause. Its deeds are often better than its words; its Bills more drastic than its promises.

No one ever accused Mr. Asquith of being a demagogue, and when his opponents charge him with falsity of word or conduct they do it knowing that no one believes them, and not believing it themselves. For he moves in the clearest atmosphere of truth of any public man of his time. Artifice and affectation are as alien to him as excess or inexactness, and the firmness of his mind enables him to preserve a singular detachment from the momentary passions of debate. Violence and recrimination find in him no response. He may utter a rebuke and it may be severe, but it is free from venom or any personal taint, and is governed by the desire not to score a mere dialectical point, but to elucidate a position.

This detachment from the pettiness and meanness of controversy is largely the source of the growing authority he has established over the House. He restores its self-respect, liberates its better emotions, and recalls it to its rational self. I have seen him, following on the most embittered attacks, change the whole temper of the House and lift the discussion to an atmosphere of dispassionate calm by the firmness with which he has put away all temptation to meet thunder with thunder, and has concentrated on the plain facts of the situation. The effect is like the shock of cold water upon an angry mob. It is not the " sweet reasonableness " of the quietist, nor is it the calculated persuasiveness of the advocate. It is the judicial quality in its highest expression, grave, aloof, indifferent to the feelings aroused, concerned only with the facts and the principles involved in them. No party leader ever conveyed a more complete sense of disinterested aims and unbiassed judgment.

His power of work is unequalled, for the strength of his mind is backed by a physique equal to any burden. His capacious intellect grasps a subject in all its bearings with an ease and comprehensiveness that never fail to win the admiration of those who approach him. There is little subtlety in his thought, just as there is little delicacy in his utterance. It is a purely masculine understanding, powerful and direct. He was in other days one of the society of "Souls"; but—*Que diable*——? One would as soon look for Cromwell, of whom in feature and in some other respects he is reminiscent, among the curled Cavaliers, as for him in a dilettante circle. That was the natural element of Mr. Balfour, who was fitted for the rôle of Mr. Bunthorne. But there is nothing "precious" or transcendental in Mr. Asquith's equipment. He is precise as a time-table. His vocabulary is abundant, but it consists wholly of plain, serviceable words, without a touch of emotion or imagination, and his vocabulary truly reflects his mental outlook. He is the constructive engineer of politics, not the seer of visions. He leaves the pioneering work to others and follows after with his levels and his compasses to lay out the new estate. No great cause will ever owe anything to him in its inception, but when he is convinced of its justice and practicability, he will take it up with a quiet, undemonstrative firmness that means success. It was so in the case of Old Age Pensions. He made no electoral capital out of them, seemed indeed to be unsympathetic. He had won the victory for you almost before you realised that he was on your side. No man in politics ever mortgaged the future less than he does, or lived more free from promissory notes.

If he is wanting in any essential of statesmanship, it is strong impulse to action. He has patience rather than momentum. He never seeks a quarrel, and does not raise issues for the joy of action. His temperament is easy-going, and, in strange contrast to his intellect, a little flaccid. Unlike Mr. Chamberlain or Mr. Lloyd George he does not disturb the sleeping dogs of politics willingly, and he would prefer a quiet life to the smoke of battle. Mr. Chamberlain's talk was wholly of the conflict. He lived on the battle-field and drew from it all the interest of his life and all the material of his talk. The conversation of Mr. Asquith, on the contrary, though it has not the encyclopædic range and devouring intensity of Mr. Gladstone, has the same scholarly flavour, the same love of the classics and of the literature of thought. In his public utterance he conceals these interests with the reticence and dislike of display which are characteristic of him and which are so largely the secret of the small hold he has upon the affections of the public. To be a popular leader one must be expansive and self-revelatory, and Mr. Asquith is neither.

It follows from all this that he owes nothing of his success to pushfulness, ambition, or intrigue. His career has been singularly free from drama and sensation. He emerged with a natural inevitableness. Wherever he came he overcame, and opportunity never found him unequal to the occasion. When in the Parnell trial Russell, owing to indisposition, left the cross-examination of Macdonald of the *Times* to him, it was felt that it was a grave misfortune, for here was the crux of the case. If this went wrong all might go wrong. When Mr. Asquith sat down he had shattered the *Times* case and made his own reputation. When in 1892 Mr. Gladstone entrusted him with the final attack on the Salisbury Government, he did so with hesitation. But after it he had no hesitation in making him Home Secretary. Mr. Asquith, in fact, is the man who never fails. He is always intellectually bigger than his task.

Two incidents in his career cannot be ignored. He, on the repeated telegraphic appeal of the Mayor, permitted military to reinforce the police in the Featherstone colliery riots and two men were shot dead. It was a regrettable incident, of which, whatever may be our view of the facts, he has been adequately reminded at a hundred meetings since. And, though he believed the Boer War unnecessary, he dissociated himself from Sir H. Campbell-Bannerman and was one of the founders of the Liberal League that gathered around the disturbing figure of Lord Rosebery. Balliol did not come well out of the Boer War. But he never embittered an unhappy situation, and when peace returned he was one of those who healed the breach. I am, I believe, revealing an open secret when I say that he stood loyally by Sir Henry when the last rally of Imperialism sought to drive him, a *roi fainéant*, to the House of Lords, and as his chief lieutenant his attitude won universal admiration, not for its cold correctitude, but for its generous and warm-hearted service. No one in the Cabinet was more loyal to the Premier than he was, and none of those who heard it will forget the noble speech he made on the occasion of his leader's death. It was a speech that sounded unsuspected depths of emotion, and seemed for once to lift the fire-proof curtain of his reserve.

Prophets, Priests, and Kings

His succession to the Premiership was a matter of course. And as Premier he is not inferior to a great lineage. He does not at present command the affection that Sir H. Campbell-Bannerman commanded, nor the reverence that was Gladstone's. But he commands in a rare degree the confidence of his party, and his handling of the Parliamentary machine, at once masterful and adroit, has won universal admiration. He is slow to take up adventurous causes, but, once convinced, he has unequalled power to give them shape and, in doing so, to carry the conviction that comes from his own secure and unimpassioned intellect to that timid public who see the dread form of " Socialism " in every effort after a more just and therefore more firmly-rooted State.

THE KAISER

WHEN I think of the Kaiser I think of a bright May morning at Potsdam. It is the Spring Parade, and across from where we are gathered under the windows of the old palace the household troops are drawn up on the great parade ground, their helmets and banners and lances all astir in the jolly sunshine. Officers gallop hither and thither shouting their commands. Regiments form and re-form. Swords flash out and flash back again. A noble background of trees frames the gay picture with cool, green foliage. There is a sudden stillness. The closely serried ranks are rigid and moveless. The shouts of command are silenced.

" The Kaiser."

He comes slowly up the parade ground on his great white charger, helmet and eagle flashing in the sunlight, sitting his horse as if he lived in the saddle, his face turned to his men as he passes by.

" Morgen, meine Kinder." His salutation rings out at intervals in the clear morning air. And back from the ranks in chorus comes the response: " Morgen, Majestät."

And as he rides on, master of a million men, the most powerful figure in Europe, reviewing his troops on the peaceful parade ground at Potsdam, one wonders whether the day will ever come when he will ride down those ranks on another errand, and when that cheerful response of the soldiers will have in it the ancient ring of doom—" Te morituri salutamus."

Prophets, Priests, and Kings

For answer, let us look at this challenging figure on the white charger. What is he? What has he done?

The Kaiser is easily the foremost man in Europe. He is a King after Charles the First's own heart, " a King indeed," the last that is left, the residuary legatee of " the divine right." The divinity of the Tsar vanished in the tumult of Red Sunday. He is an autocrat struggling with an infuriated people. His power frankly rests on physical force. But the Kaiser is still able to associate Providence with his rule, still invokes the Almighty as the witness of his authority. Democracy, which has devoured all the rest, thunders at the base of his throne. It leaps higher and ever higher. One day there will come a wave that will submerge all, and " divine right " will have passed for ever from Kings to peoples. Then the Kaiser will rule by consent, like our own monarch, or——

Meanwhile he stands, facing the modern world, the symbol of mediævalism in the heart of the Twentieth Century. The cause for which he fights could have no more worthy protagonist. He is every inch a King. Divest him of his office and he would still be one of the half-dozen most considerable men in his Empire. When the British editors visited Germany they were brought into intimate contact with all the leaders of action and thought in the country, and I believe it is true to say that the Kaiser left the sharpest and most vivid personal impression on the mind.

It was the impression of enormous energy and mental alertness, of power, wayward and uncertain, but fused with a spark of genius, of a temperament of high nervous force, quickly responsive to every emotional appeal. His laugh is as careless as a boy's, but you feel that it is laughter that may turn to lightning at a word.

The world distrusts the artistic temperament in affairs. It prefers the stolid man who thinks slowly and securely and acts with deliberation. It likes a man whose mental processes it can follow and understand, a man of the type of the late Duke of Devonshire, solid, substantial, and not the least bit clever. There is the root of the disquiet with which the Kaiser has been regarded for twenty years. He is a man of moods and impulses, an artist to his finger tips, astonishingly versatile, restless, and unnerving. He keeps his audience in a state of tense expectation. Any moment, it feels, a spark from this incandescent personality may drop into the powder magazine.

He is full of dramatic surprises, of sudden and shattering entrances, of mysterious exits. He moves amidst alarums and excursions. And wherever he goes the limelight follows him. He journeys to Tangier, and Europe trembles with the thunder of his tread. He sails away into Arctic seas on a summer cruise, and his astonishing sermons to his men echo round the world. He comes back and makes our flesh creep with his pictured visions of the Yellow Peril. He writes an opera and is off to the Rhine to wind his horn. He addresses public meetings like a party politician, and with the authority of a prophet, and he denounces the Socialists like a Property Defence League orator.

No man in history ever had a more god-like vision of himself than he has. His " cloud of dignity is held from falling " by the visible hand of the Almighty. " I regard my whole position," he tells the representatives of Brandenburg, " as given to me direct from Heaven and that I have been called by the Highest to do His work." Sometimes, indeed, even the Almighty is subordinate. " *Suprema lex regis voluntas,*" he writes in the Golden Book of Munich. He declares his omnipotence with a childish egoism that would be ludicrous if it were not so sincere. He takes nothing for granted—does not, like Montaigne, let his chateaux speak for him. " My Church, of which I am *summus episcopus,*" he says, in lecturing the office-bearers on their duties. And again, " There is only one master in this country. That am I. Who opposes me I shall crush to pieces." It is like the vain prattle of an unschooled boy.

His uncle dwells aloof from politics. The Kaiser comes down into the arena like a stump orator. " To me," he said in 1889, " every Social Democrat is synonymous with enemy of the nation and of the Fatherland." This to the largest party in the land— a party that commands three and a half million votes. And years have not taught him discretion. At Breslau not long ago, in addressing a deputation of working men, he said:

For years you and your brothers in Germany have allowed yourselves to be kept by Socialist agitators under the delusion that if you do not belong to their party you will not be in a position to obtain a hearing for your legitimate interests. That is a downright lie. . . . With such men you cannot, you dare not, as men who love honour, have anything more to do: you cannot, you dare not let yourselves be guided by them any longer.

Diplomacy and restraint, it will be seen, are not among his varied gifts in dealing with his people.

Sometimes his vaulting ambition o'erleaps itself. It was his dearest wish to be not German Emperor, but Emperor of Germany, and crowned as such. He designed all the splendours of the ceremony, taking Charlemagne as his prototype; but he found there were limits to the complaisance of the other German rulers and peoples, always intensely jealous of the dominance of Prussia and its King. They would not yield, and he remains to-day the uncrowned German Emperor, not the crowned Emperor of Germany. It is the fly in the Imperial ointment, the supreme disappointment of his career. Bismarck had cared only for the substance, and not for the shadow, when he consented to the limited title of the ruler of the new Empire. The subject was being discussed in his presence at the time of the union. Some were for German Emperor, and some for Emperor of Germany. " Does anyone know the Latin word for sausage? " asked Bismarck, using that homely imagery of his. " Farcimentum," said one. " Farcimen," said another. " Farcimentum or farcimen, it is all the same to me," said Bismarck. Sausage was sausage, whatever the name. He had welded Germany and was indifferent to titles.

The Kaiser's view of his divine function extends to every phase of life. There is nothing in which he cannot instruct his people. He will snatch the baton from the incompetent conductor and show him how to lead the orchestra, the brush from the incompetent artist and show him how to paint. He can cook a dinner as skilfully as he can preach a sermon, draw a cartoon, write an opera, play the piano, or talk in five languages. And who will forget his amazing letter to Admiral Hollmann on the " higher criticism," in reply to Professor Delitzsch? Even trade does not escape him, and the famous pottery works which he has founded and carries on at Cardinen are a source of delighted labour to him. He has established a shop in Berlin to dispose of his wares, and he will take an order on the cuff of his shirt sleeve with the promptness of a commercial traveller.

But all this is the recreation of his strenuous life. His serious task is to make Germany great. The

ambition with which he set out was to create a Navy.
He has done it. Frederick taught Germany to march;
he has taught it to swim. "Navigare necesse est,
vivere non est necesse." And if he regards his people
as children, he is anxious that they should be efficient
children. His views on education are entirely radical
and not very sympathetic towards the meticulous and
exact scholarship which is Germany's contribution to
the modern world. "Our business is to educate
young Germans, not young Greeks and Romans," he
says. He approves of Homer, "that glorious man
about whom I have always been enthusiastic," and
of Cicero and Demosthenes, "whose speeches must
have filled everyone with delight;" but he has no
sympathy with "grammatical and fanatical philo-
logists," who waste their own time and the time of
students over grammatical hair-splitting. "Away
with this tomfoolery; war to the knife against such
teaching."

He will have no rival near the throne. Does the
mighty figure of Bismarck tower to the heavens and
divide the crown? Then Bismarck must go back to
his fields and woodlands at Friedrichsruhe. He will
brook no interference, tolerate no counsel. He is
here to command, not to take advice. And yet the
revelations of the Moltke-Harden trial have shown
that the most omnipotent of Emperors is subject to
the subtlest and most insidious of influences.

Men used to talk of him in whispers in Germany, or
they did not talk of him at all, for *lèse majesté* was
the cardinal sin, and walls had ears and streets had
spies. But that is changed. Criticism is abroad and
the doctrine of divinity has received several checks
which the Kaiser has had the wisdom to acknowledge.
But he will never be a popular figure. The old
Emperor, his "never-to-be-forgotten" grandfather,

was loved. There at the palace in Berlin they show
you the window at which he used to sit in the mornings
to see and be seen by the crowd—an old, familiar
figure, human and paternal, the father of his people.
His grandson is aloof and remote. He dwells on
Olympus and sends his thunderbolts hurtling over
the astonished people. But though he does not ask
for affection, he commands respect. His people
admire his character. They are proud of his clean,
vigorous life, of his devotion to his family, of his high
sense of duty to the Fatherland. His life is a drama
that never grows humdrum. It keeps them intellectually on the move. What will happen next with
this amazing man?

No one can be more fascinating. His smile is irresistible. But if you are a bore, or if you are out of
favour, his look runs you through like a sword. His
questions are rapped out like musket shots. He does
not listen to your answers, but plays with his dogs.
He is not aware of you.

His actions are swift and unexpected. The spur
of the moment drives him. It was a momentary
irritation with Lord Salisbury that was the origin of
the Kruger telegram, perhaps the most momentous
and disastrous incident in the history of Europe in
our time, for it was the seed of all the bitterness of
after years. The telegram form, indeed, is the symbol
of his mental processes. He will become a guest at
your board at an hour's notice, and be the most light-
hearted boy at the table. When he entertained the
editors at luncheon at the Orangerie at Sans Souci he
said nothing about seeing them. The first intima-
tion they had was the vision as they sat taking their
coffee in the sunshine of the Kaiser riding up the steep
winding paths from the palace below, and in two
minutes he was among them, talking of the London

docks and the Hamburg docks, of the Lake District and Lord Lonsdale, with pleasant frankness and easy, idiomatic English. Then with a bright word of welcome to his country and his house, and with three salutes—a special mark of Imperial approval—he rode away.

Impulsive, imperious, dramatic, a militarist from his cradle, a statesman trained in " the indirect, crooked ways " of Bismarck, governed by one passion, the passion to make his land great and powerful, how can we cast his horoscope? Is he a menace or a safeguard? Let his past be his witness. For twenty years he has had the peace of Europe in his keeping and for twenty years not a German soldier has fallen in war. " We are a military people," said a Minister to me in Berlin, " but we are not a warlike people. It is you who are warlike without being military." And so we may say of the Kaiser. He is a militarist, but he is not a warrior. " There will be no war without grave cause while the Kaiser is on the throne," said the politician I have quoted. " He is distrusted by the warlike party—and remember that Germany has a considerable school of thinkers who believe in war philosophically as a national purgative. They believe he is timid. But the truth is he wants peace because it is his own and the nation's chief interest. Remember how he disappointed expectation when he came to the throne. Germany was on the verge of war with France and Russia combined, and Europe saw the accession of the youthful Kaiser, so hotheaded and impulsive, with fearful expectation. Here was a new Napoleon, filled with dreams of glory, armed with the most gigantic military weapon in history. And his first official words were words of peace; his first act to visit the European courts, returning with the message, 'I believe that, with the help of God, I have succeeded in ensuring the peace of the world for many years to come.' Set this and the record of his reign against those sudden ebullitions that seem so alarming, but are really only sound and fury, signifying nothing."

He keeps his powder dry and his armour bright. But he stands for peace—peace armed to the teeth, it is true; peace with the mailed fist; but peace nevertheless.

And so, as one watches him riding down the ranks at Potsdam in the bright sunshine, hears the morning greeting rapped out in sharp staccato, and sees his salute to the Empress watching the parade from the windows of the old palace, one feels confidence displacing distrust, and discerns beneath all this rattle of drums and love of the drama of government an undercurrent of purpose, making, it is true, for the aggrandisement of Germany, but making also for the peace of the world. If he fails in his policy of peace, it will be because of the incurable air of falsity that is the besetting vice of German policy—a policy which has been well described by the *Frankfurter Zeitung* as " incalculable, untrustworthy, and disturbing." It is a policy that always wears a mask, and a mask is a menace. Its words are smooth, but its acts are sinister and seem to have no relation to the words. It is a policy of cunning rather than of candour. It is incident to a government which is personal and secret, and Germany will not cease to be a disturbing element in world politics until the Kaiser has stepped down from his mediæval throne and derives his power from a free and self-governing people.

SIR EDWARD GREY

IF one were asked to say whose word carried the most weight in Parliament to-day, there could, I think, be only one answer. Whether in office or out of office, whether to friend or foe, Sir Edward Grey is intrinsically the weightiest speaker of his time. When he sits down in the House of Commons, it is as though discussion has ceased. Other men speak from the bar; he speaks from the bench. He does not argue; he delivers a judgment. There is no appeal, and no one asks for an appeal.

I remember a curious instance of this note of final authority. It was during the time when Mr. Balfour was holding his Ministry together by his arts of evasion and agility. The attack was hot and furious; the temper of the House high and passionate. But it seemed that nothing could tear away the veil of falsity behind which Mr. Balfour concealed his evolutions. Late at night Sir Edward Grey rose. It was as though a visitor from another planet had invaded the House. He spoke briefly, quietly, without heat, and without emotion. But it was as if the House had listened to a rebuke that was almost a sentence. Mr. Balfour was silenced. There seemed nothing to do but to go home.

If we seek for the source of this authority, we are struck, first, by the relative poverty of his equipment. There are many brilliant men in the House of Commons: Sir Edward Grey is not one of them. The stuff of his speech is plain to the point of homeliness. His thought is ordinary, almost conventional. He

Sir Edward Grey

never coins a phrase that sticks, nor wears a rhetorical flower in his button-hole. He has none of the arts of popular appeal. I remember him addressing a great provincial audience after the Fashoda crisis. It was an audience that had assembled to have its political partisanship stimulated. It sat in stony silence for an hour while Sir Edward told the story of Fashoda—about which the audience obviously did not care a rap—and praised Mr. Wyndham and the Conservatives for their conduct during the crisis. When he sat down the temperature of the meeting had fallen below freezing point, and only the fulminations of a local orator, whose poverty of aspirates was balanced by the richness of his enthusiasm, saved the occasion from utter failure. He is remarkable neither for learning nor ambition. His knowledge is limited, and his insularity a tradition. He never leaves the shores of England, and is reputed to have little French. He contrasts almost startlingly—to take an example—with Sir Charles Dilke, who is a citizen of the world, has been everywhere, knows everything, is like a well-kept office where you will find the minutest detail pigeon-holed for immediate reference. Nor has he the industry that corrects so many deficiencies in others. His love of leisure is as notorious as his love of tennis and of fishing. It is significant that the only book he has written is on the art of fly-fishing. He has no passion for politics. He seems a casual figure in the field of affairs, a spectator who is a little bored by its feverish activities and idle talk. You feel that he may leave it at any moment, and be discovered at home making trout flies.

It is this aloofness from life that is the key to his unique position. He comes into affairs, as it were, from the outside, detached, unimpassioned, bringing his own atmosphere with him. He has the large serenity of one who is at home in his own mind, draws his water from his own well, has that

> . . . inward light
> That makes the path before him always bright.

The passions of men, the cries of the market-place, the frenzy of the conflict do not touch him. He dwells outside them in a certain grave isolation. It is not that he is cold. His philosophy is not that of the Stoic, steeled to endurance of an implacable fate. It is rather the philosophy of the mind that " feeds on a wise passiveness," and finds in that food those large reserves of power that give his words their peculiar weight and his actions their stamp of authority.

There is a certain spaciousness and simplicity in his character that communicate a sense of abiding purpose to politics. He sees the landscape, as it were, from an elevation, and takes in its features in broad masses. His view of the forest is not obscured by the trees. There are richer minds in politics, more eager minds, more fertile minds; but there is no mind so secure and self-contained, so indifferent to external impulse, so firmly rooted in itself. His influence is not unlike that exercised by the late Duke of Devonshire. It is the influence of a character of absolute purity of motive and of unyielding independence of thought. It is the influence of one to whom the world can offer no bribe. There is nothing in its gift that he wants—neither power, nor praise, nor wealth. " His mind to him a kingdom is," and in that kingdom he finds full content.

In that kingdom, too, it is nature and not man which is his constant companion. He is wholly indifferent to society, and leaves the social and festive functions of his office to others, while he escapes to the quiet of that country cottage where, before his

tragic bereavement, he lived with his wife the simple
life he loves and where now he is happy in the companionship of natural things. His passion for nature
is, indeed, the keynote of his character. A colleague
of his in the Cabinet told me an incident illustrating
this rich and wholesome enthusiasm. The Session
of a certain year had been an unconscionable time
a-dying, and Sir Edward, yearning for the country,
had been held an unwilling captive to the dusty ways
of Westminster. At last he escaped, took the train
to Northumberland, and reached his home at Falloden
in the late evening. And, full of the joy of his recovered liberty, he ascended to the roof of his house
and spent the night amid

> The silence that is in the starry sky,
> The peace that is among the lonely hills,

until the dawn came up over the North Sea that beats
hard by against the rock-bound coast. It follows
almost naturally that his one literary enthusiasm is
for him who took men out " into the light of things,"
where Nature is the teacher. " I spent last night
with Grey," said a friend of his to me, " and we talked
of nothing but Wordsworth." It is significant, too,
that at a dinner of a literary club on one occasion,
the three authors he referred to as those " light-
hearted and happy " writers who give us recreation
when we are tired and have lost resource in ourselves
were Izaak Walton, Gilbert White, and Thomas Love
Peacock. Show me a man's books and I will tell
you his character.

He has the unhasting mind of the countryside. He
never flashes out in any sudden flame of enthusiasm.
He is slow to move; but he is slower still to speak.
The ball has reached the mark before you hear the
report. He is deaf alike to the prayers of friends and
the menaces of foes. He goes his own way, takes his

own time, declines to make any veiled promises in order to secure suspense of judgment. " They say. What say they? Let them say." When the thing is done he will speak—till then let the heathen furiously rage together. This reticence, so trying to the eager mind, invests him with a certain cloud of power that speech would dissipate. He is a hidden and implacable purpose. Sometimes that purpose, when disclosed, has the shock of dramatic surprise. For two years the friends of Macedonia had thundered at his gate in vain. He gave them no encouragement, was cold and apparently indifferent. Then one night, following a fierce onslaught by Mr. Masterman, which he waved aside without anger, almost with gentleness, he announced a policy which suddenly changed the whole situation, and revealed him taking a brave and high line with the Powers in the cause of a desolated people.

Less defensible was the muzzle he imposed on the House in the midst of the Denshawi shame. He represented the situation as too critical for discussion; but the truth, subsequently revealed, leaves one at a loss to understand that demand for silence from one whose tendency is to understate the facts. For it is clear that there was never any real peril. But, indeed, the whole of that dark story, with Sir Edward's defence of the officials, followed by the sudden resignation of Lord Cromer and the belated release of the wronged villagers who had escaped the scaffold, is obscure and disquieting.

Not less typical of his attitude of reserve towards Parliament was his silence as to the Russian agreement, which was never allowed to be discussed, and which, with apparently studied scorn, was published a few days after Parliament had risen. Sir Edward Grey's view of foreign affairs, indeed, is that it is a

close bureaucratic preserve into which he will allow
no impertinent trespassers. It is outside the field of
democracy. There is no right of way through his
woods, and he is the keeper with a gun. This is a
just view so far as the conduct of delicate negotiations
is concerned, but it is assailable when applied to the
spirit of national policy. Even Prince Bülow in
bureaucratic Germany seeks the endorsement of
Parliament, to which he explains his policy at least
with seeming frankness. But in democratic England
the Foreign Minister is silent as the Sphinx, looking
out over the desert of Parliament into infinity:

> Others abide our question: thou art free,
> We ask and ask: thou smilest and art still.

Sir Edward is, indeed, the least democratic, as he is
the least demonstrative of men. He belongs more
than any man to-day to the great Whig tradition—
the Whig tradition, touched by the strong personality
of Bishop Creighton, who was his tutor when that
great man held a parsonage in Northumberland, and
by the passionless spirit of the Balliol of Jowett. He
distrusts the irresponsible waywardness of public
opinion, with its quick emotions and passionate
transitions. "The public! the public! how many
fools does it take to make the public?" he seems to
say with a statesman of an earlier time. And yet,
perhaps, that is unjust, for there is no trace of bitterness in him, and his patrician view is free from the
taint of contempt or the airs of the superior person.
It sits on him naturally. He is to the manner born.
He takes his place at the high table without pushing
and without challenge. He is there by a sort of royal
authority, unconscious of itself, but imaged in the
bold sculpture of the face, the steady eye, and the
governing nose.

The unrivalled confidence which he commands in

the country is not wholly shared by those who regard
England as the banner-bearer in the cause of human
liberty.   For this cause he has done little.   His policy
is governed by a fixed idea—the idea that peace must
be preserved by having "friends" and that the Concert
of Europe is a creed outworn.   Under the inspiration
of this idea he has committed this country to the
support of the most reactionary government in Europe
and has given a tendency to events which is rapidly
hardening Anglo-German relations into a condition of
permanent antagonism.   The entente under him has
taken a sinister colour, and the inflexibility of his
mind, unqualified by large knowledge, swift appre-
hension of events or urgent passion for humanity,
constitutes a peril to the future.   His aims are high,
his honour stainless; but the slow movement of his
mind and his unquestioning faith in the honesty of
those on whom he has to rely render it easy for him
to drift into courses which a more imaginative sense
and a swifter instinct would lead him to question and
repudiate.

What of the future?   It depends partly on whether
the centre of gravity in Liberalism shifts to the right
or the left.   If to the right, then the highest place in
the State is within his scope, for though he is superficially little in sympathy with the eager spirit of the
new Liberalism, he is not essentially at variance with
it.   The Whig temperament is in him a restraint upon
the tongue rather than a restraint of thought.   His
views are often more advanced than his habit of
stating them.   But his love of the rod of the fisher-
man is greater than his love of the rod of Empire, and,
like Danton, he would probably hold that " it is better
to keep a flock of sheep upon the hillside than meddle
with the government of men."   One day, it may be,
he will shake the dust of Westminster from his feet

for ever, and then we shall know where to look for him. For he himself, I remember, pictured that happy time with delighted anticipation when replying on one occasion to a toast proposed by Mr. Churchill: " It is a time of unlimited leisure that we shall spend with old friends in a library. There is a garden outside the library, and, of course, a suitable river—not flowing too fast, nor, at the same time, flowing too slow, which is a worse fault. That will be the happiest time of all. I, in those days, shall have no thought of politics except to read the report of the brilliant speeches which Mr. Churchill will still be making in the House of Commons. Just think, those of you who are engaged in political occupations, what our libraries are now compared with what they will be when we get old—the quantities of clippings, the drawers full of opponents' speeches kept in the hope of being able to produce a quotation at an inconvenient moment; pamphlets and magazines by the hundredweight; blue books and Hansards by the ton. I think of the splendid time I shall have making a bonfire of them all. How I will stir the fire, and how I will mulch my rose trees with the ashes! "

It is a pleasant picture. We may fittingly leave him mulching his rose trees or going out with his rod to that delightful river which flows neither too fast nor too slow. A copy of the *Compleat Angler* peeps from one pocket, and *White's Selborne* from another, and around him is the great book of nature that never wearies. Perhaps in that serene solitude one will come to him as Maximian came to Diocletian, who had resigned the Imperial purple, asking him to resume the reins of government. " He rejected the temptation," says Gibbon, " with a smile of pity, calmly observing that if he could show Maximian the cabbages which he had planted with his own hand at

Prophets, Priests, and Kings

Salona he should no longer be urged to relinquish the enjoyment of happiness for the pursuit of power." I think I see Sir Edward showing his visitor his basket of trout and pointing to his rosebuds and the whispering woods as his answer to the appeal to return to the dusty strife of politics.

JAMES KEIR HARDIE

I AM not sure that when the historian of the future discusses our time he will not find the most significant event on that day in 1892 when James Keir Hardie rode up to Westminster from West Ham, clothed in cloth cap, tweed suit, and flannel shirt, and accompanied by a band. The world scoffed at the vulgarity, or shuddered at the outrage, according to its humour; but the event was, nevertheless, historic. It marked the emergence of a new force in politics. It was a prophet who came—a prophet in " ill-country clothes," wild-eyed, speaking in accents as rugged and uncouth as his garb.

A prophet you say — this dour demagogue a prophet? And why not? The prophet has always been dour and generally a demagogue. Even Cromwell, who had been to Cambridge, and was, among other things, a brewer, was both. Sir Philip Warwick, entering the House one day, and seeing him on his feet, has left his picture for all time—a gloomy-browed man, with harsh, discordant voice, dressed in ill-country clothes, and having a splash of blood on his collar. A most unamiable figure to the polite mind of the Cavalier; but a prophet, a rock on which the ship of the Cavaliers was to go to pieces. And, whether you like him or not, Keir Hardie was a rock, too, in those days when he stood, gloomy and alone, in the midst of the Amalekites. It needed such a man for such a rôle.

The prophet is never a comfortable person. He would not be a prophet if he were. " Tammas is gey ill to live wi'," said Carlyle's mother of her famous son; and Mr. Keir Hardie, who shares Carlyle's rage with the world as well as Carlyle's dialect and gloomy brow, is " gey ill to live wi'," too. He glowers at life from beneath his mournful eyebrows, and he confounds us all in one universal malediction. He shrinks from contact with Society as from the touch of contamination. It is the quality of gilt as well as of pitch to defile. He will not be defiled by the gilt of the prosperous. You will never find a dress shirt under the red tie of Keir Hardie. He will never be petted by Princes and Peers.

He is the pit-lad of politics. He refuses to be anything else, for he has none of the spirit of Smiles' *Self-Help*. It is true that, outwardly, his career fulfils all the conditions of a Smiles hero. He went down the pit shaft, a little lad of eight, to win his bread. He never had a day's schooling. His mother taught him to read, but he was seventeen before he could write his name. He taught himself shorthand, practising the characters on the face of the coal seam where he worked. He read Carlyle and Stuart Mill, and came out of the pit at twenty-three with an idea, a purpose, a vision. He would be an Ishmaelite. He would create a party of political Ishmaelites, and with them he would march into the fat pastures of Canaan and challenge the ancient tyrants—a fierce, intractable man, his hand against every man, and every man's hand against him.

To-day his dream is accomplished. Whether titular leader or not, he is the chief figure and inspirer of that group of which he was the " first begetter." But success has not been crowned with the reward that attended the Smiles hero, whose hardships were admirable because they led to plenty and the companionship of the great. Mr. Keir Hardie has had no

James Keir Hardie

visible reward. I do not think he wants reward. His home is still in the little cottage at Cumnock, where he was once a pit-lad, and in London you must still seek him in that lodging in the ancient house off Fetter Lane, where, when he first sought a room, the good landlady, scanning the rough figure, demanded references, and was placated by the names of half a dozen members of Parliament. He clings to his poverty with the pride of a Highland chieftain.

For he is proud with the secretive pride of his country. The vanity of the Englishman is flagrant and assertive. It displays itself with the frankness of a child, and expires at a sneer. But the pride of the Scotsman hugs itself close. It is like the camomile: the more it is trodden on the better it grows. It asks for no recognition. It is self-contained. Flattery cannot exalt it; inappreciation cannot wound it. It never comes to the surface, and is most happy when it is most misunderstood. When Mr. Keir Hardie was entering the House one day a policeman stopped him. "Are you at work here, mate?" he asked. "Yes," was the laconic reply. "On the roof?" "No, on the floor." And he passed in, happy in the pride that would not reveal itself. An Englishman would have wanted the policeman's number, and would have had his day embittered by wounded vanity. And I can imagine that the happiest moment Mr. Hardie ever had was when he was arrested in Brussels in mistake for Rubino, the assassin. I think he would rejoice to be hanged as the wrong man. The knowledge that he was right and his executioners were wrong would fill his last moments with a sombre joy.

He is, too, the most typical Scotsman in the House, in appearance and outlook. He is "the Knight of the Rueful Countenance." His face is cast in a tragic

83

Prophets, Priests, and Kings

mould, and his temperament has the gloom of Calvinism and the severity of the Shorter Catechism. When your eye passes from the cheerful Irishmen behind him to his sad and foreboding figure, you recall a passage in one of Scott's letters: "While a Scotchman is thinking about the term day, or, if easy on that subject, about hell in the next world—while an Englishman is making a little hell in the present because his muffin is not well toasted—Pat's mind is always turned to fun and ridicule." There is no fun and ridicule about Mr. Keir Hardie, and the perfectibility of his muffin leaves him uncheered. He has a soul too sorrowful to be moved by muffins. His figure brings up the vision of the Covenanters and that grey Galloway land, "where about the graves of the martyrs the whaups are crying." One seems to see him out-rivalling Habakkuk Mucklewrath in the dark frenzy of his declamation, and rushing to the attack at Bothwell Brig with damnatory psalms upon his lips.

The child-man of Plato's fancy who had come to maturity in some dark cave and suddenly emerged into the light of day was intoxicated by the glory and splendour of the universe. He was filled with wonder at the miracle which we have ceased to see. When Mr. Keir Hardie emerged from the pit he was filled with wonder, too. But it was wonder at the fantastic disorder of society, at a world in which realities are buried deep beneath a cake of custom and convention, where we see not the *thing*, but the appearance; not the cause, but the effect, and where the point of view is still that of the " Northern Farmer."

'Tisn't them as has money that breeäks into houses and steals,
Them as has cooäts to their backs and taäkes their regular
    meeäls:
Naw, it's them as nivver knaäws wheer a meeäl's to be had—
Taäke my word for it, Sammy, the poor in a loomp is bad.

James Keir Hardie

He has kept the freshness of that first revelation. The wonder light is still in his eye. Contact with the world has not blurred his sight. He remains a seer, not dazzled by shows; but with his eye fixed on realities. It was not rudeness that he intended when, on a memorable occasion, he spoke of bigamy in a certain connection. It was that his eye penetrated the polite fiction, and came to the plain, human fact. And when he attacked the late Lord Salisbury in connection with some slum revelations, and said, " I would not remain a member of a club which admitted his lordship to membership," he was not insolent, or even humorous, though the world laughed at the joke. He simply saw the naked fact. The circumstance that it was a Prime Minister who owned slum property did not make the fact less flagrant, but more.

I have been told by one who was present that his animus towards the Liberal Party dates from a meeting when a local Liberal of consequence refused to go on the platform if the irreconcilable miner's agent were allowed to be on the platform too, and when he was left to nurse his wrath outside. But he never was and never could be a Liberal. He is a rebel ridden by a theory. Liberalism stands for the adaptation of existing society to new needs: he stands for the recreation of society. Toryism is an ally. It stands for the old structure, crumbling and decayed. It makes his task possible; while Liberalism, by making the structure habitable and watertight, defeats his dream.

Of the three Socialist leaders of European reputation, he is the most doctrinaire. Jaurès has the statesman's outlook, and applies his theories to the practical criticism of Government. Bebel is a man of affairs. He revels in the fight. As he talks to you his eye twinkles with merriment and sly enjoyment.

Prophets, Priests, and Kings

He is always happy, always sanguine. A pleasant, human man, enjoying the drama of politics, with its cut and thrust, its humours and its gravities. Mr. Keir Hardie is solitary and menacing—an embodied theory.

He is not a politician or a statesman. He is a fanatic. The politician must temporise and compromise. He yields as little as he can, and takes as much as he can. He studies the weather, and is governed by the seasons. He equivocates and waits upon circumstance. The fanatic knows nothing of this opportunism. The thunder is always on his brow, the lightning always in his eye, the fire at his heart always smouldering into flame. He is a man obsessed with an idea. It gives him no rest, and he gives you no rest. Hence Mr. Keir Hardie's failure as a Parliamentarian. He has none of the plasticity necessary for the man of affairs. He is stiff and irreconcilable. He is indifferent to detail. He has no gratitude for small mercies. His eye is on the far-off vision. He is the only man who could have created the Labour Party, for concentration and intensity are the creative impulses. But he is almost the only man in the party who is not fitted to lead it. It is plain, common-sense men like Mr. Shackleton and Mr. Henderson, and astute politicians like Mr. Ramsay Macdonald who have made it a political instrument. His party is not as himself. He is as isolated in it as when he stood alone in the House. For no party can exist on anathema and prophecy. A cause comes into being at the breath of the prophet, and then leaves him in the desert.

It goes without saying that there is a strain of poetry in him, for no poetry, no idealism. The prophet must not only see the naked fact; he must have the visionary gleam. It goes without saying,

Alfred Tennyson

James Keir Hardie

too, that it is the poetry of Burns, with its fierce democratic passion and its exaltation of the humble and the sincere, that appeals most to him. One who heard him lecture on Burns told me that it revealed to him a world of unsuspected tenderness and emotion in the heart of this rugged, uncompromising man. But, indeed, it must be so. It is the fierce antipathies of the theorist that the world sees; but deep down in his heart these antipathies are seen to have their roots in a sympathy as fierce—the sympathy with the class from which he sprang, and which he has never deserted. He hates the palace because he remembers the pit.

LORD NORTHCLIFFE

I WAS talking one day in the garden of a friend of mine on the subject of Stevenson, when he brought forth a file of *Young Folks* for 1881, containing the " Sea Cook," and another for 1884, in which appeared the " Black Arrow." Turning the yellow pages, he casually pointed to an article, one of a series, on " Amateur Photography."

" There," said he, " are the modest beginnings of greatness. To-day the writer of that humble article is master of the *Times*, a member of the House of Lords, owner of half the papers you see in the hands of the people, the Napoleon of the Press; whether you like it or not, the most influential man in this country." For the name under the article was " Alfred C. Harmsworth." " How has it been done? " he asked. " What manner of man is this Lord Northcliffe? "

" I have," I said, " the privilege of not knowing Lord Northcliffe. I am that miracle in these days, a journalist who has never been through his mill, never written a line for him, nor met him, nor, except when he has been in the Peers' Gallery of the House of Commons, even seen him. I am therefore well qualified to answer your question, for I can view him without any personal emotion, which, I believe, is a rare thing in a journalist. Lord Northcliffe is the type of ' the man in the street.' There is no psychological mystery to be unravelled here, no intellectual shadow land. He is obvious and elementary—a man who understands material success

88

and nothing else. He has no other standard by which to judge life. Napoleon's question was, ' What have you done? ' Lord Northcliffe's question would be, ' What have you got? ' For he not only wants success himself; he admires it in others. It is the passport to his esteem. It is the thing he understands. If you will watch his career you will see that, as far as he has a philosophy at all, it is this, that merit rides in a motor-car. You become interesting to him, as Johnson became interesting to Chesterfield, immediately you have succeeded. When he went down to that memorable meeting at Glasgow at which Mr. Chamberlain formally opened his fiscal campaign, he changed his policy in a night. His papers had been full of denunciations of what he had christened ' the Stomach Tax '; but this meeting, so great and so enthusiastic, seemed the presage of success. He was going to be left in company with that dismal thing, failure. The thing was unthinkable, and he leapt the fence on the instant. For he believes with Mr. Biglow that

> A merciful Providence fashioned us hollow,
> In order thet we might our princerples swallow.

The one principle to which his loyalty never falters is to be on the side of the big battalions.

" This habit of swift decision, dictated without regard to principle, is the key to his success. He carries no intellectual or moral impedimenta, has no sentiment, is subject to no theory, holds no view of life. He simply asks, ' What will win? ' and then, to quote Mr. Biglow again, ' goes inter it baldheaded.' He is, in a word, the Stock Exchange man in the sphere of journalism. He represents the conquest of Fleet Street by Capel Court. Go on the Stock Exchange and you will find it crowded with Lord

Northcliffes, men of that rapid, decisive type who bull and bear with happy indifference to intrinsic merit, and to whom the issues of peace and war are of importance only as they affect the price of stock and shares.

"When Lord Northcliffe set out to feed the war flame in South Africa, he did so, I think, without any real feeling against the Boers. He is not, I fancy, a man who bears malice. For to bear malice involves attachment to some point of view, indicates some reality of character. Had the Boers won he would probably have written them a letter of congratulation. But the mood of the country was high and turbulent. We were full of

> Such boastings as the Gentiles use,
> And lesser breeds without the law.

And his conception of journalism is to give the public the meat it craves for. If it wants a war, then it is his duty to paint the enemy black and horrific; if it wants a sensation, then it is his task to provide it. Does the temper of the moment demand the immolation of France, then he is the fiercest of Francophobes:

If the French cannot cease their insults (he says in 1899), their Colonies will be taken from them and given to Germany and Italy. . . . The French have succeeded in thoroughly convincing John Bull that they are his inveterate enemies. . . . England has long hesitated between France and Germany. But she has always respected the German character, whereas she has gradually come to feel a contempt for France. . . . Nothing like an *entente cordiale* can subsist between England and her nearest neighbour.

Does the mood change and Germany become the object of national suspicion, then who so ready to throw faggots on the flame:

Yes, we detest the Germans and we detest them cordially (he says in 1903). They render themselves odious to the whole of Europe. I would not tolerate that anyone should print in my journal the least thing which might to-day wound France; but, on the other hand, I would not like anyone to insert anything that could please Germany.

Lord Northcliffe

" He blots out the foolish word ' consistency ' from his bright lexicon and repudiates his yesterdays with fearless indifference to criticism. He knows that the mob has no memory and only asks for its daily sensation with its daily bread. And so in the midst of the great German panic, his newspapers made our flesh creep with their revelations of Germany's designs, and Mr. Robert Blatchford was engaged to reduce us to the last pit of fear. Then, the mood of the public being exhausted, he turned and slew the monster of his own invention. He went to Berlin, and from thence sent to his paper a sublime reproof of our silly behaviour, and told us that all Germany was laughing at our panic-stricken folly. Such agility leaves one breathless.

" He, in fact, regards himself simply as the purveyor of a popular commodity. If the public taste changes, then he is the man to change with it, for he is wedded to no old clothes. He is, truly considered, a humble-minded person. His opinions are of so little consequence that he is always prepared to adopt those of other people, provided that they represent the majority. In 1904, when the Progressives looked like winning, he supported them; in 1907, when they were certain to lose, he filled his papers with fantastic stories of their misdeeds. It was not that he disagreed with them, for disagreement implies convictions of some sort. It was simply that he was with the crowd. He backs an opinion as he would back a horse—because he believes it will win. He reminds me of that story of Lord Chancellor Thurlow and the Nonconformist deputation that went to him to protest against some unjust advantage he had given to the Established Church. ' Why,' asked the deputation, ' do you always show this partiality for the Established Church? ' ' I show partiality for the

Established Church,' said Thurlow, ' because it *is* established. Get your —— sect established and then I'll show partiality to you.'

" It is this absolutely commercial conception of journalism which is Lord Northcliffe's contribution to his time. Journalism was a profession: he has made it a trade. It had a moral function: in his hands it has no more moral significance than the manufacture of soap. The old notion in regard to a newspaper was that it was a responsible adviser of the public. Its first duty was to provide the news, uncoloured by any motive, private or public; its second to present a certain view of public policy which it believed to be for the good of the State and the community. It was sober, responsible, and a little dull. It treated life as if it was a serious matter. It had an antiquated respect for truth. It believed in the moral governance of things.

" Lord Northcliffe has changed all this. He started free from all convictions. He saw an immense unexploited field. The old journalism appealed only to the minds of the responsible public; he would appeal to the emotions of the irresponsible. The old journalism gave news; he would give sensation. The old journalism gave reasoned opinion; he would give unreasoning passion. When Captain Flanagan, from the calm retreat of the debtors' prison, was drawing up the prospectus of the *Pall Mall Gazette*, he said proudly that it ' would be written by gentlemen for gentlemen.' Lord Northcliffe conceived a journal which, in Lord Salisbury's phrase, was ' written by office-boys for office-boys.' It was a bitter saying; but Lord Northcliffe has had his revenge. He, Lord Salisbury's ' office-boy ' of journalism, was raised to the peerage by Lord Salisbury's nephew.

" It was not the only case in which time passed an

ironic comment on Lord Salisbury's views on the Press. When Gladstone repealed the stamp duty and made the penny paper possible, Lord Robert Cecil asked scornfully what good thing could come out of a penny paper. A cheap Press, like an enlarged franchise, meant to his gloomy and fatalistic mind ' red ruin and the breaking up of laws.' And he lived to see himself kept in power by the democracy which he had feared, and deriving his support from the half-penny press, at which he would have shuddered. He lived, in fact, to realise that there is a better way with the office-boy than to drive him into revolutionary movements. It is to give him a vote and the *Daily Mail*.

" I have said that Lord Northcliffe is the man in the street, that is, that his mind is always in tune with the mood of the populace. You see it in this article in *Young Folks*. Amateur photography had just become popular. He, a lad of eighteen, seized on it as a stepping-stone to fortune. A little later came the boom in cycling, and Master Harmsworth, still in his teens, became a cycling journalist in Coventry. Sir George Newnes had touched the great heart of humanity with *Tit-Bits*, and Mr. Harmsworth, now a man of twenty-one, felt that here was a field for his genius also. He, too, would tell men that the streets of London, put end to end, would stretch across the Atlantic, and that there were more acres in Yorkshire than letters in the Bible. Why should he conceal these truths? Why should the public thirst for knowledge be denied? And so, in an upper room in the neighbourhood of the Strand, *Answers* came to birth, the prolific parent of some hundred, or, perhaps, two hundred—I am not sure which—offspring, ranging from the *Funny Wonder* to the *Daily Mail*, all bearing the impress of the common mind in an uncommon degree, the freedom from ideas, the love of the irrelevant and the trivial, the admiration for the flagrant and the loud, the divorce from all the sobrieties and sanities of life. The fate of the *Times* was long in doubt, and the secret of its new control was carefully concealed. But one day it appeared with several columns describing the dress at some society ' function,' Lady Midas' wonderful creation from Worth's, and the Duchess of Blankshire's rapturous pearls, and I knew the touch of the master-hand. The marvellous ' office-boy ' had no more worlds left to conquer.

" Perhaps the crucial moment of his life was that day in the early nineties, when a young man who had been a reporter on the *Birmingham Daily Mail*, and afterwards on the *Sun*, called on him with a scheme. The *Evening News* was for sale, and the enterprising young man had got the refusal of it, and gave Mr. Harmsworth twelve hours to decide whether he would buy it, his own reward being the editorship and a share in the business. So far Mr. Harmsworth had only adorned the sphere of ' tit-bit ' journalism. He seized this opportunity to serve his country in a larger sphere, and out of that day's work came the *Daily Mail*, with which the ideals of American journalism were brought into our midst, and all the multitude of daily papers with which he has endowed us. He is, you see, a man of bold and swift decisions. When he found the women did not want a women's daily paper, he changed it in a night into a halfpenny picture paper. And instantly he found his way to the feminine heart. He is doubtful whether women want votes; but he discovered that they do want pictures, ' stuck in anyhow, with hardly any words at all.'

" He has adroitness too. When the *Daily Tele-*

Lord Northcliffe

graph started a Sunday issue, he followed suit. Instantly there was a great outcry in the country against the Sunday newspaper. To that outcry Lord Burnham and Lord Northcliffe bowed with grave professions of respect for religious opinion. Subsequently Lord Northcliffe purchased two Sunday papers already existing, and nothing was said, though we may assume that Lord Burnham thought a good deal. There are few earlier birds about than Lord Northcliffe.

"He touches nothing that he does not—shall we say?—adorn. The note of his mind is over all he does. I was looking the other day at one of his multitudinous publications—a children's cyclopædia. It contained a picture of the solar system, the sun blazing in the centre and the planets careering round it. And each planet was depicted by a motor-car! He can make even the splendours of the midnight sky speak in the terms of the momentary and sordid earth. No doubt the men sitting in those motor-cars were reading the *Daily Mail*. I am told that in his office he has a favourite phrase about 'the shop window.' 'What is wrong with the shop window to-day?' he will say, as he points to the offending issue. It is an eloquent phrase. He is the "shop window" journalist. The sign over the journalist's office in the old days was 'Marchand d'idées.' Now it is 'The Latest Novelties,' and the editor is the chief shop-walker. Is your mood for conquest? Then here is the material to feed your hate or your fear of the foreigner. Is health the craze of the moment? Then 'Standard Bread' becomes a gospel more urgent than the Decalogue. Are you tired of panics and in need of nature's balm? Then the shop window is aflame with sweet peas and we are all turned out into our gardens to engage in a feverish competition for the finest blooms and the biggest prizes.

" He is all that is summed up in that desolating word 'smart,' He is a 'smart' man, the representative man of a 'smart' age. It is an age which, if it has ever heard of Lord Courtney, regards him only as a dull old gentleman who bores you with talk about principles. It delights in the man who will advertise himself in twelve-foot letters. It worships success, however it is achieved. You may be exposed as often as you like: all will be forgiven if only you will be smart. You may espouse one cause to-day and another to-morrow, one cause here and another there: it does not matter so long as you do it with effrontery and success. And its patriotism is that strange, inverted thing which makes 'Little Englander' a phrase of withering reproach, as though to love England were impious.

" It is not that it believes the wrong things: it is that it has ceased to believe anything. Its drama is the music-hall; its moral teacher Mr. Hall Caine; its instructor the inspired office-boy. As I came along in the Tube to see you, I took notice of the papers in the people's hands. The fat gentleman on one side of me was reading the *Globe*; the slim lady on the other the *Daily Mirror*; the smart office-boy in front the *Daily Mail*; the meek person next the *Sunday Companion*; the lad in the corner *Comic Cuts*. There were *Evening Newses*, and *Red Magazines*, *Puck*, and the *World*. The papers were different, but the accents were one. Where Lord Northcliffe was not, there was Mr. C. Arthur Pearson, his pale shadow. The revolution is complete. The old journalism is dead, the voice of *Answers* speaks in the thunders of the *Times*, and Lord Northcliffe 'bestrides the world like a Colossus,' the type of power without the sense of responsibility—of material success without moral direction."

.   .   .   .

" You have spoken truly," said the other, " though I think Watts has put the thing more tersely in his picture of ' Mammon.' But you paint the time too gloomily. It is a time of change and disturbance and fickleness and strange forms come to the surface; but out of the welter the new England is emerging with a new social gospel and a new vision. Lord Northcliffe, with his shop-window novelties, is but a transition phase. He is only the echo of the passing mood and the shallow craze. The great movement is coming from below and is independent of all the inanities of the press. Be of good cheer. We are a people yet. . . . And now to resume. When I met Stevenson at Bournemouth . . ."

DR. CLIFFORD

WHEN Mr. Balfour said that what he did not like about Dr. Clifford was his "style," he expressed the vital difference between himself and his critic. They are as East and West, "and never the twain shall meet." Mr. Balfour lives in an atmosphere of æsthetic emotion, delicately sensuous, soft, and languorous. One pictures him on a couch of rose-leaves in a chamber where the colour harmonies are perfect and no fierce disturbing light breaks in. The air is soft and aromatic, and from behind the curtains comes the tender breathing of lute and viol. He feels a harsh note like a blow; a false accent in voice or colour or gesture afflicts him with physical distress. One would expect him to flee, hands to ears, from the violence of Tchaikowsky's " 1812," or the poignant humanity of Beethoven, and to find refuge in the dream world of Chopin or the Watteau land-scapes of Gluck. To such a temperament, life is neither a tragedy nor a comedy: it is an emotion. It is not a battle, but a dream vision; not a shattering reality, but a tone poem.

Into that atmosphere the Puritan bursts like a bombshell in the garden of old Khayyám. He is terribly in earnest, and there is nothing so distressing to the æsthete as earnestness. You cannot have a flawless tone poem with an earnest man about. You cannot enjoy your book of verse beneath the bough if a fierce person breaks in upon you with violent gesticulations, declaring that the City of Destruction is in flames and that you have got to go and help with the fire-engine.

Dr. Clifford

To the Puritan, life is not an emotion to be enjoyed, but a conflict to be won, and he distrusts those sensuous decorations that distract the mind from the spiritual warfare. He is happiest when the battle is fiercest, and I can imagine that Dr. Clifford must sometimes lament that he was born two and a half centuries too late. Had he lived in the great days of the Puritans, how joyously would he have had his ears cropped, with what hymns and psalms and spiritual songs he would have rushed to battle, and, when the victory was won, what sermons he would have preached as the sun went down on the carnage of the battle-field! Cromwell's eye would have singled him out for swift promotion. He would have been one of those " russet-coated captains " whom he loved. He would have had him by him when he told the Rev. Mr. Hytch in Ely Cathedral to " cease his fooling and come down," and I see him in the grey dawn of that day at Dunbar turning to him to give the keynote of the battle song, and young Clifford—now a colonel of the Ironsides—lifts his voice:

> Let God arise and scatter-ed
> Let all his enemies be.

He would have sat in judgment at Whitehall upon " the man, Charles Stuart," and would have spent his old age in preaching secretly in out-of-the-way conventicles, in prison oft, in the pillory and the stocks more often, harried from parish to parish, a stern, invincible old warrior waiting for the return of the saints and keeping the lamp trimmed and burning through the riotous night of the Restoration.

For he is the last of the Puritans. When Oxford and Cambridge opened their doors to Dissenters they ended the true Puritan strain. They infused into its strenuous intensity the subtle influences of an atmosphere of taste and culture. They softened the severe outlines, added light and shade, nuance and tone, where formerly the character was simple and sharply defined. To grace in the Puritan sense they have added the graces in the Cavalier sense.

Dr. Clifford is the type of the Nonconformist minister of the old days of proscription and disability, with all the merits and all the defects of the stern school out of which he came. He is a man who has carved himself with his own jack-knife—his University, Cassell's *Popular Educator*, which he bought in penny numbers—and his rugged personality bears the splendid impress of that unaided workmanship. He came from the people, and he belongs to the people in a sense in which, perhaps, he could not have belonged had not the Catechism stood in his path to Oxford. For when the little son of the warp machiner at Sawley, in Derbyshire, was sent to the National School, the master, attracted by his capacity, promised to get him to Oxford. But the Puritan father was not to be bribed by Oxford. He would have no Catechisms taught his son. " John," he would say, " I'll not have you tell a lie. You must not talk of your godfathers and godmothers when you haven't got any." And so, instead of going to Oxford, he went, at the age of ten, into a lace mill, where he advanced from the position of a " jacker off " to that of a " thredder." " As thredder," he will tell you, " I had to work in a gang preparing the ' carriages ' and the ' bobbins ' for the big machines. If we fell behind, the machines would be delayed, so that we often had to keep at it far into the night, with the foreman setting one gang to compete with another. Our food was sent to us from home—coffee in a tin, bread with a bit of cheese, perhaps, or butter, though butter seldom, for we still felt the effect of the Corn

Laws. Meat possibly once a week." It was a hard school, in which the character was hammered out strong, real, and enduring, or shattered in the process.

But if he is the last of the Puritans in character, equipment, and temperament, he has none of the harshness of the Calvinist theology. He is all for the sanctity of conscience and the right of private judgment in the affairs of the soul. He will impose no creeds on anyone, not even on his Church. His own faith is still as clear and primitive as when, sixty years ago, he sat a boy in Beeston Chapel, in " much mental anguish," and in his own words experienced conversion in the midst of the singing of the verse:

> The soul that longs to see My face
> Is sure My love to gain;
> And those that early seek My grace
> Shall never seek in vain.

But he is for the spirit and not for the letter. He will not make his own faith the measure of his neighbour's, and when Charles Spurgeon began his " Downgrade " controversy, and sought to rivet anew the Calvinistic dogma on the Baptist Church, it was John Clifford, then President of the Baptist Union, who fought the battle of liberation and won. " I do not object to creeds as statements of belief," he said. " It is coercion through and by creeds that I object to." He was willing, and even assisted, to formulate a declaration of the Church's faith; but beyond that he would not go. He would not apply it as a test to the individual conscience. " Creed " or " Declaration " became the issue, and Spurgeon passed out of the Baptist Church with his Calvinist doctrines and his assertion of the verbal inspiration of the Bible, while Dr. Clifford remained within victorious. And so, when Mr. Campbell raised the waters with his " New Theology," it was Dr. Clifford, almost alone among Nonconformist leaders, who took his stand by him, in sympathy not with his views, but with liberty of thought.

Hatred of creeds and passion for the freedom of an awakened conscience are the two motives that actuate him. "How long is it," asks Holmes, "since religion was such an invalid that it could only go out in a closed carriage with a gentleman in a black suit and a white tie on the box?" Dr. Clifford insists that religion is an active pedestrian who wants plenty of light and moorland air. He will not sit on the box, nor wear a white tie, nor call himself "Reverend," nor name any man heretic. He believes, with Renan's Ebrew Jew, that *On fait ce qu'on veut, mais on croit ce qu'on peut.* He has no fear of consequences if only men will think. It is not unbelief, but non-belief; not the conscience that questions, but the conscience that is atrophied, that he assails. "Think for yourselves," he cries. "If you find that it is not rational to be a Christian, then be not a Christian; but reflect well before you decide." He is the antithesis of those Christians who, in Swift's phrase, have "just enough religion to hate each other." He is all tolerance. He does not deliver the law from an infallible throne; but comes down, as it were, into the market-place and talks the thing out with you, a plain man like yourself, offering you his opinion and seeking yours. Hence his attraction for all sorts and conditions of men, his long friendship with Freethinkers like Holyoake, and his monthly "Question-Nights," when he meets all assailants on a common ground, not avoiding contradiction, but seeking it. "You must understand a man's doctrine before you attack it" is his axiom.

He has the serenity and the unconquerable optimism of the man who believes in the moral sovereignty of the world. "Personalities pass and disappear," he cries, "but the principle of justice is eternal. Ignorant men may nail it to the Cross, but the third day it rises again and mounts to heaven." And this triumph of the spirit of righteousness is reflected in the life of men. "Our lecturer thinks the world is getting better," said a Social Democrat at the close of an address. "Now, I don't think it is." "But I *know* it is," replied Dr. Clifford. "I know that when I was ten I was called at six o'clock in the morning to go and work twelve or fourteen hours in a lace factory, and I know that no boy of ten will be called at six to-morrow morning to be forced to work in any factory in the land."

His mind is all daylight. There are no subtle half-tones, or sensitive reserves, or significant shadows of silence; no landscape fading through purple mists to a romantic distance. All is clear, obvious, emphatic. There is little atmosphere and a lack of that humour that softens the contours of controversy. His thought is direct and simple, and makes its appeal, not to culture, but to the primitive emotions. He is probably the best popular orator in England. The strenuousness which is so distasteful to Mr. Balfour is a battle-cry to the crowd. He keeps his passion white hot; his body works like a windmill in a hurricane; his eyes flash lightnings; he seizes the enemy, as it were, by the throat, pommels him with breathless blows, and throws him aside a miserable wreck. In the pulpit his slight, bent form moves restlessly to and fro: he fixes someone with his glittering eye; argues with him, as it were; wrestles with him; poses him with questions; draws back to make a point; leaps forward, and explodes. *Punch* declares that he wears two cravats, one in front and one behind, so that in the midst of his passionate speeches the one behind can take the place of that in front. In the case of a long speech the cravat behind recovers its position in front, having made a complete tour of the Doctor. This, of course, is an exaggeration; but he *is* energetic.

This moral and intellectual strenuousness makes him the symbol of all that is hateful to the foe. He is pictured as a bitter, intolerant, assertive man. He is, in fact, one of the gentlest, most humble-minded men I have known, simple and unaffected, merry as a child and delighting in children, easily imposed on by the melting tale, overflowing with generous sympathy, entirely free from all personal bitterness. It is the custom of the meaner part of the Press to gibe at his degree, to represent him as a charlatan flaunting a sham honour. " Dr." indeed! Does it come from Oxford or Cambridge? Not at all. From Bates University, in the United States. And at the oft-told tale there is a gust of scornful laughter. And there's an end of " Dr." Clifford.

It is a foolish and ungenerous taunt. If Oxford and Cambridge have not offered him the honour, so much the worse for Oxford and Cambridge. He does not ask it, did not ask it of Bates University, has never himself used it. But what man of our time has a higher claim to recognition from any seat of learning or worth? What story is more fascinating, more full of wholesome stimulus, than that of his eager pursuit of knowledge under difficulties—working in the mill all day, studying far into the night; taking—now a youth—his theological course at Leicester, and, having started on that fifty years' ministry at West-bourne Park, not sinking down into a comfortable rut, but setting out bravely to London University to lay the foundations that circumstances had denied him. And well he laid them, working all the time

Dr. Clifford

at his pastorate—B.A. in 1861; B.Sc., with honours in Logic, Moral Philosophy, Geology, and Palæontology, in 1862; M.A., first of his year, in 1864; LL.B., with honours in the Principles of Legislation, in 1866.

Nothing to blush for here, is there? And then add to it those fifty years spent in tireless and unselfish labour for all noble human causes; in the front rank of every fight against tyranny and intolerance, whether in the spiritual or the political sphere, whether in London or Africa; loving truth and justice even more than religion and piety; a great citizen, a great patriot; spending himself ungrudgingly for the reward of a head clerk; as poor at the end, save for the modest competence presented to him by his admirers on his seventieth birthday, as at the beginning. " What is your fee? " asked the secretary at the close of a lecture in a remote part of England. " My third-class fare," he answered.

There are few lives that one would rather have lived than this—a life rich in unselfish service that has kept his roots watered and his branches green, so true is it that " what I gave I have." You may dislike his style, you may find the note too strident for your sensitive taste, you may resent the moral maxim and the passionate truism; but do not pride yourself upon living in the atmosphere of an artificial culture in which no man of breeding talks of principles, and in which the ripeness of emotion passes insensibly into the rottenness of moral decadence. For there is a far worse cant than the cant of morality, and that is the cant of culture. No nation was ever kept sweet and vital by moral opiates, and it is because he is a bracing tonic in a time of moral slackness that John Clifford ranks among the chief assets of our day.

JOHN REDMOND

WHEN I first looked down upon the House of Commons there was one figure that above all others touched the imagination. He sat in the corner seat below the gangway, cold, isolated, silent, a man nursing his gloomy wrath and his unconquerable hope. The sad eyes looked out with a sleepless passion from under the level and lowering brows. He affected you like the thunder-cloud. Presently, you felt, the forked lightning would leap out of the gloom and strike the offending earth. He held you by the fascination of the unknown. He was a dark secret—an idea incarnate. Near by him sat a young man of Napoleonic profile, the Roman nose boldly sculptured, the chin firm, rounded, protruding, the eye full and fearless. To-day that young man, young no longer, sits in the corner seat. The thunder-cloud has vanished. Instead there is something of the warmth and generosity of frank comradeship with the House.

For Parnell was the symbol of Ireland's despair and Ireland's hate; Mr. Redmond is the symbol of Ireland's hope and Ireland's expansiveness. He is the leader in a happier day. The sky has cleared, and the end is in view. The old passions have passed away, and with the new and more humane and enlightened spirit has come the need of a new leadership. It required Parnell's fierce intensity to create the cause, and to carry it through the wilderness; it needs another strategy to enter the promised land. Parnell was the incomparable guerilla chief, mysterious, secret, elusive, touching the imagination of his followers to a sort of frenzy of devotion; Mr. Redmond is the commander-in-chief of a regular army, pursuing his campaign in the open country according to the laws of Parliamentary strategy. He is not a dictator; he is the head of a staff.

Mr. Redmond could not wear the rebel robe, for his genius is Parliamentary and constitutional. He is, indeed, one of the ablest Parliamentarians in the House. He has the spirit of Parliament in his blood. Four generations of his family have sat in the House, and he himself learned the rules as a clerk in the House, and later by breaking them in those thrilling days when the duty of every Irish member was to smash the machine of government. When he rises in his spacious, authoritative way the House has that air of silence and respect which it only wears in the presence of a master. It is difficult to remember that this grave, senatorial figure, who comes into action with waving banners and measured pomp, learned the art of war in the fierce school of faction and rebellion. His baptism was in blood. It was in 1880 that he made his first appearance in politics side by side with Parnell. He accompanied the chief on the platform at Enniscorthy, in his native Wexford, when Parnell was pelted with rotten eggs and brutally attacked. Parnell remained impassive through it all. "When an egg struck him on the head," said Mr. Redmond in telling the story, "he never even raised his hand to brush it off, but calmly went on with his speech. Afterwards in the hotel he took his lunch as calmly while a tailor stitched his torn trousers." Later on that memorable day young Redmond was attacked by a mob in the streets, knocked down, and cut on the face. Parnell met him, and remarked, "Why, you are bleeding; what's the matter?" Being told, he said with his cold smile, " Well, you have shed your blood for me at all events."

Nor was his advent in the House less dramatic. He had intended to stand for the Wexford seat vacated by the death of his father, but Parnell selected Mr. " Tim " Healy for the seat, and young Redmond loyally supported the Chief's nominee. In the following February of 1881 he was returned for Ross. " They were stirring times," he told me, " and I got a telegram from Parnell to come at once. I crossed the Channel immediately, took my seat, and was suspended with all the rest of the party the same night for refusing to vote. But not before I had made my maiden speech. It was brief, but conclusive. The Speaker called on me to withdraw, and I said, ' Mr. Speaker, I decline to withdraw.' That was all; but I had broken the ice." He took his share in many such scenes. " We were most of us high-spirited young fellows, fresh from the University, and enjoyed that rough campaigning."

To-day the House has no warmer admirer. " Putting aside its attitude to Ireland," he says, " it is the finest assembly in the world—so manly and generous. It has tenderness, too. It is remorseless to the bore, but the touch of sincere humanity goes to its heart. It came to love Biggar with his quaint figure and his interminable speeches. And you remember how, when Bradlaugh was dying, it passed a resolution cancelling the wrong it had done him. That was a fine and generous act." With all his apparent composure he has some awe of the House. " Familiarity does not breed contempt," he said to me once. " I find it harder and not easier to address it than I used. I am discovering that I have nerves. When I am going to make an important speech I am fidgety and unhappy."

John Redmond

He is the orator of the House—the last representative of a tradition that has passed. Other men rise to speak: he rises to deliver an oration. He advances, as it were, with his colours flying and his drums beating. It is no longer a skirmish, but a general engagement. All his rhetorical legions are brought into action with pomp and circumstance. His commanding presence, his strong utterance, his unhurried manner give a certain dignity and authority to his lightest word. He could make the multiplication table sound as impressive as a funeral oration, and the alphabet would fall from his lips with the solemn cadence of Homeric verse. To hear him say "Mr. Speaker, sir," is alone a liberal education in the art of saying nothing with immense seriousness. It is the oratory of the grand manner, like that of Mr. Henry Chaplin; but there is "stuff" in his speech, while Mr. Chaplin has only stuffing. With all his air of deliberation, he relies largely upon the moment. On one of the rare occasions when he wrote out his speech he "missed the points," picked up his notes, found them in a hopeless confusion, tried again and failed, had a further and unavailing search among his papers, now more hopelessly jumbled than ever, put them away, and sailed off before the wind of his portly eloquence. It was all done with perfect gravity. He is a man who can even break down with dignity and repose.

In many respects he is the least representative of Irishmen. He has none of the gay, irresponsible wit of his brother "Willie," the idol of the House, who has a tongue as swift as a Dublin jarvey's, and whose interjections explode like joyous crackers on the floor of the Chamber. Mr. "Willie" refuses to be solemn. It is enough for him to be merry and mischievous. He holds that his brother has dignity enough for both. In the hot days after the " split," when he replied with his delightful impulsiveness to some exasperating attacks by Mr. " Tim " Healy, his brother remonstrated with him on the ground that his words were not " gentlemanly." " One gentleman in the family is enough, John," he said with his delightful gaiety, and no doubt went off twirling his shillelagh.

Nor has he any of that Celtic mystery and passion which give the philippics of Mr. " Tim " Healy their touch of magic. Still less has he his spirit of impish mischief. Again, he has not the detachment of John Dillon, a patriot of the Brutus strain, simple, chivalrous, self-forgetful, a man who lives for a cause with a certain stainless purity that ennobles the House and enriches our public life. Mr. Dillon is the poetry of patriotism; Mr. Redmond is its politics. He is the plain, competent business man who has succeeded to the command of the concern and does his work with thoroughness and dispatch, but without passionate intensity or that tyrannic impulse that possessed Parnell. When Parnell was dethroned he died. If Mr. Redmond were dethroned you feel that he would simply have more leisure for sport. No one has ever doubted his patriotism; but he has none of the bitterness of fanaticism. He is above all a man of the world and of affairs. The air of the country blows about him, and he loves the wholesome entertainment of life. You are not surprised to learn that he was a good cricketer and that he still follows the game with interest, that he is happiest tramping the mountains with a dog and a gun, that he can manœuvre a salmon as skilfully as a Parliamentary motion, and sit a horse as firmly as he sits in the saddle of the chief. He is alone a sufficient answer to the foolish view that the Irish have not the gift of self-government. He is one of the ablest generals in the House. He has brought his frail barque through the wildest rapids that any statesman ever navigated. Through all the bitter war that followed the fall of Parnell he remained loyal to his old chief—loyal in the face of English morality and Irish clericalism. He marched out of the battle with his little band of nine, and wandered with them through the wilderness for nearly ten years. At last he brought all the scattered flock together, and to-day even Tiger Tim consents to bear his mild yoke—at least for a time.

He has the great virtue of never making enemies, for there is no poison in his shafts. He has about him a spacious and sunlit atmosphere in which the rank growth of personal bitterness cannot live. He can be generous even to his political foes. " I like Balfour," he will tell you. " He bears no malice. When the round is over he shakes hands. After I came out of prison in 1888 he met me in the lobby. ' I'm glad to see you back,' he said. ' I hope you are no worse for it.' And he said it in a way that made you feel he meant it. Now that is not the way with ——." He will not even admit that Mr. Balfour was wholly bad as a Chief Secretary. " The worst Chief Secretary by far was ——," and he mentions a name that fills one with mild surprise. " No man of sensitive feeling," he says, " can fill that office long. Birrell is too finely strung for it. It needs a man like Walter Long. ' I hunt three days a week and draw a fat cheque at the end of it,' he told an audience in Dublin. He is one of the good type of Tories. You know he is half an Irishman, and hunts in my country." He has, you see, a good word for everyone.

If the old ferocities of the Irish issue have vanished from the House, it is largely due to him as well as to the softening influence of time. He has no anti-British sentiment and will never talk of " cutting the painter." " Our stake in the Empire is too large for us to be detached from it," he said to me. " We Irish have peopled the waste places of Greater Britain. Our roots are Imperial as well as national." He rejoices in the new spirit that has come over Ireland. The old religious strife is dying. " When I first went to Belfast, I went carrying my life in my hand. In those days you dared not be seen in the streets and had nowhere to speak save a remote schoolroom, and even there you were not safe. The last time I went to Belfast I spoke in the Ulster Hall, the largest building in the place, and a third of the audience were Protestants. At the close one after another of them came up and shook hands and spoke cordially about my speech. The world is growing better and saner."

Unlike Parnell, he is a Catholic, but in his urbane way he has fought an heroic fight with clericalism. When the Parnell split came he elected to stand by his political chief and to defy the lightnings of the Church. It needed courage. He has sat in his pew and heard himself denounced by name from the altar as the anti-Christ. He has seen the congregation rise in a body and walk out in revolt against the priest. His ultimate triumph was won without sacrifice, and it involved the end of the political domination of the priesthood. The secular power of the priest was split on the rock of Parnellism.

There have been moments of weakness. He made a mistake in tactics when he responded to Cardinal Logue's appeal and brought his party over to support the Education Bill in the autumn Session of 1902. And his action in moving the rejection of the Irish Councils Bill at the Convention did not square

John Redmond

with his reception of the Bill in the House. His judgment is sometimes overruled by expediency. He is not the autocrat of his party, as Parnell was: he rules by consent.

When Home Rule comes, it is to be hoped that it will find him still in the saddle. It will be well for Ireland and well for England that his suave spirit should give the note to the new relationship of the two countries. For the fundamental fact about Mr. Redmond is that he stands for peace and goodwill. He is by nature the least combative of men. He has been fighting all his days, but he has always fought as though he loved his foes, and when he passes from St. Stephen's at Westminster to St. Stephen's Green in Dublin, he will not leave a single bitter memory behind him.

John Redmond

FLORENCE NIGHTINGALE

LYING before me is a manuscript. It is written on
large sheets of stout paper which have turned yellow
with the years. The writing, that of a woman, is bold
and free, as of one accustomed to the pen; but the
fashion of the letters belongs to a long-past time. It
is an obituary notice of Florence Nightingale, written
for the *Daily News* fifty-one years ago, when the most
famous of Englishwomen was at the point of death.
The faded manuscript has lain in its envelope for half
a century unused. The busy pen that wrote it fell for
ever from the hand of the writer more than thirty
years ago, for that writer was Harriet Martineau. The
subject of the memoir still lives, the most honoured
and loved of all the subjects of the Sovereign.

There are tears in that old manuscript, the generous,
almost passionate, tears of a great soul stricken by
a sore bereavement. Miss Martineau was writing
within three years of the Crimean war, when the
name of Florence Nightingale still throbbed with
memories vivid as last night's dream, and when her
heroism had the dew of the dawn upon it. To-day
that name is like a melody of a far-off time—a melody
we heard in the remotest days of childhood. Florence
Nightingale!

> It comes o'er the ear like the sweet South,
> Stealing and giving odour.

It has perfumed the years with the fragrance of
gracious deeds. I have sometimes idly speculated on
the strange fortuity of names, on the perfect echo of
the name to the deed—Shakespeare, Milton, Wordsworth, Tennyson! Why is it that the world's singers

Florence Nightingale

come heralded with these significant names? Why
is it that the infinite families of the Smiths and the
Robinsons and the Joneses never sing? And Oliver
Cromwell and John Churchill and Horatio Nelson!
Why, there is the roar of guns and the thunder of
great deeds in the very accents of their names. And
so with the heroines of history, the Grace Darlings
and the Florence Nightingales. One almost sees in
the latter case events carefully avoiding the common-
place and shaping a lustrous name for the wearer.
For her mother was named Smith, the daughter of
that William Smith, the famous philanthropist, and
member for Norwich, who fought the battle of the
Dissenters in Parliament, and was one of the leaders
of the anti-slavery movement. And her father was
named Shore, and only assumed the name of Nightingale with the estates that made him a wealthy man.
" A rose by any other name," no doubt. But the
world is grateful for the happy accident that gave
it " Florence Nightingale."

It is a name full of a delicate reminiscence, like the
smell of lavender in a drawer, calling up memories of
those from whose lips we first heard the story of " The
Lady with the Lamp." It suggests not a personality,
but an influence; not a presence, but a pervasive
spirit. For since that tremendous time, when the
eyes of the whole world were turned upon the gentle
figure that moved like a benediction through the
horrors of the hospitals of Scutari, Miss Nightingale's
life has had something of the quiet of the cloister. It
is not merely that her health was finally broken by
her unexampled labours: it is that, combined with
the courage of the chivalrous world into which she
was born, she has the reticence of a temperament
that shrinks from publicity with mingled scorn and
humility.

This rare union of courage and modesty is illustrated by her whole career. When, after a girlhood spent in her native Italy—for she was born in Florence, as her only sister, afterwards Lady Verney, was born in Naples—and in wanderings in many lands, she decided on her life work of nursing, she returned from her hard apprenticeship in many institutions, and especially in the Kaiserswerth Institution on the Rhine — the first Protestant nursing home in Germany—to take the management of the Sanatorium for Sick Ladies in Harley Street. In those days of our grandmothers, woman was still in the mediæval state of development. She was a pretty ornament of the drawing-room, subject to all the proprieties expressed in "prunes and prisms." She had no duty except the duty of being pretty and proper, no part in the work of the world except the task higher than that of seeing that her overlord's slippers were in the right place.

The advent of Florence Nightingale into Harley Street was like a challenge to all that was feminine and Early Victorian. A woman, a lady of birth and culture, as manager of an institution! The thing was impossible. The polite world thrilled with indignation at the outrage. "It was related at the time" —I quote from the yellow manuscript before me— "that if she had forged a bill, or eloped, or betted her father's fortune away at Newmarket, she could not have provoked a more virulent hue and cry than she did by settling herself to a useful work." And it was not society alone that assailed her now and later. "From the formalists at home, who were shocked at her handling keys and keeping accounts, to the jealous and quizzing doctors abroad, who would have suppressed her altogether, and the vulgar among the nurses, who whispered that she ate the

jams and the jellies in a corner, she had all the
hostility to encounter which the great may always
expect from those who are too small to apprehend
their mind and ways." But she had a dominating
will and a dear purpose in all the acts of her life.
She was indifferent to the judgment of the world.
She saw the path, and trod it with fearless steps
wherever it led.

Within her sphere she was an autocrat. Lord
Stanmore, in his *Memoir of Sidney Herbert*—the War
Minister whose letter inviting Miss Nightingale to go
to the Crimea crossed her letter offering to go—has
criticised her severe tongue and defiance of authority.
But in the presence of the appalling problem of
humanity that faced her and her band of thirty-eight
nurses, what were red tape and authority? As she
passed down through those four miles of beds, eighteen
inches apart, each bearing its burden of pain and
suffering, her passion of pity turned to a passion of
indignation at the wanton neglect of the poor instru-
ments of government, and she turned and rent the
authors of the wrong. The hospital was chaos.
There were neither hospital accessories, nor medical
appliances, nor changes of clothing, nor proper food.
It was a time for bitter speech and defiance of
authority. And Florence Nightingale, her sight
seared and her ears ringing with the infinite agony,
thundered at the War Office until the crime was un-
done and her own powerful control was set up over
all the hospitals of the East.

And now the war is over, the long avenue of death
and suffering that has been her home has vanished,
and she sets sail for England. The world is ringing
with her deeds. England awaits her with demonstra-
tions of national gratitude unparalleled in history.
She takes an assumed name, steals back by an un-

expected route, and escapes, exhausted and unrecognised, to the peace of her father's house at Lea Hurst, in the quiet valley of the Derwent. And when later the nation expresses its thanks by raising a fund of £50,000 for her benefit, she quietly hands it over to found the institution for training nurses at St. Thomas's Hospital. And with that act of radiant unselfishness she establishes the great modern movement of nursing. Mrs. Gamp flees for ever before the lady with the lamp.

For Florence Nightingale is not a mere figure of romance. It is beautiful to think of the ministering angel moving with her lamp down the long lanes of pain at Scutari, to hear those pathetic stories of the devotion of the rough soldiers all writing down her name as the name they loved, of the dying boy who wanted to see her pass because he could kiss her shadow as it moved across the pillow. But there have been many noble and self-sacrificing nurses, many who had as great a passion for suffering humanity as hers. To think of her only as a heroine in the romance of life is to mistake her place in history as well as to offend her deepest feelings.

She is much more than a heroine of romance. She is the greatest woman of action this nation produced in the last century—perhaps the greatest woman of action this country has ever produced. She is the type of the pioneer—one of those rare personalities who reshape the contours of life. She was not simply the lady with the lamp; she was the lady with the brain and the tyrannic will, and in her we may discover the first clear promise of that woman's revolution which plays so large a part in the world to-day. The hand that smoothed the hot pillow of the sufferer was the same hand that rent the red tape and broke, defiant of officialism, the locked door to get at the bedding within. Nursing to her was not a pastime or an occupation: it was a revelation. The child, whose dolls were always sick and being wooed back to life, who doctored the shepherd's dog in the valley of the Derwent, and bound up her boy cousin's sudden wound, was born with the fever of revolution in her as truly as a Danton or a Mazzini. She saw the world full of suffering, and beside the pillow—ignorance and Sarah Gamp. Her soul revolted against the grim spectacle, and she gave herself with single-eyed devotion to the task of reform.

There is about her something of the sleepless fury of the fanatic; but she differs from the fanatic in this, that her mighty indignation is controlled by her powerful understanding and by her cold, almost icy common sense. She has been the subject of more sentimental writing than any one of her time; but she is the least sentimental of women, and has probably dissolved fewer emotions in tears than any of her contemporaries. She has had something better to do with her emotions than waste them in easy lamentations. She has turned them to iron and used them mercilessly to break down the stupidities that encompass the world of physical suffering and to crush the opposition of ignorance and professional interest. All who have come in conflict with her have, like Sidney Herbert, had to bow to her despotic will, and to-day, old and lonely, forgotten by the great world that ebbs and flows by her home near Hyde Park corner, she works with the same governed passion and concentration that she revealed in the great tragedy of sixty years ago.

Truly seen, therefore, the Crimean episode is only an incident in her career. Her title to rank among the great figures of history would have been as unchallengeable without that tremendous chapter.

Prophets, Priests, and Kings

For her work was not incidental, but fundamental; not passing, but permanent. She, too, divides the crown with " Old Timotheus "—

> He raised a mortal to the skies,
> She brought an angel down.

When good Pastor Fleidner, the head of the Kaiserswerth Institution, laid his hands at parting on her bowed head, she went forth to work a revolution; and to-day every nurse that sits through the dim hours by the restless bed of pain is in a real sense the gracious product of that revolution.

She has made nursing a science. She has given it laws; she has revealed the psychology of suffering. How true, for example, is this:

> I have seen in fevers the most acute suffering produced from the patient in a hut not being able to see out of a window. . . . I remember in my own case a nosegay of wild flowers being sent me, and from that moment recovery becoming more rapid. People say it is the effect on the patient's mind. It is no such thing; it is on the patient's body, too. . . . Volumes are now written and spoken about the effect of the mind on the body. . . . I wish more was thought of the effect of the body on the mind.

She has moved mountains, but her ideal is still far off. For she wants not merely a profession of nurses, but a nation of nurses—every mother a health nurse and every nurse " an atom in the hierarchy of the Ministers of the Highest." It is a noble dream, and she has brought it within the grasp of the realities of that future which, as she says, " I shall not see, for I am old."

.   .   .   .   .   .

I put the yellow manuscript back into the envelope where it has lain for half a century. Sixteen hundred articles did Harriet Martineau write for the *Daily News*. They are buried in the bound volumes of the issues of long ago. One still remains unpublished, the last word happily still unwritten.

Randall Cantuar:

THE PRIMATE

THERE was probably never a more striking contrast in personality than when Dr. Davidson succeeded Dr. Temple at Canterbury. "They remind me of silk and sackcloth," said a witty prelate of them after a certain interview. "Davidson really rubbed me the wrong way, yet I hardly knew it, for he had a velvet hat-pad; but Temple took a scrubbing-brush, and fairly scoured away my notions."

Around this collision of temperaments so diverse there has gathered a wealth of legend. It is related that when Dr. Temple was presented to Queen Victoria on his appointment to the See of London, it fell to the lot of Dr. Davidson, then Bishop of Winchester, to introduce him. "Your Majesty," said the courtly Bishop of Winchester, "will remember that Dr. Temple has had the honour of being presented to your Majesty before." "No," said the Queen, "I don't remember having met Dr. Temple before." "Surely your Majesty," insisted Dr. Davidson, gently, "remembers his lordship being presented on his appointment as Bishop of Exeter." "No," repeated the Queen; "I don't remember." "But," began the Bishop again, "your Majesty will recall——" Dr. Temple could stand no more. "What is the use," he broke in, in his harsh West-Country accent, "of wanting her Majesty to say she remembers when she says she forgets?" And not less delightful is that other story which tells how the two prelates were seated at dinner on either side of her Majesty. "And you were appointed to Exeter in 1867?" said the Queen to Temple. "How wonderful that your Majesty's mind should retain such details!" interposed Dr. Davidson. "Not wonderful at all," growled Temple. "I've just told her."

These legends, whatever their basis in fact, illustrate the attitude of the two men to life. Temple was no courtier. He carried directness of speech to the point of brutality. When an obsequious clergyman related to him the sad loss of his aunt, adding, "Your lordship will agree that I know what bereavement is," he replied tartly, "I can't say; I didn't know your aunt." And I am told by one who was present that at some Church ceremony in the West of London he had grown weary of the excessive amiability of the vicar, and at the subsequent dinner, when the vicar sat opposite, he turned the talk to the subject of smiling people. "I hate people who are always smiling," he said to his neighbour in his most biting tones. "They smile in the morning, and they smile in the afternoon, and they smile at night. They're always smiling. Look at the vicar there—he's always smiling." The vicar became suddenly grave.

Dr. Davidson probably never said a wounding word in his life. It might even be said without offence that he, too, is "always smiling." He is clothed in the armour of imperturbable blandness. He is never betrayed into wrathful speech, for the smooth current of his thought is unruffled by fierce emotion. He has ever ready the soft answer that turns away wrath. He is an impalpable foe. You cannot come to hard grips with him, for he smothers your attack with silken words and leaves you angry and helpless, while he retires from the lists, cool and urbane as from a garden party.

Indeed, he is one of those to whom the world is a

garden party where it is one's duty to be suavely polite, and where the unpardonable sin is over-emphasis. He moves in and out among the throng with smooth words for all, and frowns for none. The sun shines aloft, a gentle breeze stirs the foliage, and on the lawn there is the motion of colour and the hum of well-mannered speech. It is a world of delicate deportment.

The polite man lives in perpetual victory. When Renan, pushed aside in the struggle to enter an omnibus, plaintively remarked that "there is no room in the modern democratic world for the polite man," he was wrong. The assertive man may have the material victory; but the spiritual victory is always with the man of unruffled good-breeding. He is never defeated, for though he may lose the prize he does not lose himself. "I never give the wall to a scoundrel," said a man meeting Chesterfield one day in the street. "I always do," said Chesterfield, stepping with a bow into the road. The one kept his boots clean, the other went away in a cloud of victory.

Dr. Davidson is the type of the polite man. He is the courtier-statesman of the Church. He is governed by policy, and not by emotion or mood. His personality never peeps out through that panoply of considered conduct. His immediate predecessors, Temple and Benson, were both men like as we are, the one brusque and practical, breaking in on the proprieties with crashing vehemence, the other swayed by emotions, introspective, and a little sentimental. Dr. Davidson is an embodied office. You never catch him without the lawn sleeves. You never surprise him out of the clerical and courtly accent.

His career is characteristic of those qualities which

have made the Scotch the most successful people in the modern world. They are the masters of themselves. They are never victimised by circumstance. They do not flame out into sudden passion. They keep cool. And it is the cool who inherit the earth. It is often said that Dr. Davidson has been " lucky." And certainly no man ever achieved more with fewer of the externals of brilliancy. His path has lain among palaces; his companionship has been the companionship of princes. Chaplain in succession to two archbishops, married to the daughter of one of them, the favourite preacher and domestic chaplain of Queen Victoria, he was raised to the episcopal bench at forty as Bishop of Rochester, refused the Primacy before he was fifty, and accepted it at fifty-three—the youngest Primate on record. For those who believe in luck here indeed is a career that justifies their theory—a career all springing from that friendship with young Crauford Tait, who, like him, was one of " Vaughan's lambs " at Oxford, and whom, when he died, he succeeded as chaplain to the Archbishop. But, after all, what is luck but the art of taking occasion by the hand, which in turn is the result of character? We would all have the Scotsman's trick of success if we could. We miss success, not because we have souls above it, but because we lack the self-possession and command of circumstance.

He is essentially a diplomatist who has strayed, as it were, into the Church. I never see him without being reminded of Velasquez's portrait of Innocent X. His kindly face has not the sinister note of that prelate; but it has the same calculating quality, the same sense of a mind delicately balancing the scales. He is the " smoother " of politics. He blurs the sharp lines of controversy. He sees both sides of a question so clearly that he takes neither. Black is not so very black, and white is really only whitish. He differs from you in sorrow, never in anger, and he leaves the door ajar for reconciliation. He wears no labels. He eludes the Ritualist as he eludes the extreme Evangelical, and embraces both in a universal benediction. He has no antipathies, and would be equally happy with Dr. Clifford or Lord Halifax, happier still with both, who would leave his presence arm-in-arm convinced that they had really been of one mind all the time. No party can claim him. He might adapt the candidate's creed to himself:

> Ez fer my politics, I glory
> In havin' nothin' of the sort.
> I ain't a Whig, I ain't a Tory,
> I'm jest an Archbish-op, in short.

But he loves to be on the side of authority and of Government, and prefers " Yea, yea " to " Nay, nay." He is not unrelated to the Vicar of Bray.

This temperament of compromise and conciliation makes for peace and pleasantness, but it fails in the hour of crisis. It does not rise to the great argument. A significant phrase is often more revealing than the most subtle portrait. Titian's " Charles V." is among the great achievements of art, but it tells so little of the Emperor compared with what he told of himself the day when he stood beside the tomb of Luther at Wittenberg, and those about him suggested that the body of the enemy that had triumphed should be disinterred and burned at the stake in the market-place. " I war not with the dead," said Charles, and by that chivalrous word we know him. So with Luther himself. He lives, one of the most vital figures in history, by virtue of those shattering phrases that leapt from his lips like thunderclaps that reverberate for ever. " The Pope's little finger is stronger than all Germany," said the Cardinal legate to him. "Do you expect your princes to take up arms to defend *you—you*, a wretched worm like you? I tell you, No! and where will you be then—where will you be then?" "Then, as now, in the hands of Almighty God," cried Luther. Dr. Davidson will be remembered by a phrase of ingenious compromise. He will be remembered as the man who, sitting in the highest seat of spiritual and moral authority in the land, said that Chinese labour was "a regrettable necessity." The moment came for a great word and he uttered a discreet evasion. The moment came to say "This is wrong," and he said "This is moderately right."

His speech wears the Court costume as naturally as Temple's wore the russet coat of the Devon moors. He thinks in crowns and sceptres. When speaking on the fundamental unity of Christians, it was characteristic that he chose as the two occasions which revealed that unity the death of the Queen and the consecration of the King. And even the stories of his wit carry us to the same atmosphere. At a meeting of the Kent Chess Association he remarked that though he was not a brilliant player, he could claim to represent all the pieces, except the pawn. He had had a great deal to do with kings and queens, had lived in two castles, and was both a knight and a bishop. "Except the pawn." It is a notable exception, for the pawn stands for plain humanity, the rest for the trappings of circumstance.

His royal progress has not been witnessed without criticism by his fellow Churchmen. His amazingly early elevation to Rochester was keenly discussed, and Archdeacon Lefroy is credited with the remark that: "If any man was born with a silver spoon in his mouth, it was Randall Davidson; but I like his pluck, although he thinks Archdeacons small fry, scarcely worth noticing." And when he went from Rochester to Winchester on the ground of health, it was a London daily journal, friendly to the Church, and friendly, indeed, to him personally, which said it preferred the candour of Sydney Smith when he said, " I must honestly say that I have been happier all my life for every additional penny I received." The thrust was tempting, but a little unjust, for the Primate's health has always been liable to collapse since, as a lad, a charge from a gun entered the base of the spine. Every autumn he is threatened with peritonitis, and for months at a time lives on nothing but milk food. And it is fair to remember that he refused the Primacy once, and accepted it with hesitation on the second occasion of its offer.

He has not touched the imagination of the country as Temple touched it, by the sense of natural force and shattering veracity, or as Benson touched it, by a certain spiritual sadness; but he has filled his great office with a high sense of its responsibility. If he has seemed timid when the occasion called for courage, it is because he conceives that office as a moderating instrument in the national life, a check upon violent oscillations, an aid to ordered development. If one misses in him the note of the passionate assertion of right, it is not because his sympathy with right is lacking, but because it is restrained by the caution of the diplomatist, anxious to wield influence without associating his office with the cause of party. And it is undeniable that this caution is at times a source of power, as well as at others a source of bitter regret. It has, for example, given his intervention in the licensing controversy singular weight—the weight which attaches to the man who takes a side with profound reluctance. And though carrying caution himself to the utmost extreme, he is not inappreciative

of courage in others. " It is a great thing," he told
a friend of mine, speaking of the Licensing Bill, " to
have a Government which dares to bring in a measure
which it knows will lose it votes." He would be a
greater personal force if he had the same indifference
to consequences: but his office might have suffered.
For until the Church is free, its head can never sound
the clear trumpet-note of spiritual challenge, but must
utter himself in the muffled accents of compromise
with the world.

DAVID LLOYD GEORGE

I was seated at dinner one night at 10 Downing Street beside a distinguished Liberal. " What a wonderful bust of Chamberlain that is in the hall," I said. " Ah," he replied; " you mean the bust of Pitt. Yes, it is marvellously like Chamberlain. I wonder," he went on, musingly, as though the question fitted in with his train of thought—" I wonder what will happen to Chamberlain's successor." I looked up. " Chamberlain's successor? You mean——" " Lloyd George, of course."

There was a faint hint of reproof in the " of course," as though I had asked solemnly for an explanation of the obvious. I looked down the table to where Mr. Lloyd George himself sat, his face lit with that smile, so quick and sunny, yet so obscure, his light voice penetrating the hum of conversation, with its note of mingled seriousness and banter, his whole air, at once so alert and self-poised, full of a baffling fascination and disquiet. Yes, here was the unknown factor of the future, here the potentiality of politics.

And here, too, was its romance. My mind turned to that little village between the mountains and the sea, where the fatherless boy learned the rudiments of knowledge in the village school, and where, in leading his school-fellows in a revolt against the Catechism he gave the first hint of the mettle that was in him. I saw the kindly old uncle, bootmaker and local preacher, worrying out the declensions and the irregular verbs of strange tongues in order to pave the path of the boy to the law. I saw that boy at twenty-one a qualified solicitor, with his foot on the ladder, fighting the battle of the village folk against the tyranny of the parson, who refused the dying wish of a Dissenter to be buried in his child's grave. "Bury him where he wished to be," said young Lloyd George, strong in the law. "But if the gate is locked?" "Break down the gate." And the old man was buried in his child's grave, and solemn judges in London pronounced a solemn verdict in support of the young Hampden. I saw him, still little more than a lad, leaping into the ring, and challenging the squire of his village for the possession of the Carnarvon Boroughs—challenging him and beating him. I saw him, with nothing but his native wit and his high-soaring courage to help him, flashing into the great world of politics, risking his fortune and even his life in support of an unpopular cause, escaping from Birmingham Town Hall in the clothes of a policeman, his name the symbol of fierce enthusiasms and fiercer hates. And then I saw him, transformed from the brilliant free-lance into the serious statesman, the head of a great department, handling large problems of government with easy mastery, moving great merchant princes like pawns on his chess-board, winning golden opinions from all sides, his name always on the lips of the world, but no longer in hate —rather in a wondering admiration, mingled with doubt. And now there he sat, the man who has "arrived," the most piquant and the most baffling figure in politics—the man, perchance, with the key of the future.

What is the secret of it all? In the first place, audacity. Danton's great maxim is with him, as with Mr. Chamberlain, the guiding principle of conduct. He swoops down on opportunity like a hawk on its prey. He does not pause to think: he acts. He has

no fear. The bigger the task, the better he likes it.
The higher the stakes, the more heroic his play. He
never fears to put his fate to the touch, and will cheerfully risk his all on a throw. When the great moment
came he seized it with both hands. He had two
motives: his love of the small nationality and his
instinct for the great game. The one gave him
passion, the other calculation. Here was the occasion:
he was the man. His business was being ruined: no
matter. His life and his home were threatened:
good. The greater the perils, the greater the victory.
And

> We roared " Hurrah! " and so
> The little Revenge ran on right into the heart of the foe—

ran on and lashed itself to the great San Philip of
Birmingham, and came out of the battle-smoke
victorious—the one reputation made by the war, the
one fortune born on the battlefield where so many
were buried.

And he has not only the eye for the big occasion and
the courage that rises to it: he has the instinct for the
big foe. He is the hunter of great game. " Don't
waste your powder and shot on the small animals,"
said Disraeli, and he hung on to the flank of Peel.
" Go for the lion " was Randolph Churchill's maxim,
and he gave Gladstone no pause. Even to snap at
the heels of the great is fame. It is to catch the limelight that streams upon the stage. There are names
that live in history simply because Gladstone noticed
them. Lord Cross and Lord Cranbrook came to
great estate merely because they beat him at the poll.
To have crossed swords with him was a career. Mr.
Lloyd George's eye, ranging over the Government
benches, saw one figure worth fighting, and he leapt
at that figure with concentrated and governed passion.
It became a duel between him and Mr. Chamberlain.

It was a duel between the broad-sword and the rapier
—between the Saxon mind, direct and crashing as the
thunderbolt; and the Celtic mind, nimble and elusive
as the lightning.

He has, indeed, the swiftest mind in politics. It
is a mind that carries no impedimenta. Hazlitt once
wrote an essay on " The Ignorance of the Learned,"
and declared that " anyone who has passed through
the regular gradations of a classical education and is
not made a fool by it, may consider himself as having
had a very narrow escape." Certainly the man of
learning, unless he wears it lightly, as Macaulay said
of Milton, and has assimilated it easily, starts with a
heavy handicap when he comes down into the realm
of affairs. He is under the dominion of authority
and the awe of the past. Mr. Lloyd George has no
such restraints. He is like a runner ever stripped for
the race. The pistol may go off when it likes: he
is always away from the mark like an arrow. And
it is not speed alone. When the hare is started he
can twist and turn in full career, for the hotter the
chase the cooler he becomes.

He is the improviser of politics. He spins his web
as he goes along. He thinks best on his feet. You
can see the bolts being forged in the furnace of his
mind. They come hurtling out molten and aflame.
He electrifies his audience: but he suffers in print
next morning, for the speech that thrills the ear
by its impromptu brilliancy seldom bears the cold
analysis of the eye. He is in this respect the antithesis of Mr. Churchill, though Mr. Churchill is like
him in daring. I once had a pleasant after-dinner
talk with them on the subject of their oratorical
methods. " I do not trust myself to the moment
on a big occasion," said Mr. Churchill. " I don't
mind it in debate or in an ordinary platform speech;

David Lloyd George

but a set speech I learn to the letter. Mark Twain said to me, ' You ought to know a speech as you know your prayers,' and that's how I know mine. I've written a speech out six times with my own hand." " I couldn't do that," said Mr. Lloyd George. " I must wait for the crisis. Here are my notes for the Queen's Hall speech." And he took out of his pocket a slip of paper with half-a-dozen phrases scrawled in his curiously slanting hand. The result is a certain thinness which contrasts with the breadth and literary form of Mr. Churchill's handling of a subject, or with the massive march of Mr. Asquith's utterance. But it has qualities of sudden eloquence, imaginative flight and quick wit that make it unique in the records of political oratory. Above all it has a quite unexampled air of intimacy. His swiftly responsive nature brings him into extraordinarily close relations with his audience, so that he almost leaves the impression of a brilliant conversation in which all have been engaged. This responsiveness, while it gives his speech its rare quality of freshness and exhilaration, is the source of his occasional indiscretions. Lord Salisbury's " blazing indiscretions " were due to his detachment from men and his remoteness from his audience. They were the indiscretions of an Olympian. The indiscretions of Mr. Lloyd George come from his nearness to his hearers. He cannot resist the stimulus of the occasion. It works in him like wine. It floods him with the riot of high spirits and swift fancy, until he seems to be almost the voice of the collective emotion.

And yet with all this sensitiveness to the external impulse, he is at the bottom the most subtle, the most resolute, and the most wilful force in politics. He has passion, but it is controlled. It does not burn with the deep spiritual fire of Gladstone. It flashes and sparkles. It is an instrument that is used, not an obsession of the soul. You feel that it can be put aside as adroitly as it is taken up. And so with his humour. It coruscates; it does not warm all the fibres of his utterance. It leaps out in light laughter. It is the humour of the quick mind rather than of the rich mind. "We will have Home Rule for Ireland and for England and for Scotland and for Wales," he said, addressing some Welsh farmers. "And for hell," interposed a deep, half-drunken voice. "Quite right. I like to hear a man stand up for his own country."

The soil of his mind is astonishingly fertile, but light. He is always improvising. You feel that the theme is of secondary importance to the treatment. You have an uneasy fear that this wonderful fluency of execution may presently reveal another *motif*. You listen. Your quickened ear seems to catch a hint of coming change. He keeps your mind on the stretch. He fascinates you, plays with you, holds you with the mesmerism of the unsolved riddle. You would give anything to know the thought behind that gay, debonair raillery.

He is, indeed, the least doctrinaire of men—as little doctrinaire as Mr. Chamberlain. No anchor of theory holds him, and he approaches life as if it were a new problem. It is a virgin country for him to fashion and shape. He is unconscious of the roads and fences of his forefathers. His maxims are his own, coined out of the metal quarried from his direct contact with life. He is not modern: he is momentary. There is no past: only the living present; no teachers: only the living facts. This absolute reliance on self gives a certain sense of lack of atmosphere. There is no literature to soften the sharp lines. There are no cool grottoes of the mind, no green thought in a green shade.

David Lloyd George

This detachment from tradition and theory is the source of his power, as it was the source of Mr. Chamberlain's power. He brings a fresh, untrammelled mind to the contemplation of every problem. It was said of Leighton that he looked at life through the eyes of a dead Greek. Mr. Lloyd George looks at life with the frank self-assertion of a child, free from all formulas and prescriptions, seeing the thing, as it were, in a flash of truth, facing it without reverence because it is old and without fear because it is vast. "The thing is rotten," he says, and in a moment his mind has reconstructed it on lines that acknowledge no theory, except the theory of practical usefulness. Thus he has swept away the old, effete Port of London, and put in its place a system as original as it is ingenious. And all the world asks, Why was this not done years ago?

Like Falstaff, he is "quick, apprehensive, forgetive," but he does not, like Falstaff, owe these qualities to canary, but to the Celtic spirit that races like a fever in his blood. His apprehensiveness, indeed, is amazing. He picks up a subject as he runs, through the living voice, never through books. He does not learn: he absorbs, and by a sort of instantaneous chemistry his mind condenses the gases to the concrete.

His intellectual activity is bewildering. It is as difficult to keep his name out of the paper as it was to keep King Charles's head out of Mr. Dick's memorial. He is always "doing things"—and always big things. His eye lights on an anachronism—like the Patent Laws—and straightway he sets it on fire. He does not pore over books to discover the facts about docks: he goes to Antwerp, to Hamburg, and *sees*. When he brought in his Merchant Shipping Bill he took a voyage to Spain and learned about ships. And

his passion for action grows with what it feeds on.
He has yet his trumps to play.

With all this energy and daring, the astonishing
thing is that he has won the confidence of the most
sensitive class, the commercial class, without losing
the confidence of the working class. Like Mr.
Chamberlain, he is essentially a middle-class statesman. He is no Socialist, for, as I have said, he has
no theories, and Socialism is all theory. "England,"
he said to me once, "is based on commerce. No
party can live by an appeal to labour alone: it must
carry the commercial class as well as labour with it."
"What can I do for commerce?" was his first question at the Board of Trade. And he took up the
Merchant Shipping Bill. "What can I do for labour?"
was his second question. And he incorporated in it
those valuable provisions for improving the life of
the seamen.

Wales looks on, admiringly and a little sorrow-
fully, at his giddy flight. He has passed out of its
narrow sphere. The Parnell of Wales has become
the Chamberlain of England. The vision of the
young gladiator fighting the battle of the homeland
has faded.

> Oh for a falconer's voice
> To charm the tassel-gentle back again—

back to the resounding hills and the old battle-cries
that have grown far-off and faint, back to the pure
idealism that stirred its pulse and its patriotism. It
is proud of its brilliant son—proud of the first Welsh-
speaking Minister to enter a British Cabinet—but it
waits with a certain gathering gloom for its reward.
Is it not thirteen years since he led a revolt against
the Liberal party on Disestablishment, and is he not
now a chief in the house of Pharaoh? Once it has
been on the point of revolt; but he had only to

appear, and it was soothed. Wales will get its reward quicker than if he had remained its Parnell; but it must await the propitious season. He is "forgetive," but he will not forget Wales. For Wales is not Birmingham.

And so I turn to the figure at the end of the table, with the smile so quick and sunny, yet so obscure. If the key of the future is anywhere it is there. If the social fabric is to be reorganised, there is the man that can do it. He stands in the furrow that Mr. Chamberlain deserted. Mr. Chamberlain put his hand to the plough—and turned back. He failed because he lost the vision of his youth, and treated politics as a game, and not as a gospel. Mr. Lloyd George will succeed in proportion to his fidelity to the inspiration, not of Westminster with its intrigues, but of Wales with its simple faith.

. . . .

I turned to my neighbour, and I said, "Yes, I wonder."

MRS. PANKHURST

It was at the memorable meeting at the Albert Hall
at which Sir Henry Campbell-Bannerman made his
first public utterance as Prime Minister that the
meaning of the women's war dawned on me. There
had been one or two preliminary skirmishes, at
Manchester and again at the Queen's Hall. But here
was the first general engagement. The time was well
chosen. The spirit of that meeting can never be
recaptured in our day. It was the hour of triumph,
a moment such as one cannot look for twice in a
lifetime. The Balfour Parliament was dead at last.
The long reign of Toryism was over and Liberalism
was born again after twenty years of obliteration,
qualified by one feeble flicker of office without power.
We stood on the threshold of a new time. All the
nightmare of the war and Chinese serfdom, of adventure abroad and wrong at home, was behind. We
looked, as it were, under

> an arch, wherethrough
> Gleamed the untravelled world.

It was like a vast thanksgiving as, after long years in
the wilderness, the exiles entered the land of promise.
Suddenly I became conscious that something unusual
was happening. There was a murmur below, as
though a light breeze had ruffled the great sea of
humanity that filled the area. All eyes were turned
from the platform to a point in the boxes near me. I
looked out and my eyes encountered, hanging from
the box next but one to mine, a banner with the legend
"Votes for Women." It was the signal of a new

E. Pankhurst

attack in the rear. Another Richmond was in the field. The Tory host was in ruins; but the Amazons were upon us.

Now, whatever may be our private views as to the campaign of the militant women, we cannot deny that it revealed quite brilliant generalship. It may not have been magnificent, but it was war. It was extremely " unladylike," the exaltation was sometimes unpleasantly like hysteria, the drama often bordered on the wildest farce. Occasionally there was the sense of an astonishing lack of humour, as when some of the Suffragettes lashed themselves to the railings in Downing Street. The world would have said that that was typically feminine, but for the fact that as an achievement in futility it was easily surpassed by the police, who, instead of leaving them in the pit they had digged for themselves, solemnly rescued them and then put them in the lock-up.

But with all its elements of comic opera, the campaign was the most brilliant piece of electioneering in our time. It discovered a masterly strategy, a sense of the moment to strike, a daring and a fertility of resource that commanded admiration, if not approval. It was a revelation of the woman in action, shrill and tempestuous, with the velocity of the wind and a sort of sleepless fury that threw every convention to the winds. It was startlingly unlike the warfare of men. Men in their ultimate political expression are brutal. If you are a Minister of whom they do not approve they will smash your windows. But the women were more subtle. They got inside the hall; they hung on to the door knob; they besieged you back and front. They made life intolerable with pin-pricks. They murdered the orator's best periods, and left his peroration in rags. They marched on the House in battalions; they stormed it in furniture vans; they penetrated the keyholes. You watched the river for suspicious craft, lest they should scale the Terrace; your eye roved the sky, lest they should descend by parachute from the clouds. It was a war divorced from all the rules of war. It was feline in its activity and cunning. It was unlovely, but it was business. It made the cause. Women's suffrage had been an academic issue for half a century: it became actual and vital, as it were, in a night. It was a pious opinion, discussed as you might discuss the Catiline conspiracy: it became an issue about which men were ready to fight in the last ditch.

Who was the Moltke of this amazing campaign? Who was it who prepared her battalions and her strategy in such secrecy that no whisper of the menace was heard until the whole cannonade burst on the new Government as it entered into office? I was presiding one afternoon at one of the sittings of the Conference on Sweating at the Guildhall when a small woman with a tired and rather sad face rose to speak. She spoke quietly in a monotone, as if she were soliloquising. It was as if an abstraction had found voice, so remote did it seem from any personal emotion. With great ingenuity her remarks drifted from sweating to the subjection of women, who are the victims of sweating, and then, before the closure could be applied, the concealed battery was unmasked in "Votes for Women." It was Mrs. Pankhurst making one of her raids.

At the first glance it is difficult to associate this slight and pathetic figure with the authorship of so much tumult and with the inspiration of a movement so bizarre and frenzied. But soon the truth is apparent. She is not a woman; she is an idea. One idea. Now the dominion of an idea, provided it is sane, is the most potent thing in the world. Most people have either no ideas or are burdened with so many ideas that they are useless. They are like the normal committee described by Mr. Chamberlain. " On every committee of thirteen persons," he once said, " there are twelve who go to the meetings having given no thought to the subject and ready to receive instructions. One goes with his mind made up to give those instructions. I make it my business to be that one." Mrs. Pankhurst does instinctively what Mr. Chamberlain did by policy. She leads by virtue of an obsession. She is the symbol of the potency of one idea held to the exclusion of every other motive and interest in life.

The idea is this, that women are the victims of an age-long tyranny imposed on them by men. That tyranny varies with time and latitude and social conditions. In its crudest form, among the savage tribes, it treats woman frankly as a slave, a beast of burden, a hewer of wood and drawer of water. In the East it imprisons her in the harem and regards her as the plaything of idle moments. In mediæval England she was held "Something better than his dog, a little dearer than his horse." In Victorian England she was the graceful decoration of life, a symbol of sweetness and innocence, a creature with pretty, kittenlike ways, but having no relevance to the business of the world. To-day she is emerging into sex consciousness and beating at the bars of circumstance. The cage is enlarged; but it is still a cage. She goes to the University and is bracketed with the Senior Wrangler; but she is denied her degree. She qualifies for the Bar, as Christabel Pankhurst did, but she is denied the right to practise. She enters the inferior walks of life, and finds that there is one standard of payment for men and an immeasurably inferior one for women. She falls, and finds that society has smiles for the betrayer and the flaming sword for his victim. At the bottom of the abyss, in the sunless court, she fights the last silent, helpless battle between starvation on the one hand and the lash of the sweater on the other. Everywhere she sees herself the chattel of men. If she is happy she may be serenaded and garlanded with jewels; if she is unhappy she may be trodden in the mire. But one thing she cannot have. She cannot have equality of treatment. She cannot have simple justice, for she is a woman in a world made by men. "Madame," said Charles XI. of Sweden to his wife when she appealed to him for mercy to some prisoner—"Madame, I married you to give me children, not to give me advice." That was said a long time ago; but behind all the changes of the centuries, it still represents much of the thought of men in relation to women.

It is not until one has entered sympathetically or otherwise into this conception of the serfdom of woman that one can understand Mrs. Pankhurst and her campaign of violence. She is a woman to whom the thought of this sex oppression is like a raging fever. It has burned up all other interests. It has driven her in turn from one political party to another, from Liberalism to the I.L.P., and from the I.L.P. out into a sort of political wilderness. She has deliberately chosen the rôle of Ishmael, her hand against the whole institution of society, whether the immediate cause be good or bad, for that institution represents to her only a single lurid fact—the dominance of one sex and the subjection of the other. She sees everything in life hinge upon that fact. At the Guildhall meeting to which I have alluded, she rose to put a question after Mr. Pember Reeves had spoken. " Was the anti-sweating legislation in New Zealand," she asked, " passed before or after the women had the vote? " And a wan smile of triumph greeted the admission that it was after. The fact covers her whole sky. It hangs like a dark pall over her spirit, shutting out the sunshine. As Mr. J. J. Mallon says in a sketch of her which appeared in the *Woman Worker* :

What she has to say springs from dark and somewhat bitter waters. Her metaphors are shapes of gloom. But at her best, as on one memorable day in Manchester, when we commemorated the Russians slain on Bloody Sunday, there is that in her voice and mien that stays in the mind for ever. Then she passes from recital of particular hardship to an impassioned contemplation of all suffering:

> " . . . The whole of the world's tears,
> And all the trouble of her labouring ships,
> And all the trouble of her myriad years."

Her sombre face glows with impersonal pity and appeal; her sad lips deliver the plaint of a sex. You no longer hear a woman's voice: you hear the voice of woman.

It is the gloom of fanaticism, of a thought gnawing ceaselessly at the vitals, and growing by what it feeds on. The spirit was inherent, for Mrs. Pankhurst comes of a revolutionary stock, and her grandfather narrowly escaped death at Peterloo. But it has been cultivated by circumstance. As a student at Paris she was a room-mate of the daughter of Henri Roche-fort, and caught from her the spirit of Republican France. Back in Manchester, she met and married Dr. Pankhurst, a barrister, whose political enthusiasm equalled her own, and who made the original draft of the Married Women's Property Bill—giving married women the control of their own property—which subsequently became law. Together they worked feverishly for many causes, Mrs. Pankhurst herself serving on the Manchester School Board and the

Board of Guardians. Then they leapt into national notice in connection with the battle for free speech in Boggart Hole Clough. They won, but the victory cost Dr. Pankhurst much, and was not unconnected with his premature death. Left with a young family, Mrs. Pankhurst became a Registrar of Births and Deaths, a position which, bringing her into direct touch with the tragedy of the poor, fed anew the flame within. Her purpose ripened. There were four children. They should be prepared, like Cornelia's " jewels," for the cause and flung into the arena. She formed the Women's Social and Political Union, and out of the little group of half a dozen unknown women who used to meet in a room in Manchester has emerged the movement which has shaken the whole fabric of politics.

She has in a high degree, apart from that intensity which is the soul of leadership, the gift of command. She has something of the aloofness of Parnell. She nurses, as it were, a fire in secret, has that independent life of the mind which seems unconscious of all external motive, and invites neither help, advice nor sympathy. She seems to have no personal life and no emotions except that overmastering one of abstract justice—a

> Stern, tyrannic thought that makes
> All other thoughts its slave.

She has the masterful will that evolves laws for herself, and is indifferent to formulas. When challenged to act on the democratic constitution of her union, she replied that democracy and constitutions are of times and seasons, and are not sacrosanct in the realm of varying impermanent groups—a declaration of thinly veiled autocracy that led to a disruption. As a debater she has a mordant humour and a swiftness of retort that make her a perilous foe. " Quite right! " shouts a voice from the gallery as she protests against the provision of the Children's Bill which makes mothers punishable in certain cases of mischance to children. " Quite right! " she flashes back. " Before the law the father is parent, the mother is forgotten; forgotten, forsooth, until there is punishment to be borne. Then they drag out the woman and it is ' Quite right.' " She is, above all, a leader in that her passion is always governed by the will. Her exaltation is kept at white heat, but never, as in the case of some of her followers, gets out of control. Her extravagances are considered: they are not touched with the taint of hysteria.

Her astuteness is evidenced as much in the limitation as in the violence of her campaign. Not a word of access to Parliament. You would gather that that was an ideal to which she was indifferent. It is, of course, the crown of her purpose, the end to which the present agitation is the preliminary. For she stands for the complete civic and political emancipation of woman, for full and equal citizenship, and out of that equality of citizenship she believes there will emerge that equality of social condition and that equal justice which will remove the wrongs that afflict her sex. Whatever we may think of her methods, we cannot doubt that they have shaken the walls of Westminster and made a breach through which future generations of women are destined to enter into undisputed possession of citizenship, with consequences fateful and incalculable. It may be that the methods will be carried too far—that their success as an advertisement will lead to their adoption as a policy. In that case the cause will suffer, for the English people are not easy to coerce.

LORD MORLEY OF BLACKBURN

LORD MORLEY is the only " double first " of his time.
He is perhaps the only double first since Burke.
Other men have won distinction in more than one
field. Canning wrote verse. Disraeli wrote novels.
Macaulay was an orator and a historian as well as
a statesman. Gladstone discussed Homer as vehe-
mently as he discussed Home Rule. Lord Rosebery
has trifled as piquantly with letters as he has with
politics. Mr. Balfour has spun cobwebs in covers as
well as across the floor of the House. But of none
of these can it be said that he was in the front rank
alike of literature and of statesmanship. It may,
with reserve, be said of Lord Morley.

" That a man," wrote Macaulay, " before whom
the two paths of politics and literature lie open, and
who may hope for eminence in either, should choose
politics and quit literature seems to me madness."
I speak from memory, but I think he wrote that letter
when he was smarting under his defeat at Edinburgh.
The dictum must therefore be taken with reserve,
for the grapes were sour. But we may be grateful
for a decision that gave us a history which Macaulay
himself compared with Thucydides' *Peloponnesian
War*, and which posterity, if it has not ratified that
verdict, has placed among the imperishable things
of English literature.

Lord Morley, with the " two paths " open before
him, came to a contrary decision. In middle age,
with a secure European reputation in letters, he rose
from the editor's desk and took a commission in the
field. " He gave up to a party what was meant for

mankind," and left "the harvest of his teeming brain" largely ungarnered. When I see him I seem to see a row of phantom volumes—books that will never be written — beginning with that Life of Chatham, the promise of which, made nearly twenty years ago, is still unredeemed. And I wonder whether posterity will endorse his decision as it has endorsed Macaulay's.

No man ever made a more dramatic entrance into office than he did. The announcement one morning that Mr. John Morley was the new Irish Secretary was the first clear indication of the most momentous departure in policy made in our time. It meant that Home Rule was the official policy of the Liberal Party. It startled the country then. If it could have foreseen all that it meant, it would have been startled still more, for it would have seen that it meant not merely a change of policy but a political revolution, the end of an epoch, twenty years of reaction culminating in the emergence of the spectre of Protection, and side by side with it the emergence into practical politics of social ideals which Lord Morley was wont to regard as the idle dreams of "impatient idealists."

For Lord Morley belongs to the past. He looks out on politics with reverted eyes. He has, it is true, more than any other man the passion of the old philosophic Radicals for liberty and political equality. He sat at the feet of John Stuart Mill and wears the mantle of that great man not unworthily, though with a difference, for the disciple has less of the optimism of logic than the master. The spirit of the French Revolution still burns in him with a pure flame. Manchester, the Manchester of the mid-Victorian time, still speaks through him with unfaltering accents. He is the high priest of liberty—

the civil and religious liberty of the individual. He stands for a cause that is largely won; but, being won, still needs that eternal vigilance which is the price of liberty, to hold as well as to win. That is his task. He is the guardian of the victories of the past. He is not a pioneer. He points to no far horizons, and stands icily aloof from all the eager aspirations of the new time. He will have nothing to do with strange idols. The gospel of social justice, that, proclaimed by Ruskin and heard at the street corners, is penetrating into Parliament and changing the whole atmosphere of political thought, finds in him little response. He murmurs "Impatient idealists," and is still. For reward he has incurred that subtlest of all rebukes—the praises of the *Spectator*.

The world of politics is a world of action, of quick resolves, and firm and sudden movement. To hesitate is to be lost. Lord Morley has the hesitation of the man of thought. Hazlitt used to say that you could see the defeat of the Whigs written in the weak, fluctuating lower features of Charles Fox's face, just as you could see the victory of the Tories imaged in Pitt's "aspiring nose." So in the deep-set, contemplative eye and indeterminate chin of Lord Morley you see the man who inspires others to lofty purpose, rather than the man of action. In his study, alone with the past or the present, he hitches his wagon to a star and rides away into the pure serene. In a set speech, face to face with a great issue, he sounds a note of moral greatness, austere and pure, that is heard from no other lips to-day. But in the presence of a situation calling for immediate and drastic action from himself, he is like Hamlet, and laments the "cursed spite" that has brought him face to face with a world of trouble. To do great things one must have a certain fearlessness of consequences, an indifference to responsibility, a fanatical faith, or the gambler's recklessness. Lord Morley has none of these qualities. The gravity and apprehensiveness of his mind revolt against the irrevocable word and make decisive action an intolerable pain.

It is this perplexity of the will, so characteristic of the philosopher in affairs, that is perhaps the secret of Lord Morley's admiration for Mr. Chamberlain, for we all admire most that which we have not. He sees in him the quality of decisive action at its highest. Mr. Chamberlain never doubts, never hesitates. He risks his whole fortune on the cast of a die. He does not pause to think: he acts. He has no yesterdays, no moral obligations. Do the principles he has professed stand in his path? Then so much the worse for his principles. He discards them as lightly as the mariner disburdens his ship of the ballast in the hold. His days are not, like the poet's, "bound each to each with filial piety." He does not care what he has said: he only sees the instant strategy, and adopts it. Action! Action! And again Action! If it is necessary to burn his boats, he burns them on the instant. If it suits his purpose to change his coat, he changes it and is done with it. If his purpose can only be achieved by a war, then war let it be. No situation so obstinate but he will unloose it, "familiar as his garter," if in no other way, then with the sword. He is a horse in blinkers. He sees neither to the right hand nor to the left, only to the goal ahead, and to that he flashes like an arrow to the mark. He knows that the thing the people love in a leader is swift decision and dramatic, fearless action. "Right or wrong, act!" Lord Morley, lost in reflection, weighing all the delicately balanced factors, sees with wonder the whirlwind go by.

Nor is the dominion of reflection over action the only bar to the leadership of Liberalism which once seemed within his scope. For his reflection upon life is touched with an abiding melancholy which differentiates him from his masters, who saw in the triumph of reason and logic the solution of all the problems of society. He cultivates no such confident optimism, but seems to detect in modern life the odour of decay, to see our civilisation not lit by the auroral light and bursting to perfect and enduring forms, but passing into the twilight whither the gods have vanished. It is of the late Lord Salisbury that he sometimes reminds one, though he has nothing of the grim acidity of that statesman. Lord Salisbury, it was well said, was " like the leader of a lost cause, resolved to fight on, though well assured that nothing but defeat awaited him." His deep-rooted scepticism about all the tendencies of what he called " our miserable life " was qualified only by the disposition to resist all change, not because the existing social order was good, but because it existed, and because his despairing vision saw nothing but deeper glooms ahead. It was the disposition to bear the ills we have rather than fly to others that we know not of. The ship was doomed and human effort an impertinence. Lord Morley's dejection is charged with a more active principle. It may be a losing fight in which we are engaged; but human effort after perfection is none the less not an impertinence but the highest duty. The ship may be doomed, but we can still steer it by the stars. With Empedocles he says:

> Fear not! life still
> Leaves human effort scope.
> But, since life teems with ill,
> Nurse no extravagant hope.
> Because thou must not dream, thou needst not then despair.

A pessimistic philosophy is not inconsistent with the

John Morley.

leadership of the Tory party, but to Liberalism it would be fatal; and even the Stoicism of Arnold—which more nearly represents the attitude of Lord Morley—would serve only as a check to dissolution. For Liberalism must be compact of dreams and inspired by " extravagant hopes."

Twenty-five years ago the future of British politics seemed bound up with three friends, the most powerful triumvirate of our time. Citizen Chamberlain provided the driving power and the popular appeal, Citizen Dilke the encyclopædic knowledge of detail and affairs, John Morley the moral motive and the intellectual foundation. Together they could have moved mountains. But the combination, for various reasons, fell to pieces, and the great hope vanished in twenty years of dismal reaction. " The pity of it, Iago, O the pity of it." It is one of the two great personal tragedies of modern politics.

Of the three, Lord Morley alone remains in effective service, and upon him, the preacher of political liberty, the irony of events has placed the burden of despotic control over a vast subject people, dimly struggling towards freedom. It seems like a jest of fate—a jest to show how far the stern moralist, the foe of the " reason of State," can resist the assaults of circumstance and of entrenched officialdom. It is too soon yet to judge of the result. The deportation of Lajpat Rai suggested that Lord Morley had begun to dig his own grave; but the victory of second thoughts still keeps him on the side of the angels. With courage he may yet make India his title to rank among statesmen of the first class secure. And then his claim to a " double first " will be established.

But whether success or failure awaits him, he cannot fail to stand out as one of the most memorable figures of our time. For he breathes into the atmosphere of public life the quality it most needs and most lacks—the quality of a lofty and instructed moral fervour. It was that quality which made Victorian politics great. It is the absence of that quality which makes the politics of to-day so inferior in spirit if not in purpose. There is no one left who can use the stops of the great organ save Lord Morley, and he in these days uses them only too rarely. Twenty years ago a speech by John Morley was an event. I recall one great utterance of his in Lancashire as the most memorable speech I have heard. Its peroration, so simple and poignant, lingers in the memory like a sonnet. He was speaking of Ireland, and he closed, as I remember it, thus: " Gentlemen, do to Ireland as you would be done by. If she is poor, remember it is you who have denied to her the fruits of her labour; if she is ignorant, remember it is your laws that have closed to her the book of knowledge; if she is excessive, as some of you may think, in her devotion to a Church which is not the Church of most of you, remember that Church was her only friend and comforter in the dark hour. Gentlemen, the dark hour is past. She has found other friends, other comforters. We will never desert her."

You will catch that thrilling note in the oratory of Lord Morley at all times, for he touches politics with a certain spiritual emotion that makes it less a business or a game than a religion. He lifts it out of the street on to the high lands where the view is wide and the air pure and where the voices heard are the voices that do not bewilder or betray. He is the conscience of the political world—the barometer of our corporate soul. Tap him and you shall see whether we are set at " foul " or " fair." He has often been on the losing side: sometimes perhaps on the wrong side: never on the side of wrong. He is

Lord Morley of Blackburn

True as a dial to the sun,
Although it be not shined upon.

There is about him a sense of the splendid austerity
of truth—cold, but exhilarating. It is not merely
that he does not lie. There are some other politicians
of whom that may be said. It is that he does not
trifle with truth. It is sacred and inviolate. He
would not admit with Erasmus, that "there are
seasons when we must even conceal truth," still less
with Fouché that "les paroles sont faites pour cacher
nos pensées." His regard for truth is expressed in the
motto to the essay "On Compromise." "It makes
all the difference in the world whether we put truth
in the first place or in the second." This inflexible
veracity is the rarest and the most precious virtue
in politics. It made him, if not, as Trevelyan says
of Macaulay, "the worst popular candidate since
Coriolanus," at least a severe test of a constituency's
attachment. It is Lord Morley's contribution to the
common stock. Truth and Justice—these are the
fixed stars by which he steers his barque, and even
the Prayer Book places Religion and Piety after them,
for indeed they are the true foundation of religion and
piety.

It is this severe loyalty to truth and justice that
is the note of his writings—this and a clarity and
invigoration of style that give one the sense of a brisk
walk on the moorlands. He is like the breath of
winter—"frosty, but kindly." The lucidity of his
thought is matched by the chasteness of his phrasing.
He does not love what Holmes called "the Macaulay-
flowers of literature." He does not burst—

Into glossy purples that outredden
All voluptuous garden roses.

But he is a well of English pure and undefiled—a well

whose waters have never served any growth save what was noble and worthy.

In personal intercourse he is singularly attractive. True, he has something of the impatience and hot temper that used to make his brother, "the Doctor," so formidable and delightful. But the lightning is harmless and soon over—if you are good and discreet —and then his smile makes ample reparation. It is the most sensitive smile I know. The famous smile of Mr. Balfour has more of the quality of the *charmeur*, but this has the same winning pensiveness without the elusiveness and uncertainty of the other. And there is one sure specific for banishing his frown. Insinuate into the conversation a delicate reference to literature and the sky clears magically. Then you discover where his heart really dwells and are admitted to the most intimate chambers of his thought. He is like one who has escaped from the prison of the present with all its fateful tasks to the free air where one may talk of the fathers that begat us and pass judgment upon all their deeds and words without the uncomfortable necessity of facing their problems and the peril of committing their errors.

He is not and could never be a popular politician. He is too eclectic, dwells too much apart for that. " I am not a gregarious person," he once said, and apart from his passion for music he has few popular tastes. But there is no man whose word carries more weight with friend and foe than his does. The old gibe at him about spelling God with a small " g " is no longer heard, for he has made men realise that there may be at least as much true religion in the spirit in which one doubts as in the most exact formulas of belief, and he has never divorced the chivalrous austerity of his teaching from the conduct of his own life. It was characteristic of him that when he lived

Lord Morley of Blackburn

on the top of the Hog's Back and kept a horse and trap to meet him at the station, he always walked behind the animal when it was going uphill. When men disagree with him they do so with searchings of heart, for he is " clear of the oak and the pine-scrub, and out on the rocks and the snow," and perchance his vision is most true. He brings to the consideration of politics that historic sense which is the most rare and valuable element in contemporary criticism. He seems aloof from the dust and heat of the conflict, watching the unfolding of a new chapter in the eternal drama of things, and making his comments, not in the spirit of one of the actors, but with the cold detachment of the Greek chorus. The alarums and excursions of politics, its subtleties and stratagems, do not appeal to him. He is not conscious of them, has not that celerity of mind that moves with ease amid the tortuous labyrinth. He is stiff and remote, irritated by the asperities of the game, scornful of its expediencies. His true place is with Burke on the back benches, applying the test of eternal principle to the momentary task, rather than with Walpole on the Treasury bench, seeking to make principles bend to the necessities of occasion, and basing his calculations on the foibles and follies of men.

RUFUS ISAACS, K.C.

I GOT a telegram one morning stating that a libel action in which I was concerned was down for hearing that day. When I entered the Law Courts half an hour later, the case was already in progress. I had expected to find the air cold and inimical. Instead, I found the court beaming with good humour. Everyone seemed cheerful. His lordship leaned back in his chair with an air of comfortable calm; the jury leaned forward with various shades of amused interest upon their faces; barristers and spectators seemed to be following a pleasant comedy. I took a seat and soon shared the prevailing spirit. My fears vanished in this easy, good-humoured atmosphere. This was not the thunderstorm which I had anticipated with black forebodings. It was a pleasant, breezy day.

The meaning of it was soon apparent. Mr. Rufus Isaacs was weaving his magic incantations. His geniality was infectious. You felt that everyone was a good fellow. His lordship—look what an amiable, cheerful old gentleman he was! He wouldn't harm a worm. And the jury — what excellent fellows they were! And the plaintiff, an honest, nice man, labouring under a little misapprehension. And the defendants, equally honourable, equally nice, if you only knew them. And his learned friend— why, he was the best fellow of all! He exchanged " nods and becks and wreathed smiles " with the judge; he talked to the jury as though he had never met twelve such luminous-minded men before; he permitted his learned friend to trip him up on the mispronunciation of a name, thanked him gaily for his correction, repeated the offence, and laughingly rebuked his own forgetfulness. It was all done with a lightness of touch, a freshness and gaiety that were irresistible.

Vainly did his learned friend try to stem the insidious tide. Vainly did he lash the poor defendants—villains of the deepest dye—vainly grow red and indignant, calling for heavy—yes, gentleman of the jury—exemplary damages. His fierce denunciation fell on deaf ears, his demand for revenge sounded harsh and discordant in this kindly world. The judge frowned disapproval at the bitter note, and the jury gave him—a farthing damages! And so home, very merry, as good Samuel Pepys would say.

" But," I said to Mr. Isaacs afterwards, " why did you alter your line of defence? You never touched on our real case."

" My dear sir, his lordship is a plain man who loves a plain issue. Your real case was complex, and would have tired him and irritated him. He would have said: ' Gentleman of the jury, you have heard the evidence. If you think it is a libel you will find for the plaintiff; if you have any doubts you will find for the defendants. Gentlemen, consider your verdict.' Or words to that effect. And down they would have come on you, for there was only one man in that box you could count on."

I saw in this scene at the Law Courts something of the secret of the most brilliant career of the time at the bar. Sir Charles Russel won his triumphs by passionate intensity and autocratic compulsion. His eye flashed fire and his tongue was an edged sword. He was like a torrent in spate, and the jury were swept along, helpless and unresisting, upon the swirling current. He dominated men by his impetuous wrath, by the energy of his mind and his manner. As he tapped his snuff-box and eyed you terribly over the pince-nez that hung low upon the nose, you felt that the storm was gathering beneath those pent brows, and you waited for the lightning that came with the flash of the stretched forefinger. To cross his path seemed a misdemeanour. To be opposed to him was, *ipso facto*, to be in the wrong. He won by sheer passion. He gained the battle by the sword.

Mr. Isaacs wins by wooing. It was said of Cobden that he was the only man who ever turned votes in the House of Commons. He did it, not by rhetoric, but by the sweet reasonableness of his persuasive talk. Mr. Isaacs has the same ingratiating faculty. He is so pleasant and amiable that it is a pain to disagree with him; so frank that you are sure that he is telling you all about it; so sensible that you feel he must be right. He does not browbeat the witness, or hector the judge, or dictate to the jury. He pervades the court with the sense of polite comedy. He makes everybody feel at ease, except his learned friend, who sees his case vanishing in wreathed smiles and urbane compliment. It is only when he leaves the box that the witness sees how he has been caught in the folds of that insinuating net. " I dreamed about you last night, Mr. Isaacs," said a surgeon returning to the box. " You have been a nightmare to me. I have hardly slept since you let me out of the box on Friday. I dreamed you had examined me and I seemed to have nothing on except bones."

He has the intellectual suppleness of the East, and something of the mystery of his race. The Jewish mind at its best has an orbit outside the Western range, at its worst a depth below our lowest deep; the Jewish temperament is for us inscrutable. We are at

Rufus Isaacs, K.C.

home with all other minds, whether they be clothed in
black skins or white, but the Jew, like the Japanese, is
eternally alien to us. He moves in other spheres; he
is motived by springs to which we have no access.
the soul of Spinoza, as he bends over his humble task
of glass-cutting at the Hague, " sails beyond the baths
of all the Western stars." Lasker, sitting over the
chessboard, seems to dwell in the unexplored vastness outside our intellectual range. Shakespeare we
grasp; but Isaiah has a vision that is not ours. Gladstone we understand, but who has fathomed the dark
mystery that was called Disraeli?

> Slaves in eternal Egypts, baking their strawless bricks,
> At ease in successive Zions, prating their politics—

they are of every nation and of none. It is one of
the greatest of living Jews who has best stated the
strange duality of Israel, the splendour and squalor
of his race. But even he has not wholly unveiled to us
the heart of its mystery.

The English mind is direct, obvious, emphatic. Its
attack is frontal. It marches up to the enemies'
batteries with bull-dog courage and breaks the line
or is broken in the attempt. You may take Mr. Gill
as the legal type of the English mind. He goes for the
witness with great, smashing blows. He knocks the
breath out of his body—if he can—and then turns,
hot and perspiring, to receive his reward from the
jury. Mr. Isaacs is all subtlety and insinuation.
You cannot come to handgrips with him. He is
intangible. A duel between him and Mr. Gill is one
of the most delightful spectacles I know. It is a duel
between quarterstaff and rapier—all the weight on one
side, all the agility on the other. It is like those
immortal combats at the " Mermaid " between Ben
Jonson, massive and slow as a Spanish galleon, and
Shakespeare, swift and elusive as an English

frigate. Down comes the quarterstaff with an immense sweep and—there is Mr. Isaacs, leaning lightly upon his sword, or gently pricking the defence-less flank of his opponent, his pleasant face more aggravatingly pleasant than ever.

It is all a gay comedy. His spirit is still the spirit of the boy who ran away to sea and served before the mast on the *Blair Athol*. He found that stowing the main skysail and cleaning the brass-work were not such fun as they seemed in fancy, and he decamped at Rio de Janeiro. But he was laid by the heels, and had to finish the voyage round by Calcutta. Two years in Magdeburg as the German agent of his father's business satisfied him that superintending shipments was little better than stowing the main skysail of the *Blair Athol*, and he turned up on the Stock Exchange, where, I believe, he lost money, and won fame with the gloves. Then, rich in worldly wisdom, he went to the Temple, where worldly wisdom is more valuable even than law, and stepped breezily out of the chambers of Mr. Lawson Walton into a practice that led to £20,000 a year, a dwelling in the paradise of Park Lane, and any office that he may choose to aim at.

He probably knows more of human nature in its crude state than any man of his time. He has seen it where it is most naked and unashamed—in ships at sea, in trade, on the Stock Exchange, and in the Temple, where its most rapacious and unlovely aspects are unveiled. And it is not surprising that one finds in him a touch of good-humoured cynicism, mixed with the breezy carelessness of his demeanour. Most lawyers have a touch of cynicism. Diogenes might find an honest man in the Temple: he certainly would not find an idealist. The law is death to dreams.

Perhaps it is this want of the atmosphere of dreams that makes the lawyer generally so arid a figure in

Rufus Isaacs, K.C.

politics. The lawyer who succeeds in politics on a grand scale is rare, and, with few exceptions, he succeeds not because, but in spite of the lawyer qualities.

Mr. Asquith is the exception to the rule. Men never thought of Harcourt as a lawyer. Russell's passion for Ireland obliterated the lawyer, and the only occasion on which Sir John Rigby touched the heart of the House was when a pipe fell from his pocket and he was seen to be, after all, a man and a brother.

Mr. Isaacs is not an arid figure in the House. His personality is too piquant, his outlook too bright and human. But he is not a great Parliamentary figure. The impression he creates is that of a light skirmisher on the fringe of the battle. There is no compelling conviction, no burning zeal that carries him passionately into the heart of the conflict. Contrast him for a moment with Sir William Robson. I have seen them both in Court, in cases in which I was involved, and—let me put it modestly—I prefer Mr. Isaacs. But in the House how different their values! Mr. Isaacs is the lightest of weights, Sir William Robson one of the most commanding of contemporary political minds. It is not perhaps, in this case, the difference between the lawyer who is primarily a lawyer and the lawyer who is primarily a layman. It is the difference between the English mind and the Jewish mind in relation to British politics. The Jewish mind is essentially outside our politics, despite the sorceries of Disraeli. The Jew is a citizen of the world. He has no patriotism, for he has all patriotisms. If he is orthodox his loyalty is to his race; if he is unorthodox his loyalty is commonly less reputable. The only Jew I can recall who had the root of the matter in him, who really thought about English politics as an Englishman thinks, was Goschen. And no one thought of him as a Jew.

Prophets, Priests, and Kings

When Mr. Isaacs' name was canvassed in connection with the Solicitor-Generalship, a barrister said to me: "There is too much work for one man, and Mr. Isaacs is the only man I know equal to the task. His energy and power of work are incredible. He is in bed at eleven and he is up at four when the Courts are sitting. Four hours he is at his briefs, and then, fresh as a lark, he is at the Courts, winding up with an afternoon and evening at the House." He carries his work as lightly as he carries his triumphs. He is wholly unspoiled by success, a pleasant, debonair figure, easy in all company, telling a bright story with droll enjoyment, the brilliant black eye of his race sparkling with fun, the mobile mouth working with the genial current of his thought. Wherever his brilliant path may lead him, whether to the Woolsack or to the seat of the Master of the Rolls, whose most famous ornament, Jessel, was, like himself, a Jew, it will lead him to no place he is not fitted to adorn.

THE BISHOP OF LONDON

BISHOP CREIGHTON wrote the *History of the Papacy;* his successor preached on *When it was Dark.* The fact is significant of much. We hear a good deal to-day of the poverty of the Church. The poverty is real; but it is not the poverty of money: it is the poverty of men. The Church shares the national bankruptcy. We may say of England, much more truly than Cassius said of Rome, that we have " lost the breed of noble blood." We are travelling across the plains. There is no peak on the sky-line of our vision. There is no personality that stirs our emotion, or excites our expectation. We have much cleverness, much energy, much talent; but we have no great men. We are an army without leaders. Johnson said of Burke that you could not meet him casually sheltering from a shower of rain without discovering that you were in the presence of a man of genius. Though the rain pelted down to-day over all the British islands, it is doubtful whether it would drive a single man of genius of this generation to shelter. " No birds were flying overhead: there were no birds to fly."

In this intellectual impoverishment the Church of England has more than its due share. Some twenty-five years ago it echoed to the sound of great voices. Lightfoot was at Durham, Westcott and Magee at Peterborough, Temple at London, Stanley at West-minster, Liddon at St. Paul's, Hort at Cambridge, Tait at Canterbury. They were like beacon lights in the land. To-day the darkness is lit with feeble and uncertain lamps. Dr. Percival, Canon Barnett, and Dr. Gore alone have the ear of the nation, and two of them belong to the past generation rather than the present, and none rises to supreme greatness. Among the younger men no figure emerges more considerable than that of the Bishop of Stepney, an astute ecclesiastic, or Canon Hensley Henson, an erratic and indeterminate quantity. The Church is poor indeed. It seems to have lost its attraction for the best minds even of an inconspicuous time.

Arthur Foley Winnington-Ingram is therefore typical of his generation. When he preached on Guy Thorne's shallow novel, he reflected the poverty of the thought of the Church, just as Mr. Hall Caine reflects the poverty of literature and drama, or Lord Northcliffe the poverty of journalism, or Mr. Austen Chamberlain the poverty of politics. We are in the backwash of the intellectual tide, and the Bishop of London is with us. We feed ourselves on thin, emotional gruel, and the Bishop of London shares our food.

And yet it might be claimed for him that though he is not a great man, he is a great Bishop. For there are two kinds of episcopal greatness. There is the intellectual greatness which stamps itself upon the mind of the Church. Such was the greatness of Tait. And there is a certain administrative greatness and personal magnetism, which quicken the diocese and touch the heart of the crowd. And such is the greatness of Bishop Ingram. Long ago Selden stated the functions of a bishop. "For bishops to preach," he said, "'tis to do other folks' office, as if the steward should execute the porter's or the cook's place. 'Tis his business to see that they and all others about the house perform their duties." Dr. Ingram offends against this law by preaching constantly; but he fulfils the latter part of it perhaps better than any man of his time. He is a great steward of the Church.

He is a great bishop, too, in the sense that he is a great Christian. His heart is filled with the love of his fellow men, but most of all with love of the poor. From the days when he left Lichfield and came to the Oxford House Settlement in the East End, he has given himself to the cause of the disinherited and the miserable. Slumming to him has been no idle diversion. It has been his vocation, his life. Into it he has poured all the wealth of a boundless joy, of a nature all sunshine and generous emotion. He as much as any man of our time has realised that if you would reach the souls of men you must first care for their bodies, heal their sores, lessen their miseries. And, full of this primitive law of the faith, he has carried the cup of cold water to the lips of the dying girl in the garret, laboured to drain the morass of the slum, lived his days and his nights among the forsaken and the hopeless. And then, his heart full of the goodness of the poor rather than of contempt of their squalor, he has gone down to Oxford to call others into the same harvest field. "It was an address he gave when I was an undergraduate," said a friend of mine to me, "that brought me here ten years ago to live in the slums. I thank God for it." Or he has gone out into Victoria Park to meet the atheists face to face; answer their pet posers with ready wit, and win their hearts by his genial comradeship.

He is not a humorist, but he has the gift of inexhaustible good-humour. "I enjoy," he says, "every minute of my work, every minute." And he has the happy answer ever ready to turn the attack. "Please, sir," said the Sunday-school child when he had asked the class for questions—"please, sir, why did the angels walk up and down Jacob's ladder when they had wings?" "Ah," said the Bishop, " very good indeed! Now would any little boy or girl here like to answer that question?" He is not afraid to stoop to conquer. Careless of his boots and his toes, he learned "the foot and door trick," as he calls it, in order to penetrate impenetrable homes. "After long hesitation," he says in his *Work in Great Cities*, " the door will be opened about half a foot by a little girl; you will hear a distant voice from the washtub in the rear, ' Well, Sally, who is it?' Then Sally will answer at the top of her voice, ' Please, mother, it's religion.'"

It is the defect of the average Church dignitary that he is remote from the people, dwells in another atmosphere, talks another language. Dr. Ingram thinks their thoughts, talks their speech, is one of themselves. He is a man who

> Hails you " Tom " or " Jack,"
> And shows by thumping on your back
> How he esteems your merit.

And he does it without offence. If he digs you in the ribs and tells you to " Buck up," you do " buck up." If he lends you his greatcoat or gives you " a lift " going down to Poplar, you have no feeling of being patronised. He is one of yourselves. He is a " pal." He does not fill you with the sense of the awful respectability of religion. He fills you with the sense of its good fellowship.

And so he warms the hearts of men where his gaitered brethren too often freeze them. Take that incident at the Church Congress at Northampton— a serried rank of solemn bishops and deans facing a crowd of Northampton shoemakers. Could the force of contrast further go? Could anything bridge the gulf between? Could anything warm this Arctic

The Bishop of London

atmosphere? Suddenly a light, athletic figure, face clean shaven, eyes twinkling with merriment, stepped forward and began to talk of his life in the East End. It was the Bishop of London.

"I remember," said he, "my first Sunday in Bethnal Green. I addressed a meeting of 500 men, and at the end of the service I said to them: 'Well, now, what shall we talk about next Sunday?' And immediately 500 voices yelled out: 'Eternal punishment.' That was a nice little subject to hurl at a young man who was out 'on his own' for the first time in his life. And then, of course, they wanted to know who was Cain's wife—they always do. Well, we settled that question, and we buried the poor old lady in Bethnal Green, once and for all." The bishops and the deans looked grave and pained, but the shoemakers were won. The gulf between platform and hall was bridged, and the solemn dignitaries could cross with ease.

It is this breezy intimacy that has made him win a hearing for religion among those who are indifferent or who regard it as an enemy. "Look at 'em! Just look at 'em!" said the 'bus driver, waving his whip towards the crowd gathered round the Bishop, preaching from the open-air pulpit at St. James's, Piccadilly. "I ain't religious, mind you, and I can't stomach parsons. They're fair pizen to me; but 'im—well, 'e's different. There's something 'uman about 'im. I've 'eard 'im down East many a time, and I tell you, when you've been a-listening to 'im for a bit, a kind of clean feeling takes 'old on you, same's if it was your day off, and you'd 'ad a bath and got your Sunday suit on."

And he has the same access to the rich as to the poor. "Bishop," said the stockbrokers who gathered round him after he had preached to them at Wall

Street: "Bishop"—and they grasped his hand—
"you've made us feel real good." Then I have no
doubt that they went back cheerfully to the business
of rooking their neighbours.

He does not divorce preaching and practice.
What is good for others is good for him. What he
would have others do he first does himself. And so,
when he preaches temperance, he does not follow the
example of Bishop Moorhouse of Manchester, who,
I remember, once opened a temperance speech with
the declaration, "I am not a teetotaler"—an affirma-
tion which effectually froze the meeting. When
Dr. Ingram, discussing temperance, was asked by a
workman, "Are you a 'tot'?" his reply was, "Of
course I am." "All right, then," came the reply;
"fire away. We'll listen to you."

He has little erudition, and less theology; but he
has the religion of service and sacrifice, and it is the
only religion that counts. "The best argument for
religion," said Mark Guy Pearse, "is six foot of
Christianity." It is the argument that Dr. Ingram
employs. And wherever he goes he carries the
sunshine with him. For he has the unconquerable
optimism of the man who in giving himself for others
finds the miasma of vain questioning vanish from
his own sky. *Solvitur laborando.* If you would be a
pessimist, sit in your study at Kensington and think
about the horrors of the East End. Do not go and
live and work in the East End. Pessimism perishes
in the East End, for pessimism is the poisonous fruit
of brooding and optimism the gracious flower of
service.

It is perhaps to be regretted that the Bishop of
Stepney ever became the Bishop of London. He is,
as I have said, a great steward of the Church. His
labours never cease. "I do all my reading and most

The Bishop of London

of my writing here," he will tell you, as you sit in his brougham in the light of his electric reading lamp. He rises early, retires late, lives sparingly, is poorer than when he had a tenth of his present income, fills every day with a hundred duties, and applies his two maxims, " Worth while " and " Don't be afraid to be human," to every one of them. But his true sphere is Bethnal Green Road, and the life of the mean streets that he loves and knows and has helped to transform. He is too light an intellectual weight for statesmanship or the leadership of thought. His excursions into politics are jejune, his point of view too narrowly ecclesiastical. One likes to think of him not in the House of Lords defending indefensible privileges, but as the parish priest in the East End, living the life, fighting for the faith, and carrying the sunshine of his happy spirit into the sunless homes of the forlorn and the miserable.

PRINCE BÜLOW

On some rising ground by the port of Hamburg there is a statue, rude, colossal, looking out over the landscape. In its suggestion of brutality and force it is incomparable. It stands out against the sky like a ruthless menace, and in fancy one sees a sea of blood surging at the base. It is the statue of Bismarck looking out over the Germany that he welded with blood and iron.

With this vision of the Vulcan of modern Europe fresh in the mind you turn out of the Wilhelmstrasse at Berlin into the Chancellor's residence and pass through into the park where Bismarck used to stride about with his great boarhounds for companions. To-day the Chancellor holds a reception. You advance through the gay throng thinking of those terrible brows and that fierce, barbaric figure with the boarhounds, and find yourself in the presence of a suave and polished gentleman with—a black poodle. He takes you by the hand and leads you aside with winning cordiality. He gives you the impression that you are the only person he really cares for in all that company. It is for you he has been waiting and watching. You gather that your affairs are his constant companion and that his interest in them is one of his really serious attachments to life. He stoops and pats the black poodle, surrenders you with an air of regretful affection, and turns to the next comer with his genial smile.

Bismarck was force: Bülow is finesse. Bismarck was the iron hand: Bülow is the velvet glove. Bismarck's tread sounded like thunder through Europe: Bülow treads softly. He is the most accomplished courtier in Europe. He disarms you by his uncon-

Prince Bülow

querable blandness and friendliness. I saw him described in an English paper recently as "worn-out and harassed, looking too tired and apathetic to be a happy man." I have never seen a man who looked less harassed, less tired and apathetic, more at ease with himself and the world. He carries his sixty years with the spirit of youth. His eye is clear and laughing, the carriage of his tall, soldierly figure erect and alert, his conversation full of an engaging sprightliness. He has none of the challenging air of the typical Prussian, and his vivacity suggests Rome rather than Berlin, the boudoir more than the battle-field. He wins by subtle address. With Bismarck it was a word and a blow—and the blow first. When Richter used to attack him in the Reichstag he would rise in a sort of apoplectic wrath, tug at the stiff collar of his uniform and hurl his thunderbolts about in blind fury. Prince Bülow meets the assaults of Bebel of the twinkling eye and the fiery eloquence with the weapons of wit and politeness, for he has brought into German Parliamentary warfare a style of oratory, polished and urbane, which is wholly contrary to the traditions of a country where politics are harsh and intolerant, and where your public foe is your private enemy.

He has the elusiveness of the diplomatist. The impression he conveys is that of an elegant trifler with affairs, one who is as free from hates as he is from passionate enthusiasms. No urgent moral or human motive governs him. He has followed Bismarck's ruthless policy in Poland, but without Bismarck's ruthlessness of spirit, for he has nothing of Bismarck's fierce intensity. His heart is never engaged. When he utters his occasional Bismarckisms, they fall from his lips robbed of their thunder. "Let the man alone," he said, replying in the Reichstag to Mr.

Chamberlain's reference to the German Army—" let the man alone. He is biting at granite." It was a fine saying; but it was an echo. The voice was the voice of Bülow, but the words were the words of Frederick the Great. The true Bülow utters himself in lighter and more airy fashion, in the language of gay persiflage. " Well, why shouldn't Miss Italy have an extra dance if she wants one? " he asks when Germany is disturbed by the appearance of a violent flirtation between Great Britain and Italy. " It would be absurd to show jealousy." And so with the Socialists. He never stamps on them with Bismarck's brutal violence. He is polite and ironical. He seeks to laugh them out of court by superior wit and pleasantry.

All parties are one to him, for he is vassal to no political theory. The machine of government is a thing apart from the life of the people. It is the property of a class—his class. " The public! What have they to do with the law except obey it? " he might say with a famous Bishop of Exeter; but he would say it with more suaveness of phrase. Democratic government is an ideal which fills him with polite scorn. The people are children to be ruled with paternal kindness and tickled with the phrases of Chauvinism. His political empiricism is exhibited in his *bloc*. The idea of ruling through an alliance of the Clericals and the Liberals could only have occurred to a mind without any fixed principle of internal political development. It could only have occurred also in a country where the spirit of Liberalism is dead and only the shell remains.

Prince Bülow's politics, in fact, are the politics of the Foreign Minister. Human rights and human wrongs do not interest him. He dwells, like his Emperor, outside them in the realm of Imperial

Prince Bülow

dreams. The Baghdad Railway is more to him than the desolation of Macedonia, and a great navy is more than the impoverishment of the people that is its price. In all this he represents the spirit of German policy, with its large ambitions and its divorce from the humanising tendency of modern politics. It is a spirit that contrasts strikingly with the spirit of France, which, now as ever, bears the banner of civilisation. France is in the Twentieth Century: Germany, with all its wonderful organisation, is spiritually still in the Eighteenth. It will remain there until the inspiration of its government comes not from the Court, but from the people.

But with all his Imperialism Prince Bülow would seem to love war as little as the Kaiser. " Wars themselves are not half so interesting as the events that cause them," he said long ago, and in these words spoke the diplomatist. And again, " War is a vulgar thing, and at this time of day the man who prevents war is greater than the man who wins battles." He will never talk like Bismarck about " bleeding France white "; but the Morocco affair left an uneasy sense that his pacificism is not wholly to be trusted. Trust, indeed, is not a quality that springs from so supple and adroit a personality.

His imperturbable urbanity and *savoir faire*, concealing a certain Machiavellian view of government, are the secret of Prince Bülow's success. They have enabled him to remain on the top for eleven years in a world of intrigue as tortuous and unscrupulous as an Oriental Court. How tortuous, how unscrupulous, the world realised through the noisome revelations of the Harden-Moltke case. It is the consequence of a government which centres not in the people, but in an autocrat. Prince Bülow, of course, denies this. When replying to Bebel on one occasion, he declared that *camarillas* and intrigues were not peculiar to absolute monarchies.

" I have," he said, " spent a portion of my life in countries which are governed on strictly Parliamentary lines. I have also lived in Republics. I can assure Herr Bebel that intrigues and backstair influences and all that sort of thing flourish in those countries a good deal more than in ours. Never has so much incense been burned before princely vanity as there is now burnt before King Demos. The courtiers of King Demos are superior to the courtiers of princes in the art of cringing and fawning."

Yet outside the realm of romance it would be difficult to find a story of political plotting to parallel that in which Prince Bülow has played so interesting a rôle. It is a story in which we see the Emperor as a tool in the hands of a subtle intriguer who weaves his plots and pulls his strings from the *coulisses* behind the scenes. There is no more sinister figure in modern European politics than that of Prince Philip Eulenburg, who has now fallen, like Lucifer, never to rise again, bringing down with him in his final catastrophe Count Posadowsky, with the long grey beard, whom I used to see taking his coffee every afternoon in the café opposite the Palast Hotel. Eulenburg has been the Warwick of Germany. Even in Bismarck's day this strange, elusive figure was a power strong enough to win the hate of the Iron Chancellor, who would have no rival near the Throne. " He has eyes that can spoil my breakfast at any time," said Bismarck of him. " He does not want to be anything — neither Secretary of State nor Chancellor. He thinks with Voltaire, *l'amitié d'un grand homme est un bienfait des dieux.* That is all he wants. He is an enthusiast, a spiritualist, and a fine talker in the style of Radowitz. For a man of the

Kaiser's dramatic temperament that kind of man is very dangerous."

Eulenburg not only did not want to be anything. He feared to be anything, for he wanted to be everything. He wanted to be the invisible power behind the throne, and he knew that if he became Chancellor his official relations with the Kaiser would destroy that power. So he contented himself with being Ambassador at Munich, from whence he pulled his strings. Bismarck fell, Caprivi fell, Hohenlohe, who hated Eulenburg also, passed, and Baron von Bieberstein, perhaps the ablest statesman in Germany, having been spirited away to Constantinople, the way was clear for Eulenburg's nominee. That nominee was Herr von Bülow, who, after a career in half the embassies of Europe, St. Petersburg, Paris, Bucharest, Athens, and Vienna, was now Ambassador at Rome, and married—he had eloped with her—to a brilliant Italian Princess of the House of Camporeale, a stepdaughter of the Italian statesman Minghetti. Bülow and Eulenburg were old friends, using the familiar " thou " in their intercourse. But Bülow's wife loved Italy and did not love Berlin, and, it is said, travelled to Vienna to plead with Eulenburg not to press the nomination. The story of this journey is denied by Prince Bülow. " It is an excellent story," he said in the Reichstag. " It has only one defect— it is not true." Whether true or false, Eulenburg had his way. Herr von Bülow became Count von Bülow and Imperial Chancellor. Then the Eulenburg web was woven at a furious speed. The Chancellor was his nominee. Eulenburg then got M. Lecomte, a friend of his Munich days, appointed to the French Embassy in Berlin, which gave him the key to Franco-German relations. Two lieutenants of his, Holstein and Kiderlen Waechter, were at the

Berlin Foreign Office, and finally he secured the appointment of his former military attaché, Count Kuno von Moltke, as Military Governor of Berlin, a position that brought him into daily contact with the Kaiser. Eulenburg was supreme. He held all the strings in his hand.

The *camarilla* that enmeshed the unconscious Kaiser ran the Empire. The world began to talk, even to print. Eulenburg fell out with Holstein, and the Morocco affair enabled him to secure his dismissal by the Kaiser. Coldness had sprung up between Eulenburg and his Chancellor, for Count von Bülow had proved too great a success to please the ambitious master of the palace. He could talk as brilliantly as Eulenburg, and his influence with the Kaiser was becoming dangerous. He was marked for slaughter. But a sudden attack from another quarter incontinently brought the whole fabric to the ground. Herr von Holstein, smarting from his dismissal, and the desertion of Eulenburg, took Herr Harden, the most brilliant journalist in Berlin, into his confidence. Conveniently, at this time, the wife of Count Kuno von Moltke divorced her husband, and this unsavoury affair became mixed up with Harden's exposure of the *camarilla*. All this time the Kaiser was sublimely unconscious of how he was ruled, and still visited the Eulenburg seat. But one day the Crown Prince placed half a dozen copies of Harden's paper in his father's hands, and the crash came. Moltke was dismissed, Eulenburg ostracised, and Posadowsky — innocent, able, grey - bearded Posadowsky—whom Eulenburg had selected as the successor of the Chancellor, deposed from his post as Minister of the Interior, where he had done more for Germany than any man of his time.

And so Prince von Bülow—Prince on the morning that Delcassé fell—survives, the last relic of the

Prince Bülow

Eulenburg system, more powerful than ever, so powerful that the Kaiser has begun to feel uncomfortable, so powerful that the fate of Bismarck already overshadows him. "His days are numbered," said a student of politics in Berlin to me. "He lasts because the Kaiser can find no one to succeed him. We are so poor in men who are at once able and liked by the Kaiser. But he will go."

When he falls there will be nothing of the tragedy that surrounded the fall of Bismarck. The old Chancellor's dismissal was like a sentence of death to him. "You take my life when you do take the means whereby I live." He had two passions whereby he lived—the passion for power and the passion for the Germany that he had created. When he was cast out of the Wilhelmstrasse he was beggared. No attachment to life remained to him. Prince Bülow will pass out as cheerfully as Charles Lamb left the servitude of the East India Company. He will smile as blandly as he smiles now when he receives you in the Wilhelmstrasse, and his black poodle will be with him. He will not be found in Prussia, nor in his native Mecklenburg, nor even in Germany. Italy is the land that holds his heart, and it is there, in Rome, that he has bought a lordly pleasure-house, the Villa Malta, which he purchased from Queen Margherita for £200,000. For Prince Bülow, fortunate in all worldly things, is a rich man. He was not rich when he went to Berlin, but an admirer had the happy thought to die and leave him a fortune which brings him in half a million marks a year. Upon that he and his wife will be able to cultivate those polite tastes which are their chief interest in life, for the Prince loves art and literature and archæology, and will quote the poets of half a dozen tongues, while the Princess, a pupil of Liszt, is devoted to music.

LORD ROSEBERY

In the early days of the Fiscal controversy I was dining with two politicians at the table of a mutual friend in the Temple. The politicians—one a Peer and the other a Commoner—had been and still were Liberal Imperialists; both are now in the Government. The talk turned, as it always did in those days, on the prospects of a "C.-B." or a Rosebery Cabinet.

"I must admit," said the Commoner, "that C.-B. has treated me very handsomely. I attacked him bitterly in the midst of the war. Most men would have remembered it; he has forgotten it, and when last week he was asked to preside at a meeting I was to address, he consented cheerfully, without a moment's hesitation. Now Rosebery is a man whom you never know how you will catch. He may be all smiles to-day and to-morrow you will find him cold and remote as an iceberg."

"Yes," said the Peer, "he came down to the House this afternoon to support my motion, and delivered an excellent speech. I met him in the lobby afterwards, stopped him, and thanked him for his support. He turned on his heel without a word and walked away."

"He turned on his heel and walked away." The phrase sums up Lord Rosebery. He is always turning on his heel and walking away—now from his friends, now from himself. He is as inconstant as the moon, unstable as water, whimsical as a butterfly. His path leads from nowhere to nowhere. He is like a man lost in the mist on the mountains and having no compass with which to guide his steps. He has all the gifts except the gift of being able to apply

them. Macaulay said of Byron that all the good
fairies brought their offerings at his christening; but
the one malignant fairy, uninvited, came and turned
the gifts of the others to bitterness. And so with
Lord Rosebery. He was endowed with all the elements of greatness; but the elements are not enough.
They must be compounded into unity by that in-
definable something, constant and purposeful, which
we call character, and it is the quality of character
which Lord Rosebery lacks. And lacking that he
lacks all. His gifts are idle ornaments; his life a
drama without a sequence and without a theme.

He is the tragedy of unfulfilment. Twenty-five
years ago he rode in the lists the most brilliant figure
in the land. The sun of Gladstone was near the
setting; but here was the promise of the dawn of
another day hardly less splendid. Genius and wealth,
wit and wisdom, fascination and the gift of incomparable speech all combined and all fused by a young
and chivalrous enthusiasm that drew all men's hearts
to him. He rode by the side of his great chief in
those memorable Midlothian days, a figure of romance
carrying the golden key of the golden future. With
what enthusiasm we saw him enter the brief Ministry
of 1886 as Foreign Minister! With what high hopes
we welcomed his splendid championship of the new
London County Council, saw him fling himself into
the great cause of a regenerated London, saw him
sitting seven hours a day in the chair, taking his
chocolate in place of a meal! Here was indeed the
man to lead us into the Promised Land.

> Was it all false, that world of knightly deeds,
> The splendid quest, the good fight ringing clear?
> Yonder the dragon ramps with fiery gorge,
> Yonder the victim faints and gasps and bleeds;
> But in his Merry England our St. George
> Sleeps a base sleep beside his idle spear.

What is the meaning of it all? For answer one recalls that saying of William Johnson, his tutor in his Eton days—" Dalmeny has the finest combination of qualities I have ever seen. He will be an orator, and, if not a poet, such a man as poets delight in. But he is one of those who like the palm without the dust." " The palm without the dust." But it is the dust which gives the palm its meaning; it is the race and not the reward that matters. Fortune, with cruel irony, gave him the palm without the pursuit. He found it an emblem of nothing, and he threw it scornfully aside. He had not paid for it in toil and devotion, and he could not value that for which he had not paid.

He has been the spoiled child of fortune—the type of the futility of riches, whether of mind or of circumstance, undisciplined in the hard school of struggle. It was as though he had the Midas touch. All things turned to gold beneath his hand. He had but to express a wish and it was fulfilled. He had but to appear and the path was clear before him. That triple ambition which is attributed to him is true in spirit if not in fact. He would marry the richest heiress in England; he would win the Derby; he would become Prime Minister. He would have the palm, but not the dust. He would have learning; but he would " go down " rather than sacrifice his racing stud at Oxford. He would have the Premiership; but he would not sit on a stool in the Home Office. He would command; but he would not serve.

It was said of Sir James Picton, that brilliant hero of Waterloo, that he would never have learned to command because he had never learned to obey. Lord Rosebery never learned to obey. He served no apprenticeship to life, and the inconstancy of the brilliant amateur is over all he does. Above all, he

served no apprenticeship to politics. Fortune, cruel
in its kindness here as always, sent him straight to
the House of Lords. Again, the palm without the
dust. " What a mind, what endowments the man
has! " said Mr. Churchill, speaking of him to me.
" I feel that if I had his brain I would move mountains. Oh, that he had been in the House of
Commons! There is the tragedy. Never to have
come into contact with realities, never to have felt
the pulse of things — that is what is wrong with
Rosebery."

There is truth in this; but it is not all the truth.
He has, it is true, the petulance and impatience of
the unschooled mind. But his real defect as a
politician goes deeper than circumstance. It is in
his nature. He has the temperament of the artist,
not of the politician. The artist lives by the intensity
of his emotions and his impressions. The world of
things is coloured and transmuted in the realm of his
mind. He is subjective, personal, a harp responsive
to every breeze that blows. The breath of the May
morning touches him to ecstasy; the east wind chills
him to the bone. He passes quickly through the
whole gamut of emotion, tasting a joy unknown to
coarser minds, plunging to depths unplumbed by
coarser minds. He is a creature of moods and
moments, and spiritually he often dies young.
The successful politician is made of sterner and
harder stuff. His view is objective, and the less
introspection he has the better, for introspection
palsies action. He applies his mind to things like
a mechanic. They are the material that he moulds
to his slow purposes. He is not governed by them,
but governs them. He is insensitive to impressions,
and, if he has emotions and impulses, has learned,
like Gladstone, to be their master and not their

slave, to use them and not to be used by them. He is, in fact, a man of business, cold and calculating even in his enthusiasms, not a poet lit with the rose-light of romance. Walpole, Pitt, Chamberlain, Asquith—these are the type of the politician. Lord Rosebery's temperament is that of Byron rather than of these.

There is in him, indeed, much of the Byronic instinct for melodrama. He rather enjoys making our flesh creep with horrific vaticinations and proclaiming " the end of all things " to our affrighted souls. There was a curious illustration of this rhetorical tendency at the dinner of welcome given to the Imperial Press Conference at the White City. His speech was couched in the most forboding vein. Deeper and deeper grew the silence and the gloom as he pictured the menace that encompassed us. And when in a thrilling whisper he spoke of the peace that hung over Europe being charged with such a significant silence that " we might almost hear a leaf fall " we felt as though the German Navy were already off Tilbury docks. And at that moment there was a roar like the roar of a hundred guns outside. For an instant we thought that Lord Rosebery had uttered his warning too late and that our doom was sealed. But then the truth flashed on us. It was ten o'clock—the hour at which the fireworks display began in the Exhibition grounds outside. It was Mr. Brock and not the German Navy who was offering his comment on the speech within. It seemed a singularly appropriate comment, conceived in the true spirit of this artist in the histrionics of public life.

It is not difficult to see that to so variable a temperament, political leadership was impossible. The public may enjoy the moods of the artist, but in affairs it demands constancy of mind and distrusts

the man of moods. In this it has the true instinct of
the child. It was a deep truth that was uttered by
the rustic who was asked whether Wordsworth was
not fond of children. " Happen he was," he replied,
" but they wasn't vara fond o' 'im. He was a man
o' moods, thou sees." The man of moods has no
welcome in the kingdom of the child and no permanent place in the leadership of men. It is this
incalculable quality that has made Lord Rosebery
the spendthrift of political friendship. No man
in our time has " run through " such a fortune in
friends as he has done. His path is strewn with
their wreckage. When, like Achilles, he went to his
tent, they gathered round him with loyal devotion.
They left the titular chief in chill isolation to fight the
battle of Liberalism through the bitter years of the
war. They sacrificed everything to woo him back
to the battle line. They became " Imperialists ";
they formed a League in his service; they kept the
way clear for his return. When the war was over,
" C. B." himself, in the historic interview, besought
him to come back. (" I liked Rosebery," he told me,
" and took the leadership always hoping to see him
back.") " No, no, C. B.," he said, " I do not belong
to your tabernacle." The more he was importuned
the more wayward and impenetrable he became.
He continued to speak; but he never spoke without
turning his guns on his old friends. Even when the
Fiscal issue arose he spoke in unclear tones. " Free
Trade was not in the Sermon on the Mount." He
flung the mantle of mystery around him, took refuge
more and more within himself. His friends hoped
against hope. The day of decision was near. Still
they waited for him. Then he went down to Bodmin
and declared: " I will not serve under that banner."
And with that final word he pronounced his political

extinction and rehabilitated Liberalism. He had squandered the last penny of his political fortune. He was left a lonely figure in his lonely furrow—a political profligate at the end of his resources.

And yet—*Tout savoir, c'est tout pardonner.* Perhaps if we knew all the inner history of that brilliantly futile life the verdict would be given in sorrow and not in anger. It is not for me to raise the curtain on the Rosebery-Harcourt feud. The two were flint and steel. They met only to clash and strike fire. Lord Rosebery would not serve under Sir William in the Home Office. It can be imagined with what feelings the great stalwart of Liberalism saw the young rebel snatch the palm from his grasp in the moment of victory. He took office under him; but the wound rankled, and Sir William could be an ill bedfellow. " It was a sorry business," said one who was in that Cabinet to me, " and my sympathies were with Rosebery. He was not well treated." Perhaps there we have the secret of the wasted life. Or perhaps it is in that domestic sorrow that robbed him of the wife to whom he was deeply attached. Or in that cruel affliction of insomnia which has pursued him for long years, making him a night wanderer in search of sleep. One thinks of him taking his carriage under the stars and driving, driving, driving, and of the cheerless dawn breaking on the unslept eyes. Yes, perhaps, to know all would be to understand all.

There he sits on the cross-benches of the House of Lords, his head leaning back on his linked hands, his heavy-lidded light blue eyes fixed in a curious, impassive stare—a sphinx whose riddle no man can read, a sphinx gazing bleakly at the

> Universal blank of Nature's works,
> To him expunged and razed.

A lonely man, full of strange exits and entrances,

incoherent, inexplicable, flashing out in passionate, melodramatic utterances, disappearing into some remote fastness of his solitary self. The light has vanished from the morning hills, the vision has faded in grey disenchantment. He is the Flying Dutchman of politics—a phantom vessel floating about on the wide seas, without an anchor and without a port. It is significant that his latest work should deal with " The Last Phase " of Napoleon, for it is that solitary figure standing on the rock of St. Helena and gazing over the sea at the setting sun of whom he most reminds us. Behind, the far-off murmur of the great world where he was once the hero, now lost to him for ever; before, the waste of lonely waters and the engulfing night.

GENERAL BOOTH

WHEN General Booth rises to receive you in his office in Queen Victoria Street, the first impression you have is of the alertness of the lithe, lean form in its frogged coat with the legend "Blood and Fire" blazing in red letters below the reverend white beard. The second impression comes from the eye. Certain men live in the memory by the quality of the eye alone. That was so in the case of Gladstone. His eye obsessed you. It seemed to light on you like a living thing. It penetrated you like a sword and enveloped you like a flame. It was as though he seized you in his masterful embrace and swept you whither he would. You did not question: you obeyed. No man who ever fell under the compelling hypnotism of that imperial and imperious eye will ever forget it. General Booth, too, dwells in the memory by the eye. It does not dominate you as Gladstone's did; but it fascinates you by its concentration. It searches the thought behind your words. It seems, with its beady brilliancy, to be burrowing in the dark places of your mind. You feel that your secret, if you have one, is being unearthed. You are sapped and mined. Your defences are crumbling beneath that subtle assault. There is nothing for it but flight or surrender.

You emerge from the interview with a new and revised version of the General. You went in to meet a saint and a visionary. You come out having met the astutest business man in the city. You feel that if the tradesman's son of Nottingham had applied himself to winning wealth instead of to winning souls he would have been the Rockefeller of England. He would have engineered " corners " and " squeezes " without precedent. He would have made the world of finance tremble at his nod. When he passes by the Stock Exchange he must say: " There, but for the grace of God, goes William Booth."

His genius for affairs is visible in the vast fabric of his creation. The world has seen nothing like this movement that in one brief generation has overspread the earth with a network of social and regenerative agencies. You may question its permanence, you may doubt its methods; but as an achievement, the achievement of one man, it is a miracle.

It astonishes by its absolute independence of motive and origin. Loyola's Society of Jesus sprang organically out of the Roman Church; Wesley to the end regarded his movement as a movement within the Church. But the Salvation Army is unique. It has no relationship with any Church or any system. Like Topsy, " it growed." It is an empire within the Empire. It is a system without a dogma and without an intellectual interpretation. It is, in fact, a revival movement converted into an organism.

It is a miracle which could only have been performed by an autocrat, and General Booth is above everything an autocrat. " L'état? C'est moi." His whole career is a record of absolute reliance on the leading of his own spirit. This quality revealed itself even as a boy of sixteen, when, left fatherless with the burden of a business upon him, he cut himself adrift from the Church of England, in which he had been baptised and brought up, and took to street preaching. He had been fired by the visit to Nottingham of the American revivalist, James Caughey, whose straightforward, conversational way of putting things, and whose common-sense manner of forcing his hearers to a decision, seized his imagination. He allied himself with Wesleyanism, gave up business, and began his campaign, gathering his crowds in the street, wet or fine, taking them to the penitent form inside, reaching the poor and the outcast if in no other way than by songs and shouting. Wesleyanism was shocked by these improprieties. It sought to make him respectable. He found himself, in his own phrase, " hooked into the ordinary rut and put on to sermon-making and preaching." He refused to be respectable. He cut Wesleyanism and tried Congregationalism. He found it bookish and intellectual and turned to the Methodist New Connexion, of which he was ordained a minister fifty years ago. But again the fetters of restraint galled him. He was put on circuit work instead of the revival work he passionately desired. The final emancipation came at the Liverpool Conference of the Connexion in 1861. Once more, despite his appeals, he was allocated to circuit work. " Never! " said William Booth. " Never! " echoed the voice of his wife from the gallery. And so, at thirty-two, without a penny of assured income, and with a wife and four young children to support, he faced the world, a free man.

And when his movement began to emerge from Mile End Waste, amid the brickbats of the Whitechapel mob and the hideous caricature of the Skeleton Army, the same masterful spirit prevailed. He found his ideas hindered by the conference, and the conference vanished like a Duma at a wave of his hand. Not even his family must break his iron law. His son desired to remain in America beyond the term allowed for service—insisted on remaining. Then his son must go. Do you question the future of the Army? The future is provided for. I, the General,

have named my successor. " Who will it be? No
one knows but me. Not even the lawyers know.
His name is sealed up in an envelope, and the lawyers
know where to get it. When my death is announced
the envelope will be opened and the new General
proclaimed."

It is magnificent and—it is war. There is the key
to the mystery. It is war. It is still the custom in
some quarters to ridicule the military aspects of the
Army. It is inconceivable that the insignia and
discipline of militarism can have any literal application to the spiritual realm. The thing is a travesty.
We sing " Onward, Christian Soldiers," but that is
only a poetical simile, and the Christian army sits in
comfortable pews outside the range of fire. General
Booth conceived a literal warfare, his battle-ground
the streets, his Army uniformed and disciplined,
challenging the world with fierce war - cries, its
principle unquestioning obedience. It is necessary
to remember this when we charge him with being a
dictator. An army in the field must be ruled by a
dictator, and his is an army in the field. " They call
me a Pope sometimes," he says. " I reply it is the
only way. Twenty people are banded together, and
nineteen are for taking things easily, and if you leave
them to themselves they will take the easy path.
But if you say ' Go; that's the path,' they will go.
My people now want and wait to be commanded."
His mistake is in supposing that a dictatorship can be
bequeathed. Cromwell made the experiment and
the Commonwealth vanished. A system which
derives all its vitality from a personality may fade
when that personality is withdrawn. For the
Salvation Army is not a Church or a philosophy or
a creed; it is an emotion.

An emotion! You look in that astute eye, so keen,

so matter-of-fact, so remote from the visionary gleam, and ask for the key of the riddle. And the truth dawns on you that there is a philosophy behind the emotion. When the artful politician sets out on an adventure he appeals to the emotion of patriotism or to the emotion of hate of the foreigner and fear of the unknown. So General Booth has a practical purpose behind the spiritual emotion. He is, in a word, a politician. He is a social reformer working through the medium of spiritual exaltation. Wesley saw only the Celestial City, and he called on men to flee from the City of Destruction. General Booth points to the Celestial City, and he uses the power generated by the vision to drain the City of Destruction and make it habitable. He is as designedly political as any Socialist, for it is the redemption of Society in the material as well as the spiritual sense that is his aim. But politics in the party meaning are forbidden to his followers as absolutely as alcohol. Change the laws by all means, he says to the politician, but I am working to change the heart. "We are tunnelling from opposite sides of the hill. Perhaps we shall meet in the middle."

He has the enthusiasm of humanity. He loves mankind in the mass after the fashion of the philanthropist. The average man is touched by the incidental and particular. His pity is casual and fleeting. His heart goes out at the moving tale; he feels for the sorrow he sees. But he is cold to misery in the mass, and generally shares the conviction of the Northern farmer that "the poor in a loomp is bad." The philanthropist, on the other hand, is often cold to the particular, but he has that imaginative sympathy that bleeds for the misery of a world. His pity is not casual; it is a frame of mind. His eyes look out over wasted lands; his ears ring with lamentation and an ancient tale of wrong. He is not so much indifferent to the ordinary interests of life as unconscious of them. General Booth's detachment from the world is as complete as if he were an anchorite of the desert. He has a single purpose. " The one prudence in life," says Emerson, " is concentration; the one evil, dissipation." General Booth has the concentration of the fanatic — the fanatic governed by the business mind. He carries no impedimenta. Politics are a closed book to him; the quarrels of creeds are unheard; literature unknown; his knowledge of golf is confined—as Bagehot said of the Eton boy's knowledge of Greek—to a suspicion that there is such a game.

Yet he is the most familiar figure in all the world. He has travelled further and spoken to more diverse peoples than any man in any time—to Hindoos by the sacred Ganges, to Japanese by the sacred mountain, in Germany often, in America and Australia and New Zealand. He flashes from Land's End to John o' Groat's in a motor car, whips across to Berlin, is heard of in South Africa. Yet all the time he seems to be in the bare room in Queen Victoria Street, talking eagerly as he walks about and stopping at intervals to take you by the lapel of the coat to emphasise a point. All this activity bespeaks the ascetic. " Any amount of work can be performed by careful feeders," says Meredith; " it is the stomach that kills the Englishman." General Booth is careful of his stomach. He lives the life of a Spartan. His income has never exceeded that of a curate, for it is wholly derived from a fund of £5000 invested for him years ago by an admirer—a fund which returns to the benefactor after the General's death. From the Army he draws nothing beyond travelling expenses.

His indifference to the judgments of the world has in it a touch of genius. It is not easy to be vulgar. Religion, like society, suffers from the creeping paralysis of respectability. The General set himself to shock the world by vulgarity, and he rejoiced in the storm he created. He had nothing to do with the world of proprieties and " good form." His task was to reclaim the Abyss, where the methods of organised Christianity were futile. " My work is to make war on the hosts that keep the underworld submerged, and you cannot have war without noise. We'll go on singing and marching with drums beating and cornets playing all the time." It is the instinct of the business man—the instinct of advertisement applied to unselfish ends. He is the showman of religion. " I would stand on my head on the top of St. Paul's cross if I thought it would bring men to salvation."

Intellectualism has no place in his life. Theology he leaves to the schools and the churches, and " Modernism " is a word that has no meaning for him. Metaphysics are not a path to the masses, and his answer to the " New Theology " would be " Hallelujah! " His creed is like Holmes'. " I have a creed," said Holmes. " It is summed up in the first two words of the Paternoster. And when I say them I mean them." So with the General. " The religion of the Army is summed up in the two great Commandments, ' Thou shalt love the Lord thy God with all thy heart,' and ' Thou shalt love thy neighbour as thyself.' " He applies no other formula. The dogmas will take care of themselves. " A man tells us he is a Catholic. We ask, ' Are you a good Catholic? Are you true to the principles of your faith? ' And so with the Protestant." His banner is as broad as the heavens.

General Booth

His methods are his own, and he will bend them to no man. He never argues: he simply goes on as if he did not hear. " I shall not reply to Dr. Dowie. I leave my work to speak for me. We must both answer to the Great Judge of all." He is charged with sweating, with not paying the trade union rate of wages. What are trade unions to me or I to trade unions? he seems to say. I am saving the lost; I am setting their foot on the ladder; stand aside. His finances have been constantly challenged, but he will not disclose them. Yet his personal probity has never been impugned, and when in 1892 the agitation came to a head and a committee consisting of Sir Henry James, Lord Onslow, Mr. Long and others was appointed to investigate the facts, it found that no member of his family had ever derived any benefit from the money raised for his " Darkest England " scheme, that the administration had been " business-like, economical, and prudent," and that the accounts " had been kept in a proper and clear manner." He is charged with indifference to the source of his money. " I was once reproached with having accepted a donation of £100 from a well-known Marquis. ' It is tainted money,' they said. What if it was? Give us the money, I say; we will wash it clean with the tears of the fatherless and lay it on the altar of humanity."

He has the unconquerable cheerfulness of the man who lives for a cause and has no anchorage in things or possessions. " My wife is in Heaven and I have no home, merely a place where I keep some furniture," he says; but no man I ever met is less weary. He has the dauntless spirit of youth. " How old do they say I am? Seventy-nine? What nonsense! I am not old. I am seventy-nine years young. I have heaps of time yet to go around fishing—fishing for

souls in the same old way with the same old net."
He is like an idea, an enthusiasm, that lives on
independent of the flesh. The flame of the spirit
flares higher as the candle gutters to the end. He will
go out with a burst of " Hallelujahs " and a roll of
drums.

LORD LOREBURN

LORD LOREBURN started life with two enormous advantages. He was a Scotsman and he was known as " Bob " Reid. To be born a Scotsman is to be born with a silver spoon in the mouth. It is to be born, as it were, into the governing family. We English are the hewers of wood and drawers of water for our Caledonian masters. Formerly they used to raid our borders and steal our cattle, but they kept to their own soil. In those happy days an Englishman had a chance in his own country. To-day he is little better than a hod carrier. The Scotsmen have captured not our cattle, but the British Empire. They sit in the seats of the mighty. Westminster is their washpot, and over Canada do they cast out their shoe. The head of the English Church is a Scotsman, and his brother of York came out of a Scotch Presbyterian manse. The Premier is usually a Scotsman and, if not Scotch, he sits for a Scotch constituency, and the Lord Chancellor, the keeper of the King's conscience, is a Scotsman too. London has become an annexe of Edinburgh, and Canada is little more than a Scotch off-hand farm. Our single satisfaction is that whenever we want a book to read we have only to apply to Skibo Castle and Mr. Carnegie will send a free library by return. It is a pleasant way he has of reminding us that we want educating.

Next to being born a Scotsman, Lord Loreburn was most fortunate in his name. Many a man's career is blasted by an ill name. When Mr. A. C. Morton rose upon the firmament of Parliament, he seemed to have a prosperous future before him. But one day a malevolent pressman in the Gallery discovered that " A. C." stood for Alpheus Cleophas. He published the fact to the world, and Mr. Morton never recovered from the blow. He vanished in derisive laughter. His fate was sealed at the font. No man can stagger to success under such a burden as Alpheus Cleophas. And half the bitterness felt towards Mr. Jabez Balfour was due to his unctuous name. It was an aggravation of his offence. It was felt to embody all the negative pieties. Lord Loreburn, on the other hand, might claim that his name was his fortune. There was a simplicity and directness of appeal about " Bob " Reid that was irresistible. It left nothing more to be said. It was like a certificate of good character. It made you trust him without knowing him. It seemed to bubble over with good humour, to radiate honesty and simple worth, to utter volumes of sound sense. A man who was known to everybody as " Bob " had disarmed the world. He simply had to enter in and take possession.

A plain, unvarnished man, large of frame and soft of voice, stiff in opinion, honest and unimaginative, loyal in friendship, immovably obstinate in purpose, he represents the British type in its stubborn devotion to justice as perfectly as his predecessor represented it in its ruthless claim to the supremacy of force. There was more geniality about Lord Halsbury than about Lord Loreburn. But it was the geniality of a merry ogre, secure of his victims, jubilant in his strength, jovially contemptuous of moral considerations. Under the Stuarts he would have whipped Dr. Clifford off to Jack Ketch with a quip about shaving his beard for him.

Nothing is more significant of the change effected by the election of 1906 than the fact that Lord

Lord Loreburn

Loreburn sits where Lord Halsbury sat for nearly twenty years. Lord Halsbury—for whose genius as a lawyer, by the way, Lord Loreburn has a profound admiration—filled his great office with a jolly cynicism that made his tenure of the woolsack notorious. He frankly regarded it as a political instrument. He reduced the Bench to a lower level than it had touched for a century. Any party hack, any necessitous relative of a Tory magnate, might look for office from the Lord Chancellor. There is a story—probably invented, but conveying the spirit of political preference with which he exercised his great powers of patronage—that when one position on the Bench fell vacant the late Lord Salisbury asked him to appoint a certain barrister to the post. Even Lord Halsbury was staggered at the proposal. " But," he said, " a Judge must know a *little* law. It would be a scandal to put —— on the Bench." " It would be a worse scandal," replied Salisbury, " for a member of an old county family to pass through the Bankruptcy Court." The plea was irresistible. Lord Chancellor Westbury, when his nepotism had become so gross a scandal as to lead to protest from his colleagues, replied, " But remember my oath. I have promised to appoint only those whom I *know* to be fitted for the duties. A dozen names are submitted to me. One of them is that of a man whom I have known for years, perhaps all my life, and whom I *know* to be fitted for the office. What am I to do? " It was an unanswerable way of putting the case; but Lord Halsbury had a certain blunt honesty that would have scorned such ingenious defences. " To the victors the spoils " was his maxim, and he acted upon it with a gay contempt for criticism which had a certain merit that adroit excuses would not have had.

The fault of Lord Loreburn is in the opposite direction. He is overwhelmed with the sense of responsibility. The solemn oath he has taken is ever present to his mind. " I saw him take it," said a friend of his to me, " and I saw the deep impression it made later. I went to see him when he was considering an appointment. When he began to murmur his oath, ' without fear or favour,' and the rest, I knew there was going to be trouble." Soon after the election I was sitting at dinner next to one of those clever women of the Tory Party who pull the strings of Government behind the scenes. " I was terribly frightened of your Lord Chancellor," she said. " I have just met him at dinner. We have nothing to fear from your Lord Chancellor." What she meant was that Lord Loreburn was so just that he could be relied on to be a little unjust to his own side.

Hence the anger, not loud but deep, that has raged around him. His speeches in the House of Lords are brave utterances of uncompromising Radicalism. The man who stood like a rock against the war now faces the serried ranks of Toryism and in suave accents delivers the most Radical speeches ever spoken from the woolsack since the days of Brougham. But when it comes to the administration of his department, then away with party. Justice, as he conceives it, shall be done though the heavens of Liberalism fall in ruins. It was he—he, the fierce enemy of the war and of Chinese serfdom—who stood for the sanctity of those 16,000 permits which the Tories issued to the mine-owners on the eve of the dissolution. It is he who has restored the full authority of Tory lord-lieutenants throughout the country to ratify the nominations to the magistracy. Every appointment shall be made on its intrinsic merits and through traditional channels without relation to politics. An excellent ideal, except that the lord-lieutenants have no legal authority, as Lord Herschel showed. An excellent ideal, if we did not start with a bench packed during twenty years with Conservatives. But to the plain man who fought to destroy this gross partiality of the bench, and who incidentally placed Lord Loreburn in the position to do him justice, this excessive correctitude seemed like a betrayal.

Lord Loreburn has faced the rebels in his own camp as unflinchingly as he faces the Lords on questions of policy and principle, or as he used to face the bowling in the days when he kept wicket for Oxford. He faces them with a certain stiffness and hauteur that treats criticism as an affront to his solemn oath. " I do not wish to be introduced to Mr. ——," he said on one occasion of a certain Liberal M.P. " I do not wish to be introduced to those associated with him. He has been very rude to me on the subject of the magistrates."

Whether we like this view of duty or not, we cannot but respect its honesty and fearlessness. It springs from a rare purity of motive, from the ideal of public service as a sacred trust. Such a tradition will make the task of future Halsburys difficult.

In his personal relations Lord Loreburn has none of the cold severity of office. He is a man of singular sensitiveness and tenderness of heart, clinging to old memories and old friendships. His devotion to the late Sir Frank Lockwood when living, and to his memory now that he is dead, is typical of this fine trait. They were the David and Jonathan of the Bar and the House. Sir Frank—as those who saw the exhibition of his caricatures will remember— satirised his friend mercilessly, pictured him in kilts holding on to a lamp-post, meeting a young lady in the dusk with the legend, " Meet me at the corner when the clock strikes nine," and preparing his speech for the Parnell Commission with the aid of a short black pipe and a huge whisky bottle. But no one enjoyed these wild extravagances of friendship more than Sir Robert. His affection for kindly John O'Connor, M.P., is a tradition of the House and of the National Liberal Club, and he never fails to preside at the frequent dinners to Spencer Leigh Hughes. " Show me a man's friends——" In these friendships we have the key to Lord Loreburn's character. He loves the plain, unpretentious man, who wants nothing, fears nothing, hates cant, and tells the truth. All the better if he plays cricket. " Does he bowl? " used to be one of his questions when a candidate for the Eighty Club came before him. For in the days of his youth he was a brilliant wicket-keeper, filling the position for Oxford against Cambridge, and in the days of his years and dignities he became President of the M.C.C. Thrice, moreover, he represented Oxford at racquets and later fought for the amateur tennis championship unsuccessfully against Sir Edward Grey. But he was far too good a Scot to allow pleasure to absorb his energies, and his industry and solid capacity secured him a double-first. And when he saw that the attractions of the playing fields endangered his career, he put bat and racquet firmly aside for ever.

The same resolute purpose and tenacity carried him to the head of his profession. When Jowett asked him what career he proposed for himself and he told him the Bar, the Master of Balliol said in his arid way, " You will do no good at the Bar. Good morning." When, years later, his reputation made and his future secure, he revisited Oxford, Jowett said, " By the way, Mr. Reid, I told you you would be no good at the Bar. I beg your pardon. Good morning." It is dogged that does it, and the Lord Chancellor's career is the most striking example to-day of what may be achieved by plain, homespun capacities governed by an indomitable purpose.

His love of the plain man was the secret of his devotion to Sir Henry Campbell-Bannerman, as it was of Sir Henry's attachment to him—an attachment not blind to his little defects. "Reid is a splendid fellow and a very good Radical," he said to me, "but if he doesn't have his own way he can be an uncomfortable bed-fellow." Through all the bitter time of the war Sir Robert stood by him with a loyalty that neither asked nor gave quarter. He was the relentless enemy of the Liberal League, stiff, uncompromising, and challenging. He burnt his boats with the Rosebery Party, and in the Temple his chances of the Chancellorship were ridiculed. But when Lord Rosebery went down to Bodmin one Saturday and said finally, "I will not serve under that flag," he incidentally placed Sir Robert Reid on the woolsack. His was the first appointment Sir Henry Campbell-Bannerman made when he came into power.

With the exception I have indicated, it has been splendidly justified. Lord Loreburn has not the learning of Gladstone's great Chancellors, Page Wood and Roundell Palmer, but he has courage, high purpose, and persuasiveness. His appointments to the High Court and the County Court have won general approval. He has set himself to reform the "law's delay" with striking success. On the bench his judgments are grave, lucid, and weighty.

He is an example of the maxim that "honesty is the best policy"—honesty backed by very plain, everyday qualities, industry, courage, unwavering purpose. A solid man, without brilliancy, imagination, profundity, or humour, he has risen to the highest place in a profession in which these qualities are more common than in any other department of life. It is the triumph of character, the reward of the " industrious apprentice " and of sterling worth. England has had more brilliant Lord Chancellors, but none who combined in a greater degree the sense of the high responsibilities of his office with perfect honesty, unaffected dignity, and rare lucidity of thought and utterance.

T. Hardy.

THOMAS HARDY

A FRIEND of mine—one of those people described by Keats as being married to a romance and given away by a sonnet—stopped in the course of a pilgrimage in Wessex at the hotel of a small market town. As he waited for lunch he discussed men and things with a farmer, a cheerful, bucolic soul, whose name may have been Gabriel Oak.

" Does Thomas Hardy ever come here? " he asked.

" Thomas Hardy! Thomas Hardy! " and the farmer's face took on the pale cast of thought. Suddenly his countenance cleared. " Ah," he said, with an air of quiet triumph, born of superior knowledge, " you mean Bill Hardy, the pig dealer, a little round-faced man wi' whiskers under his chin. Oh yes, he comes here every market day."

My friend expressed his satisfaction at the information, and sat down to his lunch with the comfortable sense of a secret possession. Farmer Oak stood before him, delightfully unconscious that he was immortal.

For Thomas Hardy shares the privilege of the prophets of old. He loves quiet and obscurity, and he has realised that to be obscure you must dwell among your own people. He knows, too, that to keep the inspiration pure you must drink at the spring whence it issues, and not slake your thirst at the muddy waters of London. And so, when, after years of London life, hovering between architecture and literature, he found that he had a career in literature open to him, he returned to his own people and there

Prophets, Priests, and Kings

—not far from the little cottage at Upper Bockhampton where he was born, where his mother died in her ninetieth year, whence, fifty years ago, he used to trudge to the architect's office at Dorchester, and whither he used to return to burn the midnight oil over the classics and the Greek Testament—he lives in the deepening shadow of the mystery of this unintelligible world. The journey that began with the bucolic joy of *Under the Greenwood Tree* has reached its close in the unmitigated misery of *Jude the Obscure*, accompanied by the mocking voices of those aerial spirits who pass their comments upon the futile struggle of the "Dynasts," as they march their armies to and fro across the mountains and rivers of that globe which the eye of imagination sees whirling like a midge in space. Napoleon and the Powers! What are they but puppets in the hand of some passionless fate, loveless and hateless, whose purposes are beyond all human vision?

> O Immanence, That reasonest not
> In putting forth all things begot,
> Thou build'st Thy house in space—for what?
> O Loveless, Hateless!—past the sense
> Of kindly-eyed benevolence,
> To what tune danceth this Immense?

And for answer comes the mocking voice of the Spirit Ironic—

> For one I cannot answer. But I know
> 'Tis handsome of our Pities so to sing
> The praises of the dreaming, dark, dumb Thing
> That turns the handle of this idle Show.

Night has come down upon the outlook of the writer as it came down over the sombre waste of Egdon Heath. There is not a cheerful feature left, not one glint of sunshine in the sad landscape of broken ambitions and squalor and hopeless strivings and

Thomas Hardy

triumphant misery. Labour and sorrow, a little laughter, disillusion and suffering—and after that, the dark. Not the dark that flees before the cheerful dawn, but the dark whose greatest benediction is eternal nothingness. Other men of genius, most men of genius, have had their periods of deep dejection in which only the mocking voice of the Spirit Ironic answered their passionate questionings. Shakespeare himself may be assumed to have passed through the valley of gloom in that tremendous period when he produced the great tragedies; but he came out of the shadow, and *The Winter's Tale* has the serenity and peace of a cloudless sunset. But the pilgrimage of Thomas Hardy has led us ever into deeper shadow. The shades of the prison-house have closed around us and there is no return to the cheerful day. The journey we began with those jolly carol-singers under the greenwood tree has ended in the hopeless misery of Jude.

And yet what a journey it has been! What companions we have had by the way—Tranter Dewey taking off his coat to the dance, Farmer Oak in the midst of his sheepfold looking up to the stars for the hour of night, Giles Winterbourne and Marty South planting the young larches amid the deep silence of the woodlands, Michael Henchard, magnificent in his rude, elemental strength, most impressive in the hour of his utter discomfiture and desolation—above all, the companionship of Nature, which is the true secret of his abiding hold. Nature is never a mere picturesque background for the human play. It is the most potent personality. Light, said the Impressionists, is the chief person in a picture. Nature is the chief actor in the Hardy drama—Nature, vast, sentient, mysterious, upon whose bosom the brief human figure is tossed like driftwood in its passage from eternity to

eternity. One feels here, as in Wordsworth's poetry
—to which the poetic prose of Hardy is the comple-
ment—that

> The mighty Being is awake,
> And doth with her eternal motion, make
> A sound like thunder, everlastingly.

Out of that immensity and mystery of Nature, poor
humanity emerges to play its part, and that a sad one.
For even the gleams of joy—and what humour is more
rich, more reminiscent of the Shakespearean vintage
than that of the Wessex rustics?—are shadowed with
the sense of doom that makes our triumphs trivial
and happiness itself a jest. " ' Justice ' was done and
the President of the Immortals (in Æschylean phrase)
had finished his sport with Tess." In that sentence
we have an epitome of Thomas Hardy's conception
of human life—a creature in the hand of an impenetrable Fate, cold, passionless, indiscriminating,
whose justice is a mockery, to whom virtue is nothing
and vice nothing, and from whose grim ironic grasp
we escape to utter darkness and silence.

I have said that Hardy's concept of nature is com-
plementary to Wordsworth's. It is the shadow of
the deep valley, cast by the mountain on whose sun-
ward slopes the light still sleeps. The spirit of Night
broods over all — majestic, mysterious, ominous.
Night and the twilight—Jupiter casting the shadow
of Tess as she digs in the allotment, the pageant of
the stars passing before the rapt gaze of St. Cleeve,
the breath of the night wind awaking the thin music
of the heath or stirring the woodlands to a richer
symphony, the primeval monoliths, terrific, awe-
some, instinct with meaning and mystery in the vast
and suggestive twilight—this is the atmosphere in
which the figures move on to a destiny as inscrutable
as Night.

Thomas Hardy

In all this and the philosophy it connotes he is the antithesis of Meredith, whose voice is of the morning, and whose vision is of the day. Meredith is the mind looking out with quick and thrilling interest upon the play of life; Hardy is the heart wrung by its agonies, "an infant crying for the light." To Meredith Nature is a joyous companion filled with the spirit of immortal youth; it is "The Lark Uprising" of whom he sings. To Hardy it is a merciless Fate, uttering itself in the hoot of the night-owl.

He is the Millet of literature, sounding the same note of the sorrow of the earth, working in the same elemental media. It is not his semi-barbaric women that we remember. They are excrescences. It is his peasants, untouched by the centuries, types of the enduring elements of humanity, as Egdon Heath is the type of the earth's ageless story, whom we love —Gabriel Oak, the glass of truth and the mould of manhood; Giles Winterbourne, tender and self-effacing, a hero in corduroys; Marty South, nursing her love in secret, and when Death has given to her the object of her devotion crooning by his grave her triumphant grief:

Now, my own, own love, you are mine, and on'y mine; for she has forgot 'ee at last, although for her you died! But I— whenever I get up I'll think of 'ee, and whenever I lie down I'll think of 'ee. Whenever I plant the young larches I'll think that none can plant as you planted; and whenever I split a gad, and whenever I turn the cider wring, I'll say none could do it like you. If ever I forget your name let me forget home and Heaven! . . . But no, no, my love, I can never forget 'ee; for you was a good man, and did good things!

It is this intense insight into the beauty of simplicity and the heart of the humble, this passion for the native and the sincere, combined with the immensity of the stage on which the drama moves, that differentiates the Wessex tales from all other literature and suggests the elemental boldness of Norse legends—Norse legends touched with the shadow of modern thought and the spirit of doom that pervades the Greek drama.

But if he is the Millet of literature, he is Millet without the " Angelus." His peasants are bowed to the brown earth in the mystic light, but no far-off bell tolls a message through the quiet air. And without that message the parallel breaks down at the crucial point, for it was with that throb of the bell in the " Angelus " that Millet rang through the heart of the world and still rings. The laborious day is over, the grey sky still shadows the sombre plain; but there is a rift in the west, and a word is borne to the tired heart on the pulsing air. Hope is not gone out of the world. But there is little hope beneath the pall that hangs over the Wessex stage. " Life is ever Lord of Death," says Whittier, and with him all those whose eyes turn to the dawn. " Death is ever Lord of life," says Hardy, and with him those whose eyes turn to the sun going down in pitiless gloom. It is the eternal conflict between the optimist and the pessimist, between " Yea " and " Nay," between the upward look and the downward. But the world is with those who, like Browning's Grammarian, are " for the morning," not with those who are of the dark and hear only the voices of the night.

In the unity of his achievement Mr. Hardy stands alone in the history of English fiction. This is due, as Mr. Lascelles Abercromby has shown, to the deliberate subordination of his art to his metaphysic. It is not necessary to accept his philosophy in order to appreciate its impressive and cohesive influence upon his work. It gives it continuity, design, a cumulative grandeur that make it unique in our litera-

ture. His vision of men—charged with aspirations
and desires—caught in the relentless toils of

> The purposive, unmotived, dominant Thing
> Which sways in brooding dark their wayfaring

may be a vision of the dark and not of the day. It
may be the vision of a recluse brooding in solitude
over his own conception of reality and shadowing
all his perceptions of the activities of life with his
painful obsession. But out of this correspondence
of conception and perception springs the unity of
Hardy's work. The note is struck at the beginning,
even in that sweetest of English comedies, *Under the
Greenwood Tree*, which closes with the hint of tragic
secrecy; it deepens through the main structure of his
creation until the implicit agony of the conflict between man and " the unweeting Will " utters itself
in the explicit rebellion of *Jude*, and it rises to its
complete summation in the " Dynasts."

The material of the Hardy drama is at once simple
and stupendous, human and cosmic—a few peasants,
types of the general sin of personal existence and
personal desire in a universe of indifferent fate. The
protagonists are nature and man—the theme, the
conflict between the unconquerable soul and that
blind Will that

> . . . heaves through space and moulds the times,
> With mortals for Its fingers.

In such a struggle man emerges splendid and abject—
splendid in his defiant resistance to circumstance,
abject in the futility of his challenge to "the all-
urging Will, raptly magnipotent." Tess paying the
debt she does not owe, Henchard stealing away to die
in solitude, the figures of the Napoleonic drama fighting
and intriguing while the spirits of the air chant their
pitying or ironic comments—all typify the eternal

struggle of the free will caught in the trap of blind circumstance. The machinery of the drama has the elemental quality that befits the theme. It moves with the rhythm of inexorable fate. It is rich in climax, yet, no matter how unexpected, the climax is always attained with the simple inevitableness of a natural law—the law that breaks the poor human figure on the wheel of doom.

Mr. Hardy would deny that a philosophy such as his, based upon an honest acceptance of facts as he observes them, has any serious relation to the capacity for personal joy. Happiness and gloom, he will tell you, are the products not of philosophy, but of individual temperament, which is unaffected by any theory of the governance or destiny of men. The Turkish lady quoted by Boswell put the view in another way when she said, " Ma foi, monsieur, notre bonheur depend de la façon que notre sang circule." Mr. Hardy has said truly that the human soul has normally less specific gravity than the sea of misery into which it is cast and emerges inevitably to the surface. So far as philosophy has any influence upon happiness, he believes that he is more truly happy who refuses the refuge of revelation he cannot prove and cultivates a reasoned serenity and fortitude on the basis of the perceived facts of life. For what he calls " the professional optimist " he has unaffected scorn. He reminds him of the smile on the face of a skull.

If you have the good fortune to meet Thomas Hardy, you will certainly find him more cheerful than his philosophy—an alert and knickerbockered man, pleasant and companionable, trotting through the streets of Dorchester, talking to its people, glad to show you the scenes his genius has made so memorable, and, having done, jumping lightly on his bicycle,

Thomas Hardy

in spite of his sixty-seven years, and riding away, leaving you a little puzzled that the wizard should be so like the plain man. But it is not the wizard you have met. Him you will meet on the spacious heath under the night sky, by the gaunt ruin of Corfe Castle, wandering among the shadows that haunt the lonely barrow or on the cliffs hard by Lulworth Cove —a presence subtle and pervasive, watching you with a thousand eyes, accompanying you with noiseless tread. For he has performed this miracle. He has printed himself so indelibly upon this Wessex country, has penetrated so deeply to its heart, that it seems to speak in his own accents. It is a world whose realities have become charged with the magic of his dreams.

HENRY CHAPLIN

I LOVE to sit in the Gallery on a sleepy afternoon and watch Mr. Henry Chaplin looking after the affairs of the Empire. Near him, on the Front Opposition Bench, Mr. Balfour reclines with an air of graceful indolence, and, beyond, Mr. Walter Long gently dozes, his arms folded, his head sunk back upon the cushion, his ruddy October face giving a touch of warmth and colour to the scene. Perhaps Mr. Austen Chamberlain sits up alert and watchful; but for the real picture of Britain guarding her own you must turn to Mr. Chaplin. There is no laxity here. The afternoon may be drowsy and the cushioned seats seductive; but the stern sentinel of Empire knows no rest. If the sun of Britain is to go down it shall not be because he slept. Let the enemy look to it:

> They shall find him 'ware and wakin',
> As they found him long ago.

His eye is upon them in stern reproof of their knaveries. He seizes some paper and makes notes, not unconscious that the enemy are trembling visibly at the menace that overshadows them. He takes off his hat under the stress of emotion, and you are surprised at the youthful hue of the chestnut hair. He returns it resolutely and firmly to his brows. A new point has struck him: more notes: more craven fear opposite.

He rises, and then what Jovian thunders echo round the House in sonorous reverberation! With what pomp the portly platitude stalks forth to combat! See the noble sweep of the right arm, the graceful handling of the cambric handkerchief, the fine fervour of the monocle. Hear the deep chest notes sink into unimaginable depths under the burden of Britain's woes and Radical iniquities. You feel that he would weep but for the Spartan spirit that sustains him.

For the splendid thing about Mr. Chaplin is that he takes himself seriously. There, as Corporal Nym would say, is the humour of it. There is the respect that fills the House with joy at his rising and makes his florid flourishes so gay an interlude. It is not vanity in any mean or unworthy sense. It is the calm, ineradicable conviction of the governing class, the *ancien régime*. He is a statesman not by virtue of so dangerous and democratic a thing as intellect; but by divine right, by right of blood and race. Brains may be necessary in business, but what you want in statesmanship, sir, is blood. It is blood that tells, sir. What is wrong with the House of Commons to-day is that there is not enough blood in it. Shopkeepers, lawyers, coal-miners, journalists, sitting here in the seats of the mighty, some of them even on the Front Bench opposite—oh, sir, the pity of it! Oh, my poor, misguided, fallen country! But, sir—and the portly frame distends with magnanimity —I will never desert her. I will never leave the burning deck.

It is this portentous gravity and detachment from reality that make him, if not witty himself, the cause of wit in other men. He is not merely " a thing of beauty," but " a joy for ever." What moment, for example, ever rivalled the hilarity that shook the House when, speaking on the Old Age Pensions Bill, he declaimed, his left hand upon his heart, his right uplifted to the heavenly witness: " It has ever been the purpose of my life to do nothing that would sap the foundations of thrift among the poor"? He paused, puzzled by the hurricane of laughter, for his mind moves with bucolic leisure, and it did not occur to him that his noble sentiment had any application to himself—he, a gentleman of blood and birth, whose career was a legend of splendid lavishness, and who, in his old age, honoured the State by receiving from it a trifling pension of £1200 a year, a mere bagatelle, a thankoffering, as it were, from a grateful public, almost, indeed, in the nature of conscience money.

The incident revealed the true workings of a type of mind so remote from the thought of our day as to be well-nigh incredible. It is a type of mind that belongs to the eighteenth century. It sees society in two clearly defined strata—a small, select aristocracy born booted and spurred to ride; a large, dim mass born saddled and bridled to be ridden. It is a divine arrangement. Does not even the Catechism support this theory of human society by bidding you "to order yourself lowly and reverently toward your betters"? He loves the poor in a fine old English way; that is, he loves them from the point of view of a kindly Providence. They are poor by the grace of God, as he is an aristocrat by the same divine authority. I think he would probably spend his pension in scattering benefactions among his retainers. But it would never occur to him that they belonged to the same hemisphere as himself, that the moral code which was for them was for him also. Thrift, for example, is a noble thing in the labourer earning fifteen shillings a week; but thrift in a gentleman of blood, sir?—God forbid! For his view of the aristocracy is the view of the French lady in the days before the Revolution, who, speaking of the vices of a certain nobleman and his prospective career

B. Chaplin

in another world, said with reverent abasement,
" But the Almighty will think twice before damning
a gentleman of his quality." If Mr. Chaplin ever
reads Carlyle, how his heart must be stirred by that
moving passage, probably the only one in all that
turgid torrent that would be quite clear to his simple
faith! It is a faith which regards the established
order of things as sacred and eternal. It is: therefore it ought to be. It is the view summed up by
Thwackum in *Tom Jones*. " When I mention religion," said Thwackum, " I mean the Christian
religion, and not only the Christian religion, but the
Protestant religion, and not only the Protestant
religion, but the Church of England."

It is this view of the divinity that doth hedge his
class that is the motive of his politics. He honestly
believes that the greatness of England consists in the
prosperity of a noble, landed caste. Hence his one
serious contribution to legislation, the Agricultural
Rates Bill, by which ingenious device the task of paying the agricultural rates fell upon the towns with
excellent results to the landlord's rent. Hence, too,
his devotion to Protection, to which——

But this is a subject which should be approached
with more solemnity. For it is here that Mr. Chaplin
must cease to be regarded as a politician. Rather he
is a prophet. Through long, long years he was as
one crying in the wilderness. The giddy world passed
him by, heeded not his message, laughed him and Mr.
" Jimmy " Lowther to scorn. " Give us a good
thumping duty on corn," was their cry, " and all will
be well. Then shall the clouds drop fatness, and
England, our brave little England, be merry England
once more." Fleeting hopes passed before their
vision. " Reciprocity " and " Fair Trade " came
like the cup of Tantalus to the lip and vanished, and

all again was dark, and the voice went on crying in
the wilderness. But a day came when he who had
been most scornful in his laughter at these antique
jesters, suddenly saw a great light, suddenly saw that
the way to make the people rich and happy was not
to give them abundance, but scarcity, not to make
things cheap, but dear. And, filled with this amazing
marvel, he launched " My Policy " and changed the
current of history. But it was the Squire of Blankney
who was the prophet of the new dispensation; it is the
Squire of Blankney who, after years of derision and
mocking laughter, sits to-day under his vine and
fig-tree, contemplating the work of his hand, thinking
over the solitary days when he was a voice crying
in the wilderness, looking forward confidently to the
time when a thumping duty on corn will make us
all happy—and hungry—and rejoicing in the rare
privilege of the prophet who has lived to see the
acceptance of his prophecy.

It is a rare revenge for the blow that was dealt him
in 1900, when, having served his Queen and country,
as he would say in that noble rhetoric of his, with
prudence, and he would hope with some success, he
was—oh, miserable, ungrateful world!—abandoned.
Yes, abandoned. He, Henry Chaplin, left out of her
Majesty's Ministry—out in the cold, like a dog. Oh,
the bitterness of that day! Not that he was sorry
for himself, not at all; but he mourned for his country,
his betrayed and desolated country.

For the sad truth has to be told that the prophet
was never appreciated by his friends at his real worth.
I am afraid that they did not take up Protection
earlier, not because they were not Protectionists at
heart, but because they feared that anything which
Mr. Chaplin advocated must be disastrous. They
loved him as their licensed jester. They were grateful

to him for his honest service, for the way he would
plant his burly form in the breach when the enemy
were nigh, as on that famous day of the Royal Hunt
Cup, when the Conservative Government were in
danger of defeat by a snap division, and he, like
Horatius of old, rushed in to hold the bridge and save
the town, and talked and talked and talked, while
messengers hurried

> forth,
> West and east and south and north,
> To summon the array,

and never ceased until the fear that was written on
the face of the Whips was turned to the gladness of
conscious victory.

But while they appreciated these heroisms, they
did not take him seriously. And yet no man ever
worked harder at his task according to his capacity
than he has done. A friend of his tells how he was
once staying with him at a country house, and in
the midst of conversation Mr. Chaplin excused himself on the ground of work. And later the friend,
while wandering in the pastures, heard from the other
side of the hedge a sonorous voice delivering itself
thus: " Mr. Speaker—sir—Little did I think, when
I came down to the House this afternoon, that I
should feel it incumbent upon me, in pursuance of
my duty to my country, and, Mr. Speaker, may I
add to myself, to address this House upon——"
and the friend fled from the august recital.

Mr. Chaplin, however, bore the whips and scorns
of colleagues with the gallant spirit with which he
took his losses on the Turf. For the decline of his
fortunes is understood to be not wholly due to the
lack of the thumping duty on corn, but to that sport
of gentlemen to which his really serious life has been
devoted. Not that he has been without his triumphs.

For is he not the Henry Chaplin, the owner of Hermit?
And who that knows the Turf finds not in that name
the music of the spheres? Who knows not the brave
story, that epic of the racecourse, of how the unknown
horse flashed on that June day, significantly heralded
by a snowstorm, to victory in the Derby of 1867,
winning for its owner £140,000 and a deathless fame?
"Easy come, easy go," and Mr. Chaplin's fortune
went easily, for he is a man of delicate tastes, a
Lucullus of the restaurant, who is reputed to know
as much about the gastronomic art as he does about
horseflesh, and more—if that be possible—than he
does about politics, with whom a noble hospitality
is innate, and in whom, as in Charles Surface, that
"hobbling beldame Economy cannot keep pace
with Generosity." He has the gift of spending, and
leaves the duty of saving to the poor. It is not that
he is a prodigal; but that he has that princely point
of view illustrated by the duke of whom Sir William
Harcourt used to tell, who, having got into difficulties,
applied for advice to Mr. Greville, a friend of Sir
William's. Mr. Greville investigated the affairs of
the duke, and he came to him and said: "Duke, I
think your establishment is larger than it ought to
be." And the duke said: "Really, Charles, do you
think so?" And Mr. Greville said, "Yes. I find,
for instance, you have got three confectioners in
your kitchen. I think that is more than is indispens-
able." And the duke looked at him in great surprise,
and he said: "You don't mean to say so! Why,
after all, a man must have a biscuit." That is Mr.
Chaplin's view. He must have a biscuit.

When Sleaford, forgetful of its long allegiance,
forgetful of the lustre shed upon it by Mr. Chaplin,
left him in the *débâcle* of 1906 at the bottom of the
poll, he, with his long experience of the vicissitudes

of fortune, took his *coup de grâce* with his habitual good temper, and gave to Wimbledon the distinction of being represented in Parliament by the owner of Hermit. It is an honour well fitted to Wimbledon.

Age cannot wither him, nor custom stale. He lingers on into these drab, prosaic times, a glorious reminiscence of the days of the dandies, defying the machinations alike of time and of the Radicals, cheerful and debonair, his ample hat sitting on his head with just a suspicion of a sporting angle, his cambric peeping from his breast pocket with a subtle suggestion of gallantry, his eye-glass worn as if to the manner born; a kindly, simple-hearted gentleman, with the spacious manners of an earlier day slightly exaggerated; a mirror in which we may see the England of long ago and the Toryism that is dead, or, if not dead, passed into a shape less reputable because less honest. Long may we see him, the last of his type, sitting on the Front Opposition Bench taking notes and watching over the Empire, a pleasant figure of industrious futility. We could better spare a greater man.

LORD CURZON

LORD CURZON would have been a great man if he could occasionally have forgotten Lord Curzon. Health is always unconscious of itself. It is not until sickness that one is aware of the body. It is not until a nation has lost its freedom that it becomes conscious of itself and the spirit of nationalism burns like a fever in the blood. And the mind in perfect health is equally self-forgetful. Lord Curzon has never enjoyed that health. He has dwelt in a house of mirrors. Wherever he has turned he has met the dazzling vision of himself. Oxford was but a setting for one magical figure, Parliament the stage for one inimitable actor, India the background for one radiant form in purple and gold. When poor Sir Naylor Leyland opposed him at Southport he turned and rent him as if he were a dog desecrating the sanctuary. When simple St. John Brodrick, forgetful of the Balliol days when he had been honoured by the notice of the Honourable George Nathaniel Curzon, dared to veto his action in India because he feared Lord Kitchener even more than he feared Lord Curzon, he forbade him his presence. Where he went Mr. Brodrick must not be. He would not have him in the same social hemisphere. He must get a hemisphere of his own. " God may forgive him," he is reported to have said; " but I never will."

It is one of Mr. Chesterton's jolly maxims that a man should be able to laugh at himself, poke fun at himself, enjoy his own absurdity. It is an excellent test of mental health. Man is a tragi-comedian. He should see himself the quaint " forked radish " that he is, fantastic as well as wonderful. He should see his mind ready to do battle and die, if need be, for an idea, but equally ready to get into a passion because his egg is boiled too hard. He should, in a word, see himself not as a hero, but as a man of strange virtues and stranger follies, a figure to move him to alternate admiration and laughter. Lord Curzon has never laughed at himself. He has only admired. And from this immense seriousness, this absence of the faculty of wholesome self-ridicule and self-criticism, issue those mistakes with which his career is strewn, a type of which was his appeal to the sympathy of the world for having asked for and been refused a seat in the House of Lords. It seemed to him an insult to majesty. It seemed to the world a joke. It kept the satire of his Oxford days true to the mature man. It made credible all those strange stories of the pomp and circumstance of the Durbar—of the Viceroy who would not touch swords with the chiefs, but left that menial function to the Duke of Connaught, and who turned the wild extravagance of that colossal show into a triumph in which he filled the rôle of Imperial Cæsar.

This grandiose vision of himself as Cæsar was at the root of most of his mistakes in India. It was responsible, for example, for that adventure into Tibet—an adventure without motive and without consequence, except the motive of personal *réclame*, and the consequence of shooting down a defenceless people like a flock of sheep, and burdening the Indian peasant, with his income of £2 a year, with new taxation. A high price to pay for the glory of being the first Viceroy to penetrate to Lhassa. It was responsible for that costly folly of the Durbar. The people were dying of famine and of plague, and he gave them a circus, for which they had to pay out of their misery. It was responsible, too, for that stupendous white elephant, the Victoria memorial, which is sinking into the mud of the Maidan at Calcutta. The people asked for a memorial that would regenerate their industry—a great scheme of technical and scientific education. Mr. J. N. Tata, the wealthy Parsee, offered to start such a scheme with a quarter of a million of money. It was refused, and the people were offered an idle show-place—in Lord Curzon's grandiloquent phrase, " a snow-white fabric " arising from the green expanse of the Calcutta Maidan, " the Taj of the Twentieth Century." He might have given India an instructed people: he promised it a pretty toy.

It was this view of the mild Hindoo as a child, to be amused and paternally governed, that was the vice of his method. He was aloof on Olympus. India had no access to him. Hindoos like Mr. Gokhale, one of the ablest men and noblest characters with whom I have ever come in contact, and Mr. Surendra Nath Banerjee, were ignored. They were " natives " —children like the rest. Had he listened to them, that fatal partition of Bengal would never have been carried out, or would have been carried out differently. It was carried out ruthlessly, and no more momentous act was ever accomplished. It has set India alight with a flame that will never die down. " When I went out to India in 1902," said a well-known Englishman to me, " there was no national movement. To-day all the land ferments with new national ideals. We owe that to Lord Curzon's provocative policy. He has created the New India." It is good that there should be a new India: it is not good that it should come to birth with the bitter feeling of British injustice.

The exaggerated sense of one's own place in the scheme of things involves depreciation of the place of

others. Lord Curzon always under-rated the Indian
intelligence, and always forgot that the Indian was a
man with the sensibilities of a man. " If you prick
him, will he not bleed; if you tickle him, will he not
laugh? " He often laughed at his lordship, sometimes good-naturedly, as when at the time of the
Durbar Lord Curzon organised a show with the
admirable idea of promoting native industries. He
denounced those who got their furniture and their
artistic ideals from " Tottenham Court Road." The
retort was crushing. It was pointed out that his
residence at the Durbar had been furnished by Maple's,
whose business is actually in Tottenham Court Road.
Sometimes the laughter had a ring of anger. Everyone remembers that blazing indiscretion at the Con-
vocation of Calcutta University, when, addressing
the Bengali students and the cream of intellectual
India, he spoke of truth as a Western virtue, and more
than hinted that the Orientals, like the Cretans, were
liars, and that they were given to flattery, and other
heinous sins. A shudder went through society. How
would India take this insult? The situation was
saved by a Hindoo with a characteristically tenacious
memory. He went home, took down *Problems of
the Far East*, by George N. Curzon, and a day or two
later there appeared in the *Amritsa Bazar Patrika*,
side by side with the offending passages in the speech,
the following extract from Lord Curzon's book:

Before proceeding to the Royal audience I enjoyed an interview with the President of the Korean Foreign Office. . . .
Having been particularly warned not to admit to him that
I was only thirty-three years old, an age to which no respect
attaches in Korea, when he put to me the straight question
(always the first in the Oriental dialogue), " How old are
you? " I unhesitatingly responded, " Forty." " Dear me,"
he said, " you look very young for that. How do you
account for it? " " By the fact," I replied, " that I have
been travelling for a month in the superb climate of his

Majesty's dominions." Finally he said to me, " I presume you are a near relative of her Majesty the Queen of England?" " No," I replied, " I am not." But observing the look of disgust that passed over his countenance I was fain to add, " I am, however, as yet an unmarried man," with which unscrupulous suggestion I completely regained the old gentleman's favour.

India was dissolved in laughter. It almost forgave the insult for the sake of the jest.

Coupled with his exalted view of himself, Lord Curzon has an energy, industry, and capacity that are probably unrivalled. They showed themselves at Oxford, where he missed his First in " Greats." The indignity cut him to the quick. It must be wiped out by heroic means. He must win the Lowthian Prize. He went away to Egypt with his books of reference. He worked incessantly; came back to London, spent a fortnight at the British Museum putting the finishing touches on his work, and at midnight on the last day for receiving the essays dashed up in a cab to the schools, awoke the porter, handed in his essay, and won the prize. With a similar fury of industry he, later, won the Arnold Prize. This power of work he has always shown. In India he was the wonder of the Service. His hand was everywhere. Nothing was delegated. No subject was too microscopic to escape him. He instructed the Government proof readers in the correct use of the comma and called the Bengal Government to book for three errors in the inscription placed on Macaulay's Calcutta house. I remember one incident of this abnormal industry and personal sensitiveness. An article criticising him had appeared in a London paper. It came back to the editor neatly pasted on foolscap sheets of paper. In the margin he had written for private information an elaborate and detailed reply to every sentence.

He was not loved by the officials. That is not

Lord Curzon

necessarily to his discredit. No Viceroy who did his duty to India would be loved by the officials. He had gone out with the gospel of " Efficiency," and he was imperious in his reforms, and in the insistence on his supremacy. The famous Note on Departmentalism is still a classic in Indian official circles. It is read o' nights over the pipe and the glass, and such passages as " Departmentalism is not a moral delinquency. It is an intellectual hiatus " still make the rafters ring.

There was never a Viceroyalty so full of the drama of action. Every day had its new sensation. In every scene the limelight was upon him, and India to-day, for good and evil, is largely what he made it. Many of his reforms were excellent, many of his practical schemes admirable. He held Commissions and inquiries, and, what is more, acted on them. His Irrigation scheme was a great and worthy effort to combat famine. He made a brave stand for the right of the Indian to equal justice. His action in regard to the 9th Lancers was high and courageous. The evidence pointed to one of them having been guilty of the murder of a native cook—a common enough occurrence. They refused to disclose the murderer. He degraded the regiment. When it marched past at the Durbar all official India applauded loudly. It was meant as a rebuke to Lord Curzon, sitting there silent upon his horse. I hope he saw that it was not a rebuke, but the proudest compliment of his career. Nor do I think he was wrong in the final rupture with Lord Kitchener. At any rate, he stood for a great principle—the civil control of the Army.

No estimate of Lord Curzon would be complete which omitted the fact that he has fought his battle with the handicap of physical weakness. He has lived his life, as it were, on broken wing. To that we may trace the defects of temperament and outlook. Nor can one forget the tragedy of his domestic life—the loss of the brilliant partner of his career in circumstances full of pathos.

A brilliant man, full of energy, full of ambition, full of capacity, still young — though more than " forty "—burning to be in the heart of the fight, he finds himself with no path open, no rôle to play, his career closed ere it has well begun. The brilliant Indian episode left him stranded on the political shore. For a time he cast longing eyes upon the House where he had once been the best-graced actor and where his eager temperament could alone find scope for play. Then he turned sadly to the House of Lords, and the shades of that decorous prison-house closed on his imperious spirit.

WINSTON CHURCHILL

It was a quarter to twelve, midnight. Mr. Balfour was once more at bay, defending his tottering Ministry from collapse. The immediate point was a certain closure resolution. What were the terms? It was vital to the Opposition that they should know, and know to-night. Mr. Balfour fenced and feinted. He would not give the conditions. He would hand them to the Clerk on the adjournment. Once in his hands they were unpublished and undiscussable until to-morrow. The moment of adjournment had almost come, and Mr. Balfour had gained his point. He threw down the document on the table, and the Opposition sank back defeated. In the moment of discomfiture a figure moved towards the table—the figure of a youth, fair, slight, with head thrust forward, eyes protuberant, eyebrows lacking, the whole air that of boyish audacity. He seized the document, turned back to his seat, and, before the House had quite realised what had happened, was disclosing, on the usual nightly motion that this House do now adjourn, the whole scheme in the form of a rain of questions addressed to Mr. Balfour. The secret was out. The Speaker rose, the House adjourned, and the members poured out into the lobbies, excitedly discussing Winston's audacity and what it had disclosed.

It was the Churchill touch. It carried the mind back to those brief years when another Churchill was the storm centre of the House, bearding the mighty Gladstone with calculated insolence, ridiculing the

" Marshall and Snelgroves " of his own party, and leaping on to his seat in the hour of victory, waving his hat and shouting with schoolboy glee. What a meteor it was! How brilliant its path, how dramatic its climax, how tragic its eclipse! And now his son leaps forward into the arena, with the same daring, the same aplomb, the same incomparable insolence. Again the cry is " A Churchill! A Churchill! " and to that cry the street responds as to no other. For it is the call to high adventure and careless gallantry. It suggests the clatter of hoofs in the moonlight, the clash of swords on the turnpike road. It is the breath of romance stirring the prosaic air of politics.

" When Nature has fashioned a genius," says Emerson, " she breaks the mould." It is true of genius, in spite of the possible exception of the Pitts; it is not true of talent. A Cæsar does not follow a Cæsar, nor a Shakespeare a Shakespeare, nor a Cromwell a Cromwell. But to-day we have remarkable evidence of the transmission of high talent. Mr. Harcourt, Mr. Churchill, and Lord Hugh Cecil are not inferior to the fathers that begat them.

Mr. Churchill, indeed, is superior to his father. For to Lord Randolph's *flair* and courage and instinct for the game he adds a knowledge and industry his father did not possess. He works with the same fury that he plays, attacks a subject with the intrepidity with which he attacks an opponent in the House. " What are all those books on Socialism? " asked a friend of mine who was calling on Mr. Churchill just before his departure on a tour to East Africa. " They are going to be my reading on the voyage," he replied. " I'm going to see what the Socialist case really is." And so with his speeches. " The mistake you young men make," said Mr. Chamberlain to some rising politicians, " is that you don't take trouble with your

speeches." That is not Mr. Churchill's way. I have
been told by one who was in Scotland with him when
he was campaigning that he never appeared at his
hostess's table until tea time. All day he might be
heard booming away in his bedroom, rehearsing his
facts and his flourishes to the accompaniment of
resounding knocks on the furniture. It is not that
he is without readiness. No one is more intrepid in
debate. But he is too wise to rely on that faculty
in a set speech. He has the genius which consists
of taking infinite pains. The speech with which he
leapt into Parliamentary fame was that in which,
while still the youngest recruit of Toryism, he shattered Mr. Brodrick's army scheme. It electrified the
House by its grasp of the problems of national defence
and its spacious movement in the higher realm of
moral purpose. " I wrote that speech out six times
with my own hand," he told me.

The courage which that speech displayed sustained
him throughout the transition from Toryism to
Liberalism. There is no parallel in our time to the
intensity of the feeling which that transition aroused.
His rising filled the Government ranks with visible
frenzy—a frenzy which culminated one day in the
whole party, two hundred and fifty strong, getting
up as one man and marching out of the House as he
rose to speak. It was the highest tribute ever paid
to a Parliamentary orator. It was as though the
enemy fled at his appearance from a literal battle-
field. And, indeed, the whole spirit of his politics
is military. It is impossible to think of him except
in the terms of actual warfare. The smell of powder
is about his path, and wherever he appears one seems
to hear the crack of musketry and to feel the hot
breath of battle. To his impetuous swiftness he joins
the gift of calculating strategy. His eye takes in the

Prophets, Priests, and Kings

whole field, and his skirmishes are not mere exploits
of reckless adventure, but are governed by the purpose of the main battle. He would not, with Rupert,
have pursued the flying wing he had broken: he
would, like Cromwell, have turned and smashed in
the enemy's centre from the rear.

This union of intrepidity and circumspection is
accompanied by an independence of aim and motive
that must always keep him a little under suspicion.
He is a personal force and not a party instrument, and
he will never be easily controlled except by himself.
He knows nothing of the loyalties which have governed
other contemporary leaders of the party. " C.-B."
was anchored to a simple faith in democracy, Mr.
Asquith is the authentic vehicle of the collective
purpose, Mr. Harcourt is governed by tradition, even
Mr. Lloyd George, with all his personal energy and
initiative, is too sensitive to the popular judgment to
run amuck. But Mr. Churchill knows no sanction
except his own will, and when he is seized with an idea
he pursues it with an intensity that seems unconscious of opposition. " I will go to Worms though
there are as many devils in Worms as there are tiles
on the roofs of the houses," said Luther. And that is
Mr. Churchill's frame of mind.

It follows from this combination of daring and
astuteness that his oratory has the qualities of the
writer as well as of the rhetorician. There is form
and substance as well as flame and spirit. Like the
hero of his novel *Savrola*, in which, at twenty-three,
he foreshadowed his career, he burnt the midnight
oil over his brilliant impromptus. He will tell you
that his father not only learned his speeches, but
studied his gestures and his pauses, would fumble in
his pockets for a note he did not want. Mr. Churchill
is not indifferent to the same arts to heighten his

effect, but with the consciousness of power he is tending to rely less upon mere artificialities of manner and more upon the appeal to the intelligence. Nor does his oratory need extrinsic aids. It is rich and varied in its essential qualities. The architecture is broad and massive. The colouring is vivid, but not gaudy. He does not worry a humour to weariness. He strikes the note of gravity and authority with a confidence that one can hardly reconcile with the youthful face. And his satire can be quite in the leisured eighteenth-century style, as when, attacking Mr. Balfour's Cabinet on the Fiscal issue, he said:

> They are a class of right honourable gentlemen—all good men, all honest men—who are ready to make great sacrifices for their opinions, but they have no opinions. They are ready to die for the truth, if they only knew what truth was. They are weary of office; they wish anything would relieve them of its cares; but their patriotic duty compels them to remain, although they have no opinions to offer, holding their opinions undecided and unflinching, like George II. at the Battle of Dettingen, *sans peur et sans avis*.

He is extraordinarily youthful even for his years. He has the curiosity and animation of a child—a child in fairyland, a child consumed with the thirst for life. He must know all, taste all, devour all. He is drunk with the wonder and the fascination of living. A talk with him is as exhilarating as a gallop across country, so full is it of adventure, and of the high spirits and eagerness of youth. No matter what the subject, soldiering or science, religion or literature, he plunges into it with the joy of a boy taking a " header " in the sea. And to the insatiable curiosity and the enthusiasm of the child he joins the frankness of the child. He has no reserves and no shams. He takes you, as it were, by the arm on the instant, and makes you free of all the domain of his mind. You are welcome to anything that he has, and may pry into

any corner you like. He has that scorn of conceal-
ment that belongs to a caste which never doubts itself
and to a personality that is entirely fearless. And
he is as frank with himself as with you. " Yes," he
said, " I have read James' *Immortality*. I have read
it three times. It impressed me deeply. But finally
I came to the conclusion that I was lacking in the
religious sense, and put it away." He has coupled
with this sense of deficiency, a real reverence for the
spiritual man. His admiration for Lord Hugh Cecil
is sincere and unaffected. He speaks of him as one
who dwells within the Palace of the King, while he
stands without the gate.

His school was the barrack-room; his university
the battle-field. He has served in two regiments of
the line, fought with the Spaniards in Cuba, and held
a commission in the South African Light Horse. He
knows life in four continents, and has smelt powder
in three. He has seen more wars than any man of his
years; written more books than any soldier living.
He has been a war correspondent; he has been
taken prisoner; he has escaped from prison. And he
showed the same address in war as in politics. General
Smuts told me that when he held up the armoured
train on which Mr. Churchill was captured he was
struck by the energy and capacity of a fair-haired
youth who led the defence. When they surrendered
this youth modestly claimed special privileges in
telegraphing to his friends on the ground that he was
a war correspondent. The General laughed. " You
have done all the damage that's been done," he said.
" You fight too well to be treated as a civilian." " And
now," added the General in telling me the story, " I
am going to the Colonial Office to see if I can get a
favour out of that fair-haired youth in memory of our
meeting on the veldt."

Winston Churchill

When, hot from campaigning on Indian frontiers and Egyptian sands, he galloped up to Westminster with his breezy " stand and deliver," he found Mr. Balfour lacking in enthusiasm. Mr. Balfour knew his father—indeed, followed his father in the jolly Hounslow Heath days of the early eighties. But while it was capital fun to go tiger-hunting with a Churchill, it was another affair to have a Churchill worrying you in office. He remembered his uncle's famous *mot*. When, after the memorable resignation, he was asked if he did not want Lord Randolph back, Lord Salisbury replied: " When you have got rid of a boil on the neck, you don't want it back again." Mr. Balfour determined that he would not have a boil on the neck.

His coolness did Mr. Churchill a service. It hastened his inevitable development. Like his father, he has the instinct of democratic appeal. His intellectual fearlessness carries him resistlessly along the path of constitutional development. The fundamental vice of Conservatism is that it distrusts the people. Its fundamental policy is to hoodwink the people, bribe them, drug them, use them as tools. Lord Randolph saw the folly of this. He saw that no party could be vital without the sanction of an instructed people, and that the modern State was healthy in proportion to the development of a healthy democratic opinion. He tried to hitch the democracy to the Tory chariot by making Toryism a real instrument of reform. It was a gallant dream, and he was broken on the wheel in the attempt. Mr. Churchill is happier in his fate. He was fired out of the Tory tabernacle before he had eaten out his heart in a vain service.

His future is the most interesting problem of personal speculation in English politics. At thirty-

four he stands before the country one of the two
most arresting figures in politics, his life a crowded
drama of action, his courage high, his vision un-
clouded, his boats burned. " I love Churchill and
trust him," said one of his colleagues to me. " He
has the passion of democracy more than any man I
know. But don't forget that the aristocrat is still
there—latent and submerged, but there nevertheless.
The occasion may arise when the two Churchills will
come into sharp conflict, and I should not like to
prophesy the result." We may doubt both the
democrat and the aristocrat, and suspect that his real
political philosophy is the philosophy of Cæsarism.
If we could conceive him in a great upheaval,
he would be seen emerging in the rôle of what
Bagehot calls " a Benthamite despot," dismissing all
feudal ideas and legitimist pretensions, sweeping aside
all aristocracies, proclaiming the democratic doctrine
of the " greatest happiness of the greatest number "
and seating himself astride the storm as the people's
Cæsar—at once dictator and democrat.

But Cæsarism, however picturesque and in certain
conditions even unavoidable, is never more than a
temporary episode, a stop-gap expedient, in a society
shifting to new foundations. Our foundations are fixed
and Mr. Churchill's genius will have to find its scope
within existing limits. There his detachment from
the current philosophies, his impetus of mind and his
personal force make him a not easily calculable factor.
More than any man of his time, he approaches an
issue without mental reserves or the restraints of
party caution or calculation. To his imperious
spirit, a party is only an instrument. *Au fond*,
he would no more think of consulting a party
than the chauffeur would think of consulting his
motor car. His magnificent egotism takes refuge

in no concealments. You see all the processes of his mind. It may be said of him, as Lord Russell said of the British Constitution, that he is like a hive of bees working under a glass cover. He leaves you in no doubt. He does not " hum and ha." He is not paralysed by the fear of consequences, nor afraid to contemplate great changes. He knows that to deal in millions is as simple as to deal in pence and that timidity is the unpardonable sin in politics.

Has he staying power? Can one who has devoured life with such feverish haste retain his zest to the end of the feast? How will forty find him?—that fatal forty when the youth of roselight and romance has faded into the light of common day and the horizon of life has shrunk incalculably, and when the flagging spirit no longer answers to the spur of external things, but must find its motive and energy from within, or find them not at all.

That is the question that gives us pause. For, with all his rare qualities, Mr. Churchill is the type of " the gentleman of fortune." He is out for adventure and follows politics as he would follow the hounds. He has no animus against the fox, but he wants to be in " at the kill." It is recorded that when, a fiery-headed boy at Harrow, he was asked what profession he thought of taking up, he replied, " The Army, of course, so long as there's any fighting to be had. When that's over, I shall have a shot at politics." He is still the Harrow boy, having his " shot at politics "—not so much concerned about who the enemy may be or about the merits of the quarrel as about being in the thick of the fight and having a good time. With the facility of the Churchill mind he feels the pulse of Liberalism with astonishing sureness, and interprets it with extraordinary ability. But the sense of high purpose is not yet apparent through the fierce joy of battle that possesses him. The passion for humanity, the stern resolve to see justice done though the heavens fall and he be buried in the ruins, the surrender of himself to the cause— these things have yet to come. His eye is less on the fixed stars than on the wayward meteors of the night. And when the exhilaration of youth is gone, and the gallop of high spirits has run its course, it may be that this deficiency of high and abiding purpose will be a heavy handicap. Then it will be seen how far courage and intellectual address, a mind acutely responsive to noble impulses, and a quick and apprehensive political instinct will carry him in the leadership of men.

THE REV. R. J. CAMPBELL

WHETHER to friend or foe, the Rev. R. J. Campbell is one of the most arresting personalities in the London of our time. He is the voice of disquiet and of challenge. He is the disturber of our comfortable peace. He hurries with breathless eagerness from point to point, the lighted torch ever in his hand, the trail of conflagration ever in his wake. He follows no lead, except that of his own urgent, unquiet spirit. He is indifferent to consequences, will brook no interference, drives straight forward, deaf to appeals from the right hand or the left. Friends cannot persuade him; parties cannot hold him; creeds cannot limit him. He is like the wind that bloweth where it listeth.

If stagnation is death and discontent divine, then he is one of the best assets of our time. He flings his bombs into the stagnant parlours of our thought, and thrills the air with the spirit of unrest. Acquiescence and content vanish at his challenge. The sleeper rubs his eyes. He is awake. The vision is before him. The air is filled with the murmur of many voices. He, too, must be up and doing.

In the great, dim, industrial cities of the North, where, in the dark of the winter and the grey dawn of the summer mornings the women, clothed in their shawls and clogs, go forth to their labour in the mills, there is a familiar figure. He is known as the " knocker-up." At four o'clock the clatter of his clogs rings down the silent street, and the thunder of his knock echoes from every door. He passes,

237

and soon in the darkness there is the sound of a people awake. Doors bang, and voices ring out on the still air, and there follows the harsh music of a thousand clogs, pattering in shrill chorus to the mills. The battle of life has recommenced.

Mr. Campbell is the " knocker-up" in the dawn of the twentieth century. The chimes of the great cathedral surge dreamful music on our slumbers; but across from the City Temple comes the sound of a bell, violent, clangorous, insistent, that shatters sleep, and awakes the City. You may not like it. You may find it harsh and discordant. But at least it makes you leap to your feet, if only to take up its challenge.

Nonconformity does not know what to make of this apparition that has suddenly burst into its midst. It finds its throne, as it were, in the hands of the revolutionary. It finds the old flags that waved from the keep hauled down, and the twin flags of the " New Theology " and Socialism flying defiantly in the breeze. It finds its doctrines vaporised into thin air, diffused into a kind of purple mist, beautiful, but intangible. It finds itself indicted in its own cathedral for the sin of Pharisaism, pictured to the world as Mrs. Oliphant loved to picture it—as a system of smug content, caricatured in the bitter sneer of Swift:

> We are God's chosen few;
> All others will be damned.
> There is no place in heaven for you:
> We can't have heaven crammed.

It has borne the scourge with singular restraint. It knows that there has been a certain truth in the charge in the past. It knows that there is less truth in it to-day than at any time since it was born out of the purging fires of persecution. It has been the Church

The Rev. R. J. Campbell

of the middle classes; but its future, as Sir Compton Rickett has said, is with the people, and it is to them that its appeal is directed to-day. The work of men like F. B. Meyer and John Clifford, Silvester Horne and Ensor Walters, Campbell-Morgan and Thomas Phillips, reflects the new spirit that has been breathed in these days into the dry bones of Nonconformity.

It is otherwise with the challenge to its faith. Here Mr. Campbell has done a real service. He has done the service to the religious world which Mr. Chamberlain did to the political world when he challenged the economic structure of the State. He was wrong; but he made us discover that we were right. He set the whole nation to think out the problem of its economic existence. We had accepted the faith as final, and had forgotten its very elements. We were in servitude to a theory that we did not understand and did not want to understand. He made us dig down to our foundations and see if they were true. He put us on our defence, and taught us our case. And so Free Trade was born again. It was a fetish: it has become a faith. This we owe to Mr. Chamberlain.

And so with Mr. Campbell. He has challenged our religious structure at its centre and has set the mind of his time seething with unrest and inquiry. He has lighted a fire which will burn up the refuse and leave the residue pure and vital. He has made the man in the street think about ultimate things, and no one can do a greater service to his time.

" But," says the Divinity Student, " think of the danger."

" The danger to what? " asks the Autocrat.

" The danger to Truth," says the Divinity Student.

And the Autocrat answers, " Truth is tough. You may kick it about all day like a football, and it will be round and full like the moon at evening, while Error

dies of the prick of a pin." We need not worry about
Truth. It comes out of the battle-smoke unharmed,
leaving the Lie dead upon the plain.

The Churches needed this challenge. They had
ceased to face those obstinate questionings of the
intellect which will not be stilled, or, if they are stilled,
are stilled only as the restless strivings of the fevered
patient are stilled—with the drugs of a deathly indifference. The world was passing them by. Mr.
Campbell has made them dig down to their foundations. He has put them upon their defence, and out
of the dust and heat of the conflict it may be that
faith will be born again.

It is not uncommon to hear him dismissed as a
rather crude mind rushing in where wiser men fear to
tread, and fighting out his doubts in the public eye.
There is a certain truth in the criticism. He is the
ordinary man thinking furiously aloud. He is the
preacher wrestling with the plain man's doubts in the
pulpit. He is not so much fighting for the souls of his
hearers as for his own soul, and in that intense drama
the man from the counting-house and the shop sees
mirrored his own disquiet and his own hunger. Perhaps he, too, out of this conflict may catch a vision of
the Promised Land. It is this fact that makes him
the most attractive pulpit personality of the day to
those outside the churches. The orthodox view him
with coldness or alarm. He shakes the pillars of the
temple and brings the familiar fabric tumbling about
their ears, without providing another stucture equally
solid and secure to receive them. He invites them out
into the open in pursuit of the rainbow. But to the
soul adrift from the churches, yet consumed with the
hunger for some revelation that the world cannot
provide, the pursuit of the rainbow offers an emotion
and a vision that stimulate if they do not satisfy.

The Rev. R. J. Campbell

This visionary fervour is expressed with unaffected sincerity and simplicity. In the oratory of Dr. Parker there was always a suggestion of the stage. It was not that he was insincere, but that the instinct of the drama was ineradicable. He could not forget the limelight, and loved the echoes of his own thunder. Mr. Campbell delivers himself up to his emotion with absolute self-surrender. He goes out of himself, as it were, into space. There is no strain either of thought or diction, no effort after effect, no flowers of speech. He speaks as the spirit moves him, without literary consciousness and without any thought of consequences. It is not without spiritual relevance that the pulpit of the City Temple used to be filled by an old man with a black mane and is now filled by a young man with a white.

For the leader of a great crusade, he has one serious defect. He is intensely sensitive to criticism. He plays at bowls, but does not look for rubbers. He "comes through," as they say on the green, with crashing force, scattering the "woods" in his path, and he seems surprised that the woods do not get out of the way, with polite apologies for their presence. "They don't burn you at the stake to-day," he said not long ago; "they stab you in the back." Few men have invited reprisals more; few men have been treated with more generosity by those who find their beliefs, their errors, if you will, suddenly and furiously assailed from within.

He has another defect. It is a certain feverishness of the spirit. There is about him the sense of the hot, uneasy pillow. The raw edges of life chafe him. He cannot escape from the hair-shirt of this mortal vestment, and he cannot endure it. Whatever is, is *wrong*. The Churches are wrong, society is wrong, Free Trade is wrong. It is this irritation with his environment that gives him the touch of perversity which is so noticeable in him. Nonconformity is definite; he is mystical. Nonconformity is individualistic; he is a member of the I.L.P. The I.L.P. is for Free Trade; he, I gather from a conversation I had with him, is for Tariff Reform. He conforms to no system, accepts no shibboleth, either spiritual or temporal. When Sir David Baird's mother heard that her son was captured in India and chained to natives, she remarked, placidly, " I pity the puir laddies that are chained to oor Dauvit." She knew the imperious waywardness of her son. The way of one chained intellectually to Mr. Campbell would be not less trying. He has the impatience of the idealist in the presence of realities. The vision fades when he touches it concretely. " Now," as Lowell says, " now ain't just the minit that ever fits us easy while we're in it." The son of a United Methodist minister, brought up in the Presbyterian atmosphere of his grandfather's home at Belfast, he turned instinctively from the appeal of Nonconformity, with its lack of sensuous attraction, to that of Anglicanism, with its sense of historic continuity. In the conflict between loyalty to the Free Church traditions of his ancestry, and the call of a more æsthetic system, his mind turned away from the pulpit. He married and took up the teaching profession. Then, with the impulsiveness that always drives him, he set out for Oxford, his mind still under the influence of Anglicanism. But the atmosphere of Oxford was Anglican, and that fact —so subversive of the Nonconformity of the normal man—headed him back to the original fold. It was not lack of sympathy, for the singular charm of his personality made a deep impression on Dr. Paget, and Dr. Gore was especially anxious to secure so powerful a recruit for the Church. It was the instinct

The Rev. R. J. Campbell

of the nomadic spirit to escape from the encompassing fold. It was the operation of what the psychologists call " contrarient ideas." The one way to prevent him going in a given direction is to urge him to go. The one way to enlist him in a cause is to prove that it is contrary to all tradition and propriety.

When men reflect upon Mr. Campbell's astonishing career, one question rises to their lips: Whither? There is no answer. I question whether Mr. Campbell himself has an answer. He belongs to no planetary system. He is a lonely wanderer through space—a trail of fire burning at white heat, and flashing through the inscrutable night to its unknown goal. His head grey in his youth, his eyes eloquent with some nameless hunger, his face thin and pallid, his physique frail as that of an ascetic of the desert, he stands before us a figure of singular fascination and disquiet, a symbol of the world's passionate yearning after the dimly-apprehended ideal, of its unquenchable revolt against the agonies of men.

THE SPEAKER

WHEN Murray complained to Byron that some of his poetry was dull, Byron replied: "You can no more have poetry all gems than a midnight all stars." So it is with the House of Commons. Ordinarily it is a very dull place. There is a general air of lassitude and weariness. The benches are thinly peopled with men who seem tired of each other's company. They lounge about in every attitude of negligent inattention. Someone is droning away on a back bench, but he is unheard amid the babble of idle conversation; for, though you may not read a book or a paper in the House, you may chatter as fluently as a parrakeet at the Zoo. Superficially it is a gathering of the comfortable unemployed, waiting for something to turn up. Occasionally something does turn up, and then the House leaps to life as if by magic. It has moments more dramatic, more intense than any stage.

There was such a moment one afternoon in 1903. Mr. Chamberlain had just flung his bomb into the astonished country, and the House was reeling and reverberating with the concussion. It was as though the familiar continent of politics had been engulfed by the sea, and all the submerged politicians were struggling to find a footing in the new one that had suddenly come from the depths. On this afternoon the air was electric with a suppressed excitement; the benches crowded, the faces of men flushed and expectant. Most flushed of all was the swarthy face of Mr. Ritchie, Chancellor of the Exchequer. He had come down to deliver his soul—a plain, bluff,

The Speaker

honest man, conscious of the keen, unnerving presence of the bomb-thrower in the corner seat behind. A question was put. No, said courtly Mr. Speaker Gully, the general fiscal question could not under the rules be discussed. It was as though a cold douche had suddenly descended from the ceiling. The drama, then, was to be strangled by red tape. Mr. Ritchie moves from his seat along the front bench, whispers to the Chair, gesticulates to the Chair. A moment later the prim, clean-shaven lawyer quietly retires, and a jovial-looking country gentleman, ruddy and bearded, takes his place. And when Mr. Ritchie rises to speak, and plunges boldly into the fiscal question, there is not a murmur of rebuke from the Chair. When he sits down, Mr. Speaker returns with his red tape, and the House subsides into the atmosphere of formality that he loves.

The incident illustrates the difference between Mr. Speaker Lowther and his predecessor. Under Mr. Gully the House lived in a strait-waistcoat of legal technicality. It crackled with parchment. It was " cribb'd, cabin'd, and confin'd." Its air was the air of a lawyer's office, and Blackstone sat heavy upon its chest. It was a dry, arid place.

When Mr. Lowther succeeded to the Chair, he opened the windows and let in the fresh air. He came bringing a jolly breeze with him from the country. It is true that he wears a wig and knee breeches, and silver buckles on his shoes; but all that is make-believe. In his pocket, you suspect, there is a pipe, and you feel convinced that he has just come from tramping the moors in very thick boots, with a gun and a dog for company. Or, if that is impossible, then he has been having half an hour at the nets at Lord's, or a little sword practice with his maître d'armes, for he is still young enough to enjoy the matchless sensation of a "late cut" and the swift pleasure of the foils. The fact probably is that he has been stewing since nine o'clock over the "Orders of the Day," and the way he shall parry the strokes of those terrible Irishmen whose wits are swords. But I speak of the impression he conveys. It is the impression of the fresh air and the sunshine, of league-long furrows, and of the open sky on the rolling moor. He seems to be a casual presence in this dim chamber. He has strolled in in a moment of aberration, and has taken the seat nearest at hand— a cheerful, bucolic man, sound in wind and limb, digestion excellent, brain clear and cool, temper unruffled.

The Speaker stamps his own personality inevitably upon the House. If he is acrid, the temper of the House will be acrid; if he is stiff and formal, the House will be stiff and formal; if he is jolly, the House will be jolly. To-day it is jolly. Mr. Peel ruled by awe, Mr. Gully by law, Mr. Lowther rules by a certain bluff common sense and good humour which communicate themselves to the members. He makes them feel at home. He is one of themselves. It is not a chill, rebuking figure that sits up there in wig and gown, ready to pounce on you and send you to the Clock Tower. It is a man and a brother. If he raps you across the knuckles, he does it with so much geniality that you feel that you ought to thank him.

> He kicks you downstairs with such infinite grace,
> You might think he was handing you up.

"Grace" is perhaps not the word for that heavy voice and solid manner. It is rather the hearty good-will of a jovial companion who really loves you in spite of your frailties, and scourges you for your own good. Even when he came down with such a heavy hand on Sir Howard Vincent, that garrulous knight was able to share the enjoyment of the House. The question was the deportation of Lajpat Rai, and Sir Howard interpolated, *sotto voce*, " Why not shoot him? " Low though it was spoken, it did not escape the terrible ear of Mr. Swift MacNeill, the watch-dog of the Parliamentary proprieties. " Mr. Speaker " —and the whispered words were boomed out on the ears of the indignant House. " I was only speaking to myself," said the discomfited Sir Howard. " The observation did not reach my ears," said the Speaker; " that is all I am prepared to say as to that. I should like to add this—that if the honourable and gallant member for Sheffield would control the observations which he is always interjecting, not only during question time, but during debate, it would be to the general advantage of the House." It was severe, it was just, and it was kindly said. That is the special grace of the Speaker. He is the antithesis of the gentleman in the song of whom it is said that " it is not so much the things he says as the nasty way he says them." He says unpleasant things in a pleasant way.

He is at his best when the waves run highest. Then he is like oil on the troubled waters. Take that memorable afternoon when the militant Suffragists stormed the Ladies' Gallery, which is over the Chair and invisible to the Speaker, and flourished their banners, with the legend " Votes for Women," in the face of the astonished House. There followed a sound of scuffling and disorder behind the grille which effectually screens the ladies from the vision of the members. Everyone knew what it meant. The police were dislodging the invaders. Instantly the storm reacted on the House. Brave hearts below answered to the cry of distress from above. " There

were girls in the gold reef city," and Mr. Willie Redmond was not the man to hear their cry of agony
unmoved. Up he sprang like a knight of old romance.
" Mr. Speaker, Sir, is it in accordance with your will
that a barbarous police should be called in to assault
our wives and daughters? " and his voice shook with
chivalrous passion. It was a great moment. The
House was rent with the passion of a sudden issue.
Forked lightnings flashed about the Chamber. Anything might happen. There was a breathless pause.
What would the Speaker say? Would he defend
the police? Would he denounce the women? Would
he——? Whatever happened, the storm must break.
" Unfortunately," said the Speaker, rising with great
solemnity, " I seem to be the only member of the
House who is unable to see what is taking place,"
and he looked up pathetically at the canopy that
overhangs his chair. The tension broke in a roar of
universal laughter, and the storm passed in summer
lightnings. There will never be a fight on the floor
of the House while Mr. Lowther is in the Chair.

I do not know what the quality of his fencing, which
he practises twice a week with his French maître
d'armes, is, but I should imagine that, if he has less
Gallic swiftness than Sir Charles Dilke, who is the
swordsman of the House, he is nevertheless a difficult
man to disarm. For he never loses his head and he
never loses his temper. The harder he is pressed
the cooler he becomes. A duel between him and
Mr. " Tim " Healy, the maître d'armes of political
fencing, is the greatest luxury the House affords.
The thrusts of Mr. " Tim " are sudden as lightning,
flashing now from that region of the sky, now from
this. You look to see whether the stroke has fallen.
Ajax, in his full-bottomed wig, stands solid and
imperturbable. He takes his time, coughs drily,

The Speaker

starts perhaps a little haltingly, but he comes round with a heavy sweep of his weapon and the thrust is turned. It is the English and the Irish mind in conflict, directness against swiftness, stubbornness against subtlety, rock against flame. I think the Speaker enjoys these moments. And it is the best tribute to his impartiality that he commands the entire respect of the Irishmen, as of the whole House.

It is said that when he was offered the Speakership he replied, " The Speakership will give me three things I don't need. It will give me a peerage, which I don't want; it will give me a house in town: I have that already. It will give me a salary of £5000 a year, and my income is already sufficient." It gave him something else that he did want. It gave him the fulfilment of a wholesome ambition. It enabled him to put the crown upon a Parliamentary record which is, I believe, without parallel. A Lowther has come from Westmorland to Westminster more or less continuously for some six centuries. During a century and a half there has been no break in his direct Parliamentary ancestry. Mr. Lowther's great-grandfather sat for half a century, his grandfather for half a century, his father for a quarter of a century; he himself entered the House in 1883 for Rutlandshire, after a few years' practice at the Bar. He is a hereditary legislator in the best sense. The spirit of Parliament is in his blood, and the honour of Parliament is to him something of a personal possession.

He will abandon none of its ancient forms or etiquette, but he tempers them with thoughtful concessions. When the poorer members of the House appealed to Mr. Speaker Gully to make the wearing of Court dress at his functions optional, they were met with refusal. When they made the same appeal to Mr. Speaker Lowther, they were met with refusal too; but he promptly took the edge off the refusal by inaugurating a series of luncheons where the democratic " sansculottes " might be free from the tyranny of velvet and gold buttons and silver buckles. It was a wise compromise. No man in broadcloth and trousers can feel quite happy beside a man who is a sartorial poem. It is like pairing a stump speech with a song of Herrick.

Mr. Lowther's success is comforting to the plain man, for it is the success of his own russet-coated virtues. It is the success of one like himself—of a plain man without a touch of genius, almost without a touch of brilliancy, but with all the qualities of the average man in perfect equilibrium. He has culture, loves painting almost as much as stalking the deer, has—since the Cambridge days when, as Mr. Lowthian R. Cade, he used to share the theatrical exploits of Lord Crewe, Mr. Alfred Lyttelton, and others—retained his interest in the drama, tells a good story, enjoys a good book. But he is essentially the ordinary man—that is, the ordinary man in an extraordinary degree, his mind full of daylight, the range of his thought limited by the daylight vision, his instinct for justice sound, his spirit firm and masculine as the strong, well-tended hand that he rests upon the arm of the Speaker's chair. He is not one of those who bring new light into the thought of men or add to the sum of human effort. He is the type of the practical man who does his task honestly, firmly, and good-humouredly. That is why, taken all in all, he is the greatest Speaker of our time. For the office of Speaker does not demand rare qualities. It demands common qualities in a rare degree.

HERBERT SAMUEL

At an Eighty Club dinner not long ago I was seated beside the Chairman, who chanced to be Mr. Herbert Samuel. It was what is known as a House Dinner—an occasion of more or less informal debate on a given political subject of the moment. Those who desire to speak are requested to send up their names to the steward, who, on this occasion, was myself. As invariably happens at Eighty Club functions, there was an abundance of men ready to talk, for political speaking is the *raison d'être* of the Club. The names were put down in order and handed to the Chairman. He took them, and, turning to me, said, " You will speak." I replied that I had no intention of speaking. " Oh yes," said Mr. Samuel, " you must speak." And he inserted my name high up on the list. I laughed and took an opportunity of putting my pen through the name. He smiled, took up his pen, and restored it. " I am serious," I said. " So am I," he replied. When the list was exhausted as far as my name I said, " Please pass my name." Without turning he announced me to follow. And I obeyed.

I do not mention this incident in any spirit of retaliation, but because it illustrates the character of Mr. Herbert Samuel better than anything I can recall. He is implacable and masterful—a man clothed in a suit of impenetrable mail. It is his golden rule to have his own way, not for selfish reasons, but because it is the right way. Argument is wasted on him, entreaty breaks helplessly at the foot of his frozen purpose. He hears your arguments with a polite air of having heard all of them from the beginning and found them worthless. He listens to your appeals with the chill calm of an iceberg. It would be easier, I think, to extract tears from the Cromwell statue than to extract from Mr. Samuel a concession which he did not wish to make.

If one were asked to find the antithesis of Mr. Balfour in the House of Commons, one would turn, I think, to Mr. Samuel. With Mr. Balfour all is speculative and formless. There is nothing fixed and absolute. He is stricken with the paralysis of indecision. Mr. Samuel, on the other hand, makes decision a habit of mind. I imagine he has a settled conviction about everything under the sun. If there is anything about which he has no settled conviction then it is outside the range of his interests and does not exist for him. He is one of those men whose minds are always " made up." You do not see them in the process of being " made up." It is as though they were " made up " to start with on the basis of some absolute formula which leaves nothing more to be said. Everything is *chose jugée*. In Mr. Samuel's precise and profusely pigeon-holed mind there is no room for hesitation about conclusions, because there is no room for doubt about facts.

There is nothing of the Oriental man of mystery about Mr. Samuel; but one would have to search long and industriously to discover the reality that dwells behind this perfectly equipped defence. Most men have their moments of unofficial freedom—moments, after dinner, for example, when they throw off the mask and delight to be gloriously indiscreet. Holmes says that every man has two doors to himself, one which he keeps open to the world, and another through which only the privileged are permitted to enter, or which is opened in moments of deep feeling or generous confidence. In the case of Mr. Samuel one feels that the key rusts in the lock of that secret door. "He has made discretion into a fine art," said one of his colleagues to me.

He is the type of efficiency. There is no more industrious man in the Ministry, none whom you find more completely equipped in knowledge or in clear-cut, decisive opinion. No matter what subject you raise bearing on his department, you find that this undemonstrative, wise young man is prepared to crush you with Blue Books you have never heard of, and experiences of places where you have never been. When I met him at the Sweated Industries Exhibition, the impression left was that of a man who had nothing to learn on the subject. He had studied it in the East End; he had studied it on the Continent years before; he could tell you more than you could ever hope to know. You felt humbled and cheap.

In this enormous capacity for mastering the details of a subject, this enthusiasm for the letter, as it were, he is typical of his race. The genius of the Jew is the genius for taking infinite pains. He may lack inspiration, but his power of application, his mastery of the letter, gives him a knowledge that is more potent than inspiration. Where the " book " is concerned, he is unrivalled. He stakes out a " claim " with calculating confidence, and develops it with an unremitting industry and an unimpassioned concentration that assure success. He gets up his subject with a thoroughness that the Englishman rarely imitates. Lasker has not the fascination of Morphy, or even of Pillsbury; but he is the greatest chess-player that ever lived, for he " knows " chess as no man ever knew it before. The Jew rarely produces great art or great music; but he is supreme in his knowledge of those realms. It is nearly always a Jew who is the expert Shakespearean scholar, just as it is always a Jew who will decide the authenticity of a Van Eyck or a Botticelli. When one of the Rothschilds advised Buxton on his career, he warned him against scattering his energies. " Concentration," he said, " is the one road to success in business; dispersion the one certainty of failure. Stick to brewing and you will be the first brewer in London. Take up banking, shipping, commerce, and your name will soon appear in the *Gazette*." It was the Jew revealing the secret of the astonishing success of his race.

Mr. Samuel's faculty for mastering detail was revealed in the Children's Bill, which Mr. Herbert Gladstone surrendered entirely to his hands. No more humane measure has ever been before Parliament, and certainly Parliament never saw a measure more ably handled, both in the House and in Committee. It was impossible to find a flaw in the workmanship, and Mr. Samuel's skill in Committee won the rare distinction of a dinner in honour of his success. It was the success of one who has in remarkable combination the *suaviter in modo* and the *fortiter in re*. He is thrice armed, for he adds to knowledge rare astuteness and blameless temper. It is impossible to trip him up, either in fact or in feeling. He has the enormous advantage of always knowing more about his subject than his opponent, and that is a great aid to serenity of temper. " There are two ways of governing men," said Disraeli in one of his novels. " Either you must be superior to them, or despise them." Mr. Samuel has adopted the better way.

His philosophy of conduct, I take it, is similar to that of Mr. Chamberlain. It was the practice of Mr. Chamberlain to come into counsel with everything cut and dried. It was his rôle to " put things through." He knew that men are always ready to follow anyone who will tell them what to do. "I see how things go in the Cabinet," said Sir Henry Campbell-Bannerman on one occasion, after he had been called in by Lord Salisbury to advise in regard to some Royal and non-party question. "Lord Salisbury explains that nothing can be done, and that, even if anything could be done, it would probably be a miserable failure. And then he calls on Mr. Balfour to say a few words, and Mr. Balfour's head ascends into the clouds and he invests the subject with a delicate haze, after which: 'Perhaps the Colonial Secretary has a suggestion,' says the Premier. And Mr. Chamberlain comes forward prompt and practical, with his scheme down in black and white, and his mind made up, and—the thing is done." As in the Cabinet, so on committees and councils of all sorts. One of the governors of the Birmingham University tells that on one occasion Mr. Chamberlain startled the meeting by saying that what the University wanted was a Siena tower. "A Siena tower!" exclaimed his colleagues in alarm. "What we want is a chair for this and a chair for that, and——" "What we want is a Siena tower," said Mr. Chamberlain icily, as though he were speaking through the twittering of sparrows, "and "—putting his hand in his pocket—" to save time I have had some drawings prepared." And, says the informant, we found ourselves outside half an hour later, having agreed to the erection of a Siena tower which none of us wanted, at a cost of £50,000, which we hadn't got, and which we needed for the equipment of the University. Those who have acted on committees with Mr. Samuel will recognise the likeness. He also comes, as it were, with his design for a Siena tower in his pocket. He does not say much. He is quiet and unobtrusive as the talk wanders on around him. Then, at the perfectly chosen moment, he interposes with chill incisiveness and enormous gravity, and you feel that an end has come to the vapourings of irresponsible frivolity. Perhaps you feel that the incisiveness is studied and the gravity a little excessive; but that does not diminish the impression. A keen blade has been suddenly run through a bag of idle wind. He conveys no impression of enthusiasm and is as free from passion as an oyster. He will never give his leader or his party a moment's disquiet, for he will never depart a hair's-breadth from the path of strict correctitude. He says exactly the right word in exactly the right accent. His work is done without a flaw, and if his manner lacks a little the spontaneous warmth that takes men captive, it has the unruffled and considered courtesy that sheds a certain grave decorum, not to say solemnity, over your intercourse. "Manners," said Emerson, "were invented to keep fools at a distance," and though Mr. Samuel would not put it so crudely as that, he probably agrees with the sentiment.

I have been told by one who was a comrade of his in childhood that his favourite amusement was politics, and that when other boys were reading Ballantyne he was reading Blue Books. For him, indeed, one can conceive no

> youth of roselight and romance wherein
> He dreamt of paynim and of paladin—

no time when he cherished a sentiment or coquetted with an illusion. One can imagine him as a boy at University College School planning out his future with the quiet certitude of a mathematical mind engaged on an easy negotiable proposition, and, having planned it, working silently and unceasingly for its accomplishment. It is characteristic of his assured restraint

that, ambitious as he is, he has never sought to force
the pace of his progress. No extravagance of speech
or action is ever associated with his carefully considered career. He does not thrust himself into the
limelight. He is content to be forgotten. He knows
the power of discreet silence as the man of taste knows
the value of the blank space on the wall.

Among the potentialities of the Liberalism of
the future he and Mr. Masterman are among the
most considerable. They represent respectively the
science and the sentiment of politics—sense and
sensibility. The one is intellect; the other emotion.
It would be hazardous to cast the horoscope of Mr.
Masterman. He is the wind that bloweth where
it listeth, indifferent to theories, impatient of slow
processes, governed only by a compelling passion for
humanity—the dreamer of dreams and the seer of
visions. It remains to be seen what effect office will
have upon a temperament which seems better fitted
to inspire than direct. Mr. Samuel's path is as
defined and absolute as a geometrical line. He is the
artificer of politics, confident of his aim, master of
himself and his materials, secure in his opinion, inflexible in purpose—a splendidly efficient instrument,
but never an inspiration.

THE TSAR

I WAS sitting in my room one day in March last year when Miss Clementina Black and Madame Stepniak called on me with a young man dressed in the garb of a workman. He was very fair, and his light blue eyes had that look of childlike simplicity and frankness that goes straight to the heart. It was a look that seemed to leave nothing to be told. A decent, sober, industrious young artisan, you would have said, and passed on. But he was indeed the most significant figure I have ever met: when I think of Russia I see it through those mild blue eyes.

He was a Lithuanian workman, Peter Pridrikson his name. He had been a member of a political organisation and had been arrested with others in the midst of the Riga horrors, had been flogged and tortured, and finally sentenced to be shot. He was detained for the night in a village near Riga, in a wooden shanty, for the prisons were so full that accommodation had to be extemporised. In the darkness he was taken outside by the gaolers to the lavatory. The irons were on his leg and the gaolers carried rifles. Escape seemed impossible. But to-morrow he was to die. When to-morrow means death, men do not shrink from the risk of a rifle shot. The drowning man snatched at the last straw of life. In the lavatory he managed with a stone to loosen the nut of one of the irons. Then, bursting through the door, he made one wild rush for liberty. The gaolers fired, but the night was dark and they missed their aim. And the time they gave to firing should

258

have been given to pursuit, for the forest was close at hand. Perhaps, too, they had mercy; felt, like Hubert, some touch of pity for those trustful, appealing eyes. However that may be, the youth, dragging his irons with him, reached the cover of the woods and safety. He freed himself from the irons, wandered for two days and nights in the forest, then, hidden in a hay cart by a friendly driver, reached the home of a friend, where he remained in hiding for three weeks before escaping across the frontier, and—here he was in Bouverie Street telling his thrilling story quietly and simply through the mouth of Madame Stepniak.

His back still bore the cruel marks of the lash, and he unlaced his boots and showed me his toe-nails broken in the torture. What was he going to do? He was going to Switzerland to join other refugees for a short time.

" And then? "

" Then I am going back."

" Back? But you are sentenced to death."

" I must take my chance."

He spoke with the calmness of that fatalism that is so deeply rooted in the Russian character. I have never seen him since; but three months ago I received a letter from Madame Stepniak. " You remember," she said, " the young Lithuanian I brought to see you some time ago. I have just heard of his death. He returned to Russia, was recaptured, and shot."

Multiply that pathetic figure by thousands and tens of thousands, see in it the symbol of a system controlling a hundred and twenty million lives, and you have the Russia of the Tsar. What of the Tsar?

Mr. Heath, the English tutor of the Tsar, relates that one day he and his pupil were reading together *The Lady of the Lake.* They came to that spirited description of the scene in Stirling when the castle gates were flung wide open and King James rode out amid the shouts of the populace, "Long live the Commons' King, King James!" "The Commons' King," exclaimed the boy, with sparkling eyes, "that is what I should like to be." The emotion was sincere. For Nicholas II. is one of those unhappy figures in whom emotion is divorced from conduct, an idealist faithless to his ideals, a visionary doomed to violate his visions. He has a feminine shrinking from war and plunges his country into the bloodiest war in history. He looks towards England and yearns for its free air and its free institutions, its Commons' King and its happy people, and every day throughout his wide realm the hangman's noose is round the politician's neck and the gaoler's key is turned upon the cry of liberty.

What is the mystery behind this perplexing personality that seems at once so humane and so merciless, that expresses itself now in a Peace Rescript, now in approval of the infamous doings of the Black Hundreds, that is compact of the shyness of a girl and the intense fanatical spirit of Philip II., that would be "a Commons' King" and yet a despot? There is no need to question the sincerity of his moods on the ground that they are mutually destructive. Even the best of men are conscious of that duality which Leighton referred to in one of his letters to his sister, in which he said, "for, together with, and, as it were, behind, so much pleasurable emotion, there is always that other strange second man in me, calm, observant, critical, unmoved, blasé, odious." There is that other self, too, in the Tsar, fanatical, terrible—and, alas, triumphant. Perhaps the wonder is that, with such an ancestry and such a tutelage, there should be any generous human emotion at all. For the history of his house is like a nightmare of blood. His father was as superstitious as a mediæval warrior. He would cross himself and even fall on his knees in prayer if a cloud obscured the sun while he was looking through the window, and he died in the arms of that miracle-monger, Father John of Cronstadt. His grandfather was assassinated in the public street; his great-grandfather is supposed to have committed suicide under the pressure of the disasters in the Crimea; the Emperor Paul was murdered in 1801; and the vices of Paul's mother, Catherine II., place her among the greatest criminals in Royal history. Her husband was " removed." Ivan VI. was buried in a dungeon for twenty-four years and then murdered. But why pursue the story? It is stained with blood right back to that pagan author of the Romanoffs, the chieftain Kobyla, who was driven from Lithuania into Russia in the fourteenth century for refusing to adopt Christianity. The contemplation of such a family history would shadow any life. It ought also to have taught the lesson of the futility of despotism.

It did, in fact, teach it, as we see in that emotion of the boy stirred by the cry of the " Commons' King." But it was the emotion of a mind ungoverned by character and subject to fanatical obsession. Had his impressionable temperament been moulded by generous influences the course of Russian history would have been happier; but he fell at the beginning under the mediæval spirit of Pobiedonostseff, the Procurator of the Holy Synod, the Torquemada of modern times, who instilled into him his doctrines of Oriental despotism, chilled by the frost of his bloodless philosophy. Under the baleful guidance of Pobiedonostseff and Prince Meshkershtsky, he became imbued, as the writer of an article in the *Quarterly Review* pointed out long before his character was realised, with the conviction that he was God's lieutenant, the earthly counterpart of his Divine Master. That obsession, working on a mind naturally occult and timorous, has driven, as it were, the disease of despotism inward, withering the feeble intimations of a more humane emotion, isolating him from his people, and converting every expression of popular thought into revolt against the divine will embodied in his own person.

This perverted intensity is the natural product of a superstitious mind in a febrile body. For he has none of the animalism and physical ebullience of his race. His tastes are domestic and simple. He is devoted to his wife and his children, the last refuge of his solitary life, and loves to sit and read to the Empress from the English authors while she is engaged in her embroidery in the evening. He has a passion for cycling; but for sport he has neither the taste nor the nerve. In the language of the old keeper who was in attendance on him when he was the guest of Lord Lonsdale in Westmorland, the Tsar " did not know enough to hold a gun straight nor to hit a bird." His lack of physical daring was exhibited in the attack made on him by an assassin when, as the Tsarevitch, he was touring in Japan with the Crown Prince of Greece. The latter wrote to his father a letter describing the incident, and in it used the phrase, " Then Nickie ran." By some indiscretion that phrase leaked out, and all Russian society went about shrugging its shoulders and murmuring, " Then Nickie ran."

Perhaps it was this timidity that was the cause of the most fatal act in his career. No monarch in history was ever faced with a more splendid occasion than that which offered itself to Nicholas on the 22nd of January 1905. The war was ending in disaster,

the country was in revolt against its own misery and
wrong and against the corruption and incompetence
of the bureaucracy. But it still had a remnant of
faith in the Little Father. It would go to him at his
Palace with a petition to him to make its cause his
own against the tyranny that oppressed it. The
people gathered in tens of thousands before the
Palace. It was the moment for a hero. It was the
moment to win the love of a people or to lose it for
ever. And Nicholas was not there! He had fled
overnight to Tsarskoe Selo, and left the Duke Vladimir
with his Cossacks to greet his subjects with sword and
musket. The streets ran with blood. More people
fell that day than in any battle of the Boer War.
And Nicholas fell for ever with them.

The lack of physical courage is companioned by
the infirmity of will, illustrated by the story of a
conversation between the Tsar and the Empress
which delighted Russia last year, and which ran as
follows:

The Empress: My dear Nicholas, you must not always
agree with everybody. Now, this morning M. Stolypin
made a report, and after he had finished you said, "M.
Stolypin, you are quite right. I quite agree with you."
Five minutes later Durnovo came. What he told you was
absolutely opposed to what Stolypin had said, but again you
remarked, "My dear Durnovo, you are quite right. I quite
agree with you." Finally, M. Schwanenbach came and told
you something different from what the other two gentlemen
had said, and again you replied, "M. Schwanenbach, you
are quite right. I quite agree with you."

The Tsar (after a moment's reflection): My dear Alexandra,
you are quite right. I quite agree with you.

This infirmity of purpose gives that sense of confusion that pervades all his actions. He yields and
withdraws, creates a Constitution and destroys it,
sets up a Duma and throws it down, yearns for
universal peace and blunders into war. He is always

under hypnotic suggestion, now faltering between the rival feminine influences of his Court, now subject to the cold, inhuman philosophy of a Meshkershtsky, now dominated by the mystical charlatanry of M. Philippe, with his miracles and spirit messages.

For superstition is the essential atmosphere of his mind, and he dwells in the realm of wonder-working relics. One of the saints, Seraphim of Saroff, he ordered to be canonised, in spite of the disconcerting fact that though he had been buried only seventy years the saint's body was decomposed. The Orthodox Bishop Dmitry of Tamboff protested on this ground against the beatification as contrary to Church traditions; but he was deprived of his see and sent to Vyatka for venturing to disagree with the Tsar. For his Majesty holds that the preservation of the bones, the hair, and the teeth is a sufficient qualification for saintship.

With these views it follows that his devotion to the Orthodox faith is as intense as it is narrow. It has resulted not only in the merciless suppression of the Armenian Church and of the Dissenters, but even in the harrying of the Old Believers, who are an important branch of the State Church, and the bodies of whose saints have been disinterred and burned. The cruellest episode of the persecution of the Old Believers was that of Bishop Methodius, who administered the sacraments to a man who, born in the State Church, had joined the Old Believers. Methodius, a man of seventy-eight, was arrested for his " crime," and condemned to banishment to Siberia, whither, with irons on his feet, and penned up with criminals, he was dispatched. At Yakutsk he remained some time, but a dignitary of the State Church intervened and he was ordered to be sent on to Vilyuisk, in North-Eastern Siberia, a place inhabited by savages.

The Tsar

The aged Bishop was set astride a horse to which he was tied, and told that he must ride thus to his new place of exile, about 700 miles distant. " This sentence is death by torture," said Methodius' flock. They were not mistaken. The old man gave up the ghost on the road (1898), but when, where, and how he was buried has never been made known. This and other persecutions, says the writer of the *Quarterly Review* article to which I have referred, " were brought to the notice of his Majesty without eliciting even an expression of regret."

It is the tragedy of the infirm will, always to become the prey of the most virile influences. It treads the path of least resistance. And in turn the fanatical obsession inculcated by those influences sanctifies every action with the divine imprimatur. From this vicious sequence we have the phenomenon of merciless oppression emerging from a personally shy and timid source. In the field of such a mind the victory is always to the most intense and ruthless and subtle. Weakness takes refuge in strength and timidity in terrorism. The boyish emotion that cried out, " A Commons' King: that is what I should like to be," ends in a political gospel founded on the maxim of de Plehve—" Severity, served up cold, is the only way with Empire wreckers." Everywhere the Autocracy takes on the aspect of vengeance and repression. " The massacre of Jews, the banishment of Finns, the spoliation of Armenians, the persecution of Poles, the exile of Russian nobles, the flogging of peasants, the imprisonment and butchery of Russian working men, the establishment of a widespread system of espionage, and the abolition of law are all measures which the Minister suggests and the Tsar heartily sanctions." That was written before the mockery of a Constitution was granted; but the spirit of the Government is the same to-day. The de Plehves and the Bobrikoffs have gone to their doom, but their successors are like unto them. The hand that conferred a star upon Prince Obolensky for his energy in flogging the peasants of the Government of Kharkoff until many of them died is the same hand that decorates the Tsarevitch with the badge of the Black Hundreds, that terrible instrument of vengeance, formed almost at the moment that the Constitution was granted, and already drenched in a sea of innocent blood.

Nor is it only the fierce, barbaric spirits to which he is subject. He has the credulity that makes him the easy instrument of the impostor and the visionary, whether of the spiritualistic type of Philippe or of the type of the eccentric adventurer Bezobrazoff, whose vast speculative scheme for developing the Yalu forests fascinated first the Grand Dukes, eager for plunder, and then the Tsar, who became an investor, gave him plenipotentiary powers, subordinated Kuropatkin and Lamsdorff to him, allowed him to make the incompetent Alexeieff Viceroy of Manchuria, and so drifted into the catastrophe of the war.

He will live as the man who made the great refusal of history. He might have been the founder of a new and happier Russia—the Commons' King of his youthful vision. He has chosen to be an Autocrat and a prisoner in his forty palaces. In ten years his rule has exiled 78,000 of his subjects and driven all the best of the nation's sons that have escaped Siberia to take refuge in other lands. But he himself is the saddest exile of all, for he is exiled from the domain of our common humanity—a prisoner in body and in spirit, hedged round by his guards, suspecting the cup that he drinks, forbidden to dine anywhere save in his own palace, receiving his guests at sea, for he dare

The Tsar

not receive them ashore, a hapless, pitiful figure that
sits

> perked up on a glist'ring grief
> And wears a golden sorrow.

Which would one rather be—the prisoner of the
palace, or that young Lithuanian carpenter with the
blue appealing eyes and the toe-nails broken in the
torture, who gave his blood in the sacred cause of
human liberty?

DR. HORTON

WHEN you enter the church at Lyndhurst Road you are conscious—if you happen to be sensitive to "atmosphere"—of a certain subdued note of expectancy. The impression grows as the service advances. There is a breath on the face of the waters—the subtle breath of personality. Perhaps the key is minor, appealing, poignant. The preacher is in the grip of some strong emotion which colours hymn and prayer and lesson, peeps out from the little fable he addresses to the children, and is fully revealed in the sermon. It is as though he has come from some sudden vision of the world's wickedness and the world's wrong. It is visible and audible. He hears the world thundering by to destruction in a frenzy of luxury and pleasure and heedless riot. The rush of motor-cars and the clatter of wheels on Haverstock Hill break in on the tense strain. They are like the voice of the doomed world drowning the cry of the prophet. He leans forward with outstretched hands, pleading, pleading. He is torn with bitter agony. His voice is shaken by the tumult of his feelings. A moment more, and the tense bow must break. But he draws himself up, closes the Bible, and the troubled sea sinks down in the calm of a hymn and the peace of the benediction. Outside some one touches you on the shoulder with a light greeting. It is like the breaking of a spell.

Or perhaps it is a bright morning in spring. The song of birds is heard on the heath, and out in Golder's Hill he has seen the snowdrops bursting from their winter prison—the first syllables in the poetry of the

Dr. Horton

year, the heralds of the pageant of the earth. And his heart sings with the glad tidings of the new birth. He has seen the finger of God in the woodlands. He has heard the voice of the eternal by the sea-shore. He has picked up a shell, and found in it thoughts that do lie too deep for tears. For the earth is filled with the whispers of the Most High.

> I find letters from God dropped in the street, and each one is signed by God's name.
> And I leave them where they are, for I know that wheresoever I go others will punctually follow for ever and ever.

And, full of this gracious assurance, the service flows on golden wings to a golden close. The rush of motor-cars and the clatter of wheels break in on the melody; but not harshly nor discordantly. Almost they seem like a part of the universal song of the reawakened earth.

But a day comes of bitter self-abasement. He is bowed down with the sense of failure, due, you will discover, to some quite small and isolated incident. He is stricken with remorse, with the passion of weakness and futility. A word, a breath, has set all the chords vibrating to the miserere. The sorrow of the world is his, and the sin of the world too, for what has he done to alleviate the one and wash out the other? He is the unfaithful servant. He is the bringer of a message which he has failed to deliver. The world is deaf because he has not unstopped its ears; the world is blind because he has not unsealed its eyes. He stands, like Whittier, in the presence of his soul and arraigns it like a felon.

Dr. Horton is the type of the poet-prophet in the pulpit. He has the poet's intensity of vision, the poet's quick emotional response, the poet's imaginative fervour. Tennyson said of Swinburne that " he is a tube through which all things blow into music."

Prophets, Priests, and Kings

It is the music of the senses, poured from old Triton's "wreathéd horn." Dr. Horton is a voice through which the emotions of the soul issue in impromptu passion, now "breathless with adoration," now flaming with wrath. He draws from a direct well of inspiration. He comes, as it were, from some journey of the soul, filled with a message which is not his own—a message urgent, tyrannical. He has seen a vision, and hurries from the road to Damascus to proclaim the thrilling tidings. He is consumed with the agitation of the spirit and cannot rest till the vision is revealed.

It is this emotion that makes his appeal so poignant, so disquieting in its intensity, so healing in its more placid moods. You cannot be indifferent under him. He touches you to the quick—to a responsive passion of revolt or acceptance. His whole message is a challenge to you—you personally, you alone. It is you to whom the moment has come to decide between the "bloom and blight," you for whom "The choice goes by for ever 'twixt that darkness and that light." You shall make the choice here and now. You shall not escape. He will not let you go until you have chosen either for "The goats upon the left hand, or the sheep upon the right."

There is in this overmastering urgency and this swift changefulness of mood a certain loss of sustained power. He does not see life steadily or whole, and lacks the fundamental quietude of spirit that would give harmony to the varying moods. And this subjection to the emotion reacts upon his thought, which is sometimes singularly narrow and at others as broad as the heavens. He is, in a word, not so much a thinker as a spiritual impressionist. He sees truth, as it were, by flashes of lightning where others arrive at it by the slow operation of intellect, and if the truth,

as he sees, is sometimes a little out of drawing, that
is usually the case with impressionism. A sermon
by Dr. Hunter delights you by its mental power.
It is the appeal of the mind to the mind. Dr. Horton's
is the appeal of the heart to the heart. He has a
feminine fervour and impatience of fetters. He
surrenders himself to his emotion, and soars with
wings. He does not argue; he proclaims. An
incident, a phrase, a thought has opened a sudden
window into the spiritual world, and he is unconscious
of all save the vision.

This sensitiveness to impression, the faculty of
seeing the infinite in the infinitesimal, has always
characterised him. As a little boy at a dame-school
he heard a lad of hard, bad face and blasphemous
tongue answering the question, " Who gave you that
name? " with the words of the Catechism, " My
baptism, wherein I was made a child of God and an
inheritor of the Kingdom of Heaven," and the shock
of that unconscious satire sealed the impressionable
child for Nonconformity. And later, at Shrewsbury,
he arrived, by the same sensitive response, at another
far-reaching conclusion. He and two others, a
Ritualistic Churchman and an Evangelical Churchman, anticipating the union of the Churches, established a prayer meeting in the study just before
evening call-over. A flame of enthusiasm passed
through the school, and the study became crowded.
But persecution came. The world, symbolised by
the rest of the school, blocked the passage, crowded
the exit, cuffed, kicked, and cursed these daring
innovators. The uproar reached the ears of the
headmaster, who threw his cold protection over these
young dissenters. " Some of us," he said, " may
think that the prayers in chapel and in top schools
are sufficient, but if there are boys that desire more

Prophets, Priests, and Kings

and wish to pray together in their study, they shall not be interrupted." The invasion of authority in the sphere of religion was fatal. The persecution ceased, but so also did the prayer meetings, and young Horton's mind leapt to another truth—that Christianity does not require the countenance or support of the State, and is only vital when it can defy persecution and is independent of the powers of the world.

He has the defects of the impressionist when he comes down into the world of affairs. He is perplexed by its ingenuities and cunning, impatient of its restraints, entirely unsophisticated, and without any of the worldly but necessary qualities of suspicion or distrust. It is surprising to learn that when, at Oxford, the invitation came to him to take charge of a new church at Hampstead, he was contemplating a career at the Bar. His mind would have fretted itself to death in the chill prison of legal forms and amid the dry detail of precedent. For of all the theatres of the world's conflict there is none so passionless and calculating as the law. And Dr. Horton is all passion and no calculation. Impulse governs him and governs him aright; but in affairs he is at sea, and his impulse is checked and chilled by the calculations of others. Thus, as President of the Free Church Council, he wrote in the midst of the education controversy a powerful appeal for the secular solution. It was a critical moment. With courage he would have carried the day, and that truth which came to him at Shrewsbury would have won an enduring triumph. But he was overborne by the counsels of worldly caution and recanted. Like all prophets, he is an indifferent politician.

" The defect of men like Horton and Meyer," said a friend of both—himself the son of a great Church-

Dr. Horton

man of other days, "is the excess of their high qualities. They live in an atmosphere of unceasing spiritual exaltation. The strain is never relaxed. They would be more powerful if they were more earthly." There is some truth in the criticism. The soul needs its fallow seasons like the body. If it never descends from Sinai to the common ways of men it sacrifices some of its fellowship with life. It may even lead men astray on great human issues, as it led Dr. Horton astray in regard to the true inwardness of the Boer war.

And yet without that aloofness the peculiar value of Dr. Horton would be lacking. He is a voice crying in the wilderness of the world. Around him he hears the sound of the tumult of life, whirling in giddy mazes of pleasure about the gods of the market-place, shot through with cries of pain, watered with hopeless tears, and ringing with idle laughter. It is a world that has broken from the ancient anchorage. He sees it drifting over uncharted seas beneath a starless sky. We are

> like corpses in a charnel,
> Fear and grief convulse us and consume us day by day,
> And cold hopes swarm within the living clay.

And, filled with the sense of a sick world, he comes with the passionate reassertion of the faith as the only cure of its ills. Reform society by all means, he says to the Socialists; but the most perfect organisation will never make the world whole. For the Kingdom of God is within you, and outside that Kingdom there is no peace.

He is a Puritan engrafted with Oxford culture— a Puritan with the atmosphere of a liberal scholarship and the graces of taste and sensitive feeling. Oxford has no more devoted son, and no better justification for opening her doors to Dissenters.

273

Prophets, Priests, and Kings

"In those days," he says, "it was good to be a Nonconformist at Oxford, for everyone was bent on showing that the position involved no disqualifications." Oxford gave him a Fellowship, and almost claimed him for her own. And out of that tender memory of his Oxford days springs the affection he always shows towards the Church whose system nevertheless seems to him so far removed from the essential principles of Christianity.

But the cool seclusion of Oxford, any more than the dry atmosphere of the law, could not have satisfied that urgent temperament. He was born to preach. One of his earliest memories is that of standing on a dining-room chair in his grandfather's house near Covent Garden Market, with his grandparents and certain guests and domestics for audience, and preaching, armed with a ball to hurl at any who should laugh. It was his grandmother who laughed first and loudest, and at whom, more in sorrow than in anger, he hurled his missile. The dream of the child was the true foreshadowing of the man—his vocation the fulfilment of his mother's hope. "It shapes itself to me," he has said, "as the thought and the wish of my mother, wrought out silently in her heart, and carried, just as I was leaving school for the University, over into the land beyond death, and there working ceaselessly and effectually, so that it would not surprise me if at any time my eyes were opened, and I found that she, an invisible spirit, had remained by my side all the way to complete the purpose with which she started me on the journey."

PHILIP SNOWDEN

It was the eve of the General Election of 1900. The Khaki fever was at its height, and Liberalism at the lowest ebb of its fortunes. Nowhere was it lower than at Blackburn. For twenty years the capital of the weaving trade had been a stronghold of Conservatism, and now there was no Liberal with sufficient courage even to challenge it. Suddenly there appeared on the scene a stranger out of the West Riding. So feeble he seemed that he moved the foe to pity more than anger. He came limping into the lists on foot—a pallid, hatchet-faced young man, small of stature, and leaning heavily on a stick, one foot dragging helplessly along the ground. His face was scored with the brand of suffering and bitter thought. He had, as the result of a bicycle accident lain twelve months motionless upon his bed, and had stolen back to the ways of men a maimed and stricken figure. He came unattended. There was no one to receive him save a few eager working men who had been preaching Socialism to deaf ears in the market-place. There was no organisation to work for him. There was no money at his command. He seemed like David going out with his pebble and his sling against the hosts of the Philistines. It was the battle of " the one and the fifty-three."

Thousands of their soldiers leaned from their decks and laughed,
Thousands of their seamen made mock of the mad little craft Running on and on—

But that was at the beginning. Later on, as in the fight at Flores, soldiers and seamen had other work

275

to do. By the end of the battle they were fighting for dear life.

For Philip Snowden wrought a miracle. That election will never be forgotten by those who witnessed it. It was like a sudden wind stirring the leaves of the forest. It was a revival movement gathering momentum with each hour. Philip Snowden's name was on every lip, his sayings ran like rumour through the weaving sheds and the street. Men in their greasy caps, and carrying their " kits," hurried from the mills to his meetings, and sat as if hypnotised under the spell of revelation. He fought the battle absolutely single-handed, and he fought it with a dignity of spirit rare in politics. " Snowden is an Atheist " was chalked on a hundred walls. He ignored the slander. " Snowden was dismissed from the Excise " passed from lip to lip. Again he was silent. He was urged to tell the real facts, which were entirely honourable to him. " No," he said, " I have resolved to fight this battle on politics and not on personalities, and from that I will not move." In a fortnight, in spite of the crushing odds against him, in spite of the war fever, in spite of the Church and the brewers, wealth, influence, and the popularity of the two Tory candidates, he had shaken the Gibraltar of Toryism to its foundations. To-day he sits for Blackburn, the first member other than a Conservative who has represented the constituency for a quarter of a century.

I take Philip Snowden to be the typical Socialist in Parliament. He is the man of the *idée fixe*. You see it in the drawn face, the clenched mouth, the cold, uncompromising grey eyes. Other men of his party will yield a little to gain much. He yields nothing. He is the steady, relentless foe of society as it is constituted. He will have no half measures, no

Philip Snowden

coquettings with the enemy. His theory or nothing. He owes his seat largely to Liberal votes; but he makes no sign of recognition or thanks. Liberalism is to him as Toryism. Nay, it is more detestable than Toryism, because it is more dangerous to his aims. He stands for revolution—a bloodless revolution, but still a revolution. Toryism, with its reactionary impulses, paves the way to revolution; Liberalism, with its moderate reforms, defeats revolution. Hence Toryism is in some sense a friend, while Liberalism, blunting the edge of popular demand, is the real enemy. And so when Mr. Snowden goes about the country, it is Liberalism which is the target of his bitterest attacks. He will acknowledge no good thing in it. He will take nothing from it with thanks, for its best gifts are only intended to make existing society tolerable, and he wants it to be intolerable.

One evening I was talking after dinner with a group of Liberal politicians and the conversation turned to the strength of absolute, uncompromising Socialism in Parliament. "Keir Hardie," said one, "calculates that there are ten Socialists in the House." We set ourselves to find them. Ramsay Macdonald? "Not a Socialist first, but a politician," said one. "Not a Socialist, but an Opportunist," said another. Pete Curran? "Not a Socialist first, but an Irishman," said a third. "Let John Redmond say 'Home Rule to-day; the Social Revolution to-morrow,' and Curran would follow the banner of Ireland." Victor Grayson? "The wine is too new in the bottle; give him time." And so the weeding-out went on. At each name some qualifying circumstance of sympathy or outlook was recalled. Only at two names was there no pause—the names of Keir Hardie and Philip Snowden.

They are Socialists *sans phrase*. Others subscribe to the economic theories of Socialism. They alone live for them and for nothing else. Others join in the political fray; they stand aloof from what they regard as idle trifling: their eyes fixed on the ultimate goal. To them the House of Commons is not a place for petty skirmishes and paltry triumphs. It is a platform from whence to preach the Social Revolution. They will not prune the tree: they will uproot it.

Most men who go to the House of Commons, no matter what their views or their social rank, soon fall in with the spirit of the place. They share its common life and enjoy its social comradeship. Many of them, indeed, find the spirit of the place a solvent of principle. They find the virgin enthusiasm they brought with them from the country languishes in this atmosphere of geniality and compromise. The principle that was so clear on the platform, where you had it all to yourself, is not so unchallengeable here. The Tory with whom you have smoked a pipe down below is quite a pleasant fellow and in his way just, and the Liberal or Labour man with whom you had a chat on the terrace seems really an honest man—misguided, of course, but still with a good deal of reason in him. The sharp lines get blurred, and black and white tend to shade away into varying tones of grey.

Philip Snowden stands aloof from all this tendency —lonely, unyielding, consumed with one passionate purpose. This House of Commons through which he moves with painful steps, what is it but the mirror of the social system that he hopes to see shattered? "Propputty, propputty, propputty"—that's what he hears it say. He is in it, but not of it. He looks out on it with cold, bitter scrutiny. A faint, wistful smile flits across his pale face as he talks to you;

but it is the smile of polite formality. It has no relation to the fierce fire that burns within, steadily, unchangeably, a fire that would consume you with the rest of the régime of wrong.

He is the stuff of which revolutions are made. I have not been in the House when he has spoken; but I am told that he has not been a Parliamentary success. It would be strange if he were. The House loves the atmosphere of sympathy: here is no sympathy, but bitter challenge. It loves light and colour and easy raillery, playing upon the surface of its purposes: here is nothing but fierce intensity, ruthless and implacable. But I doubt whether there is any man living to-day with an equal power of moving great bodies of men to a certain exaltation of spirit, of communicating his own passion to others, of giving to politics something of the fervour of religious emotion. He is doctrinaire and academic in the extreme; but he fuses his theories with an enthusiasm that burns at white heat. If ever there were a revolution in this country, I do not know who would be its Danton, but I should have no doubt as to who would be its Robespierre—not the Robespierre of the September massacres, but the Robespierre of the concentrated and remorseless purpose.

Constancy is a rare virtue in politics. There are few men of whom it would be safe to forecast their intellectual and political point of view ten years hence. But, whatever happens, Philip Snowden will be where he stands to-day. He will neither ask quarter nor yield it. He will fight his battle out on these lines though it takes all his life, and he has nothing to record but defeat. I am told that he will lose Blackburn at the next election because of his bitter attitude toward Liberalism. One thing is certain; he will do nothing to conciliate the Liberals.

Prophets, Priests, and Kings

He must be taken on his terms, if taken at all. Compromise is not in him. He is one of those rare men who live for an idea, and who have neither aim nor ambition outside it. He would wade through slaughter to achieve it; he would go to the stake rather than surrender the least fragment of it. If you want to realise the purpose and the passion of Socialism, he is the man to watch. He is worth watching as a study of intensity and idealism. He is still more worth watching as one of the potentialities of our national life. For if Socialism ever came to power—and that depends largely on whether Liberalism is a sufficiently effective instrument of reform to keep it at bay—it will be Philip Snowden who will be largely the architect of the new social structure.

... ...

ROBERT BURDON HALDANE

LIFE, it has been said, is a comedy to him who thinks and a tragedy to him who feels. Judged by this axiom, Mr. Haldane is the man who thinks. He bathes the world in wreathed smiles and floods it with infectious good humour. He seems to go through life humming softly to himself. "Toujours bien, jamais mieux," is his motto. What a delightful world it is, he seems to say, and what a capital fellow you are, and what capital fellows we all are! It is like the comfortable purring of a cat on the hearthrug. It fills you with the ecstasy of a quiet content. Everything is snug and warm, the kettle is singing on the hob, the fire burns brightly in the grate, and though the wind howls and moans outside, it serves only as a foil to the comfort within. It is the best of all possible worlds.

"He has always been so," his mother, with whom he lives, will tell you. "He is always cheerful, never worries, and works incessantly." This unconquerable good humour is perhaps less the result of philosophy than of a good digestion. He comes of a hardy strain. The Haldanes were fighters in the brave days of old. One fell at Flodden, and others also found immortality on the battlefield. For generations they have been remarkable for their pedestrian powers. Mr. Haldane's grandfather thought little of an eight-mile walk even in his eighty-third year, and there is a story that his granduncle, having been prayed for by one of his clerical friends as "Thine aged and infirm servant," suggested

a little stroll, from which the clerical friend returned
in such a state of exhaustion that he fell into a deep
slumber, from which he could hardly be aroused in
time for the service he was to perform. Mr. Haldane
himself is credited with having frequently walked
sixty or seventy miles in a day; while his brothers
are said to have established a record of 103½ miles
under thirty-one hours. His big, alert frame and
his massive neck suggest those physical resources
which have made his powers of work and endurance
possible. " Nothing in the way of work can be done
without a big boiler and a bull-neck," said a sea
captain to me long ago. Mr. Haldane has both, and
his capacity for work has always been remarkable.

This physical energy is matched by a similar
mental energy. He has lived four careers—philosopher, lawyer, politician, and man of the world,
and has spared himself in none of them. He is an
intellectual steam engine. When once he has started
talking, there seems no reason why he should ever
leave off. There is no end to him. His oratory is
like an interminable round of beef—you may cut
and come again. One feels that the river of his
rhetoric will flow on for ever, fed by a thousand inexhaustible rills. The smooth, wooing voice inun-
dates the House with a flood of words. The enemy
attempts to dam the torrent in vain. In vain does
Mr. Arnold-Forster raise his head above the flood and
utter an angry interjection. He is engulfed by a
wave from the rhetorical ocean, and the waters flow
on in copious unconcern.

He has been known at the end of the second hour of
a speech to start afresh with a pleasant remark on
" these preliminary observations." On one occasion
he went to a Volunteer dinner and came away telling
his friends that everyone had approved his scheme.

Robert Burdon Haldane

He did not know that the company had come together seething with objections and had been literally talked into silence and surrender.

It was said of Gladstone that when it suited his purpose no one could wander more widely from his subject. It may be said of Mr. Haldane that no one can invest a subject in a more lucid fog. A lucid fog, I know, seems like a contradiction in terms; but no one who has heard Mr. Haldane speak for, say, three hours will deny that there is such a thing. The lucidity of his mind is as conclusive as the fog in yours. The clearer he becomes to himself, the more hopeless is your bewilderment. If only one could feel that he himself was getting a little lost in this amazing labyrinth of locution, one would feel less humiliated. But it is obvious that the less you understand him the more he understands himself. He smiles urbanely upon you, and points the fat didactic finger at you with pleasant intimacy. He does you the honour of pretending that you follow him, and self-respect compels you to accept the delicate tribute to your penetration. It is a comedy which saves him a lot of trouble.

There are some men who seem never to have known a joy in life, and there are few who do not have their variations of temperature and their moments of depression. Mr. Haldane gives the impression that he has never known a sorrow—that there was never a moment in which he was not walking on air in sheer exaltation of mind and body. The atmosphere of flagrant enjoyment that he exudes must be an offence to the man of a melancholy habit of mind. He cannot help distrusting such an apparently inexhaustible reservoir of cheerfulness. No man, he feels, can be really so happy as Mr. Haldane seems, and since that is so it is clear that he is playing a part. " As for professional optimists," said a distinguished philosopher of the opposite school to me, " one is always sceptical about them: they wear too much the strained look of the smile on a skull." Nothing could be less true of the optimism of Mr. Haldane. It is simply a huge capacity for enjoyment, fundamentally physical, and having no relation to his conclusions about the universe. It is customary to poke fun at his Hegelianism and to treat his philosophic interests as a disqualification for politics. If Being and Non-Being are identical—so runs the quip—it obviously does not matter whether we have an Army in Being or an Army in Non-Being. But to Mr. Haldane philosophy is only an intellectual exercise, as chemistry was to the late Lord Salisbury, or as theology and Homer were to Gladstone. It springs from his sympathy with the German genius.

For Mr. Haldane is Teutonic in his love of abstract thinking, and in his enthusiasm for thoroughness and exactness. He turns always to Germany for inspiration. He went thither after graduating at Edinburgh, and his first literary enterprise was his translation of Schopenhauer. His dinner table talk is full of German reminiscences, and he never misses an opportunity of addressing German visitors on the Terrace in their own tongue. He is as great a favourite with the King as Lord Cross used to be with Victoria, but that fact does not exclude the Kaiser from his opulent affections, and the Kaiser returns the feeling, always receives him with enthusiasm, and loves to show him his army. And it is to the German Army that he goes for ideas. On one of his visits to Berlin he said, " Germany, as all the world knows, has much to teach military students, and I am here simply to avail myself of the opportunity of studying her institutions before engaging in any tinkering of our own." It is from Germany that he brought the idea of a General Staff with which he began his reform of the British Army.

It must be admitted, too, that the type of his Liberalism is German. It is vague and indeterminate. It breathes expediency rather than the compulsion of principle. It approaches politics purely as a business proposition, and seeks to establish national greatness on scientific and material rather than moral foundations. It follows naturally that he was the standard-bearer of Lord Rosebery through the years of disunion, and that during the war he was the chief author and inspirer of the Liberal Imperial schism. His strategy was opposed to the strategy of Mr. Harcourt, and the pair were not unequally matched, though in one memorable struggle for the soul of the Eighty Club I think Mr. Harcourt showed the more masterly tactics. That he is not Lord Chancellor is due less to himself than to the perversity and indecision of his leader. Lord Rosebery played a part similar to that which Eachin played in the great fight on the North Inch described in *The Fair Maid of Perth*. The Stalwarts of the Clan Quhele surrounded him with loyal devotion. " Death for Hector " (*Bas air son Eachin*) was the cry as they went into the combat; but at the crisis of the fight, after prodigies of heroism had been performed by others, Hector turned, plunged into the Tay and fled from the battle. And Hal o' th' Wynd, in the person of stout C.-B., was left master of the field. His first act was to appoint Sir Robert Reid to the Woolsack. He did not love the Clan Quhele.

It was a bitter disappointment; but Mr. Haldane bore it with his imperturbable air of enjoyment and took up his task at the War Office with a passion of zeal that suggested that this was the ambition of his life. There had been many new brooms at the War

Office; but never such a new broom as this. He swept, as it were, incessantly, and as he swept he talked, now to the public, now to the Army, now to Parliament. His breezy confidence won confidence. The world always believes in a man who believes in himself. It is the first condition of success, and Mr. Haldane's faith in himself amounts to inspiration. The world also loves a man who pays it the compliment of taking it into his confidence. That is largely the secret of Mr. Haldane's popularity. He is always taking you into his confidence. Queen Victoria's objection to Gladstone was that he talked to her as if he were addressing a public meeting. Mr. Haldane talks to you as if you were the British Empire and must be placated at all costs. You may doubt his scheme; but you cannot doubt his enthusiasm. You may dislike his politics; but you cannot help being moved by the deference he pays to your judgment.

It is by these methods that he has conquered the Army. You cannot resist a man who bursts with such enjoyment into the mess, smokes bigger and stronger cigars than anyone else, and obviously enjoys them more, knows as much about explosives as he does about the Westminster Confession, and with all these accomplishments does you the delicate honour of discussing his scheme with you as if your approval were the one thing in the world necessary to his complete happiness. One of his predecessors at the War Office, speaking to me on one occasion about the difficulties of his task, said: " What can you do with these infernal colonels, who know less about war than they know about virtue? " Mr. Haldane knows very well what to do with them. He does not lecture them or hector them. He talks to them as if he were consulting them, and they surrender to his blandishments. " He yields on small things with

Robert Burdon Haldane

such bonhomie that out of sheer chivalry they can't help yielding to him on big ones," said one who works with him to me. " Moreover, they have had such an experience of War Secretaries in the past, that, by comparison, Haldane is a jewel, and they think that any change would probably be for the worse." There is the reason why Mr. Haldane has got his schemes through with such success. He greases the wheels well. These schemes may be good or bad. Time alone will prove them. But to have got them through with so little resistance and to remain relatively popular with the colonels is an achievement in the art of managing men. Even when he disbanded the 3rd Battalion of the Scots Guards, there were tears, but few reproaches. It was a courageous act, for it brought him into conflict with the King and with his old leader. The King pronounced a funeral oration on the Guards and said he hoped to see them revived, while Lord Rosebery—forgetful of all the loyal service of his old lieutenant and remembering only that he dared to be happy without him—tore a passion of indignation to tatters and then fell into dramatic silence, to awaken later on in a passion about something else.

I am not sure whether Mr. Haldane invented the word " efficiency," which has become the hardest worked vocable in politics. When Humpty Dumpty explained how much he meant by " Impenetrability," he added, " When I make a word do a lot of work like that I always pay it extra." On that just principle, " efficiency " ought to-day to be the most prosperous word in the language. It represents the political gospel opposed to the fine old English doctrine of " muddling through," the phrase in which Lord Rosebery summed up the Boer War. But whether he invented it or not, Mr. Haldane is its recognised exponent. " Efficiency, and again efficiency, and always efficiency." It is the German spirit that he opposes to the French spirit of Danton's axiom: efficiency and ideas. " We have won a magnificent victory," he said, after the General Election of 1906. " What is it that we need? What is it that has been wanting in the past? I answer in a word—ideas! We have got the majority. Have we got the ideas? " One sees him pausing for the obvious reply. " Not numbers but efficiency " is his maxim in the making of an army. And he pays himself a modest compliment when he adds, " I have never had a more congenial occupation than this attempt at reorganisation and the introduction of science into the business."

It remains to be seen whether the German doctrine of " thorough " can be engrafted on the English stem of hand-to-mouth practicality, and whether English Liberalism could survive the infusion of bureaucracy which is the basis of Mr. Haldane's clear thinking. But whatever the fate of Mr. Haldane and his Army reforms may be, we may be sure that nothing will ever destroy his indestructible complacency. Ministries may rise and fall, Army schemes come and go, but his exuberance will remain. " Toujours bien, jamais mieux " will be his motto, and through all the cataclysms of politics he will still go his way humming softly to himself in sheer spiritual revelry.

JOHN BURNS

I WAS walking one evening along the Embankment when I overtook John Burns. The night was cold, but he wore neither overcoat nor gloves, for he scorns both as the trappings of effeminate luxury. He carried under his arm a huge bound volume of the *Phalanx*, a Labour journal of long ago, which he had just picked up at a bookstall. He plunged at once into a stream of that buoyant, confident talk which is so characteristic of the man.

" Here," he says, and his hand seizes me like a vice, bringing me up short before a tablet of the late Queen, let into the fence before the Temple. " Look at it. Been up five years. Not a scratch on it. I tell you there's not a country in Europe where there is a higher standard of public conduct than here."

A young couple of the working class pass us arm-in-arm. His iron grasp is once more on me, and I am swung round to take note of them. " That's not the sort of couple the people who vilify the working classes picture. Believe me, sir, the courting of the working classes is as pure and chivalrous as anything I know. You take it from me—the working classes are morally as sound as a bell."

A flower girl stops us, and with whispering humbleness proffers chrysanthemums. " Well, my lass, it's a cold night for your job." He puts money in her hand, but waves aside the blooms. " No, no, my girl, keep them. Do I look like a man that wants flowers? "

" Sir," he says, in reply to some remark, " I go my own way. I trust to my own eyes and ears. When

Ibsen said, ' The strongest man is he who stands alone,' he had J. B. in his eye." And he watches my merriment with quizzical good humour.

At Waterloo Bridge that terrible hand grips me again. He opens a door in the hoarding, commandeers a foreman, and crashes his way over masses of masonry and débris through the tramway tunnel which is being driven under the Strand to Kingsway, his big voice booming out questions and comments all the time.

Out on the Embankment again, he pulls up before a man, whether workman or loafer it is difficult to say. " Well, Higgins, what are you up to now? " And as Higgins proceeds with his apologia I escape.

There is the man, boisterous, confident, gaily aggressive, honest as the day, full of the egotism of the child, with the child's delighted interest in the passing show of things—Cabinet Minister and working man—proud of his present, proud of his past, most proud of all that he has " done time " in one of his Majesty's prisons.

He stands four square to all the winds that blow, solid as a pedestal of granite, short and mighty of limb, like Hal o' th' Wynd, his great eyes flashing scorn and challenge from under the terrific eyebrows, his nostrils swelling with defiance, his voice bursting in upon the tranquillities like a foghorn, thick and hoarse from thundering in the open air, his grey hair and beard belying the enormous vitality of mind and muscle. A man indeed, virile and vehement, dogmatic as a timetable, with an argument as heavy as his fist—" the powerful, natural man " of Whitman's ideal. Plain living and high thinking his maxim— no alcohol, no tobacco, no rugs and mufflers, no weak concessions to the flesh; but cold water and plenty of it within and without, early rising and hard walking, a game of cricket, a swim in the bath, and then—out sword and have at you! A glorious swashbuckler of romance.

His life an ebullient joy. There is not a page in it that he slurs over. There is not an hour when he has not found it good to be alive. His boundless exuberance fills you like a gale at sea. His optimism seems to fill the whole world with the singing of birds and the laughter of children. There never was such a world. There never was such a country as this England of ours. There never was such a city as this glorious London. Do you doubt it? Do you talk of your Germany and your France? Sir, do you know that the average number of inhabitants of a house in London is eight and in Berlin eighty; that the mortality in London is 15, and in Berlin 17; that the average rent per room in London is so and so, and in Berlin so and so; that—in fact, that an avalanche of statistics has suddenly descended on you, reducing you to abject and humiliated silence. Never was there such a man for statistics. He is a Blue Book in breeches. My brain reels at the thought of a conversation between him and Mr. Chiozza Money, each bringing up battalions of figures to crush the other, millions of figures, figures on horseback and figures on foot—a perfect Armageddon of averages and tables and percentages. Oliver Wendell Holmes says that some men lead facts about with them like bulldogs, and let them loose upon you at the least provocation. John Burns' facts are bulldogs that leap at your throat and shake the life out of you.

And the marvel is that with all this welter of facts his thinking is so clear and his judgment so sound. The reason is that he knows life at first hand. And by life I mean the life of the common people to whom he belongs and whom he genuinely loves. He has worked with them in the engine-room at sea and ashore; he has thundered to them on Tower Hill, in Hyde Park, and Trafalgar Square. He has lived among them, and never deserted them. He is easy in any company, but most at ease with them. He knows the London of the people as perhaps no other man knows it. He has spent, and still spends, months in tramping its streets, talking to the people, talking to the policemen, dipping into sunless alleys, peering into back yards. This vast metropolis is like an open book to him. It is as though he could not only name the streets, but could tell you the story of the people in the houses, and the contents of the kitchen pot.

This insatiable thirst pursues him abroad. He goes to Germany, sees its sewers and its sanctuaries, marches with its army, talks with the cabmen in the street, comes back laden with invisible imports of precious facts—more bulldogs for the unwary.

He is probably the best known man in the country —certainly the best known man in London, for which he has done magnificent service as the embodiment and the driving force of the Progressive movement. Popular enthusiasn has dowered him with the properties of his namesake. Someone was declaiming at a meeting that " A man's a man for a' that," adding, " as Burns says," whereat the audience rose with cheers for " good old John." And he dominates his enemies as much as his friends. In a 'bus during the last L.C.C. election two Moderates were discussing the "Wastrels." "Look at the Poor Law," said one. "Costs four millions a year. Nice pickings there." " Yes," said the other. " I wonder what John Burns' share is." " One million sterling, sir," thundered a voice from the other end, and the menacing eye of John Burns gleamed over the paper he had been reading unseen. Living ever in the crowd, ready

John Burns

Prophets, Priests and Kings

ever to cross swords with whomsoever will, his life is full of comedy and episode. Adventure dogs him as it did the knights of old. He is always snatching children from the imminent deadly hoof, or plunging into the river, or stopping runaway horses, or carrying "accidents" to the hospital. Members never fall ill in the House except when John Burns is there to carry them out, and at fires he is sublime. His voice frightens the flames into miserable surrender.

His honesty is above suspicion. Money cannot buy him, threats cannot coerce him. For eighteen years he was the mainstay of the government of London, a working engineer, living upon his grant of £200 from his Society, and never a breath of suspicion against his honour. No "job" could abide his wrath. A Battersea official told me that one was contemplated in his department of the borough. He went to Burns and told him. In five minutes he was away on his bicycle like the wind. By noon he had smashed the intrigue. Such passion for the public interest is magnificent. Think of it beside the appalling municipal corruption of America. Think what such an example means to us, not only in cash, but in the wholesome ideals of citizenship. See, too, how he is cleansing the Augean stables of Poor Law administration. His claims as a legislator on the grand scale yet remain to be proved; but as an administrator he is worth millions to us.

Like Sir Anthony Absolute, no one is more easily led—when he has his own way. You cannot argue with him any more than you can argue with a sledgehammer. He has no subtleties either of thought or of conduct. He is plain as a pike-staff. What is in his mind must out, and if he doesn't understand a thing he damns it. He has no secrets and no cunning, and when he is attacked he hits back with his fist. His oratory has never lost the fortissimo of his Trafalgar Square days, but he loves the finery of words—words of "wondrous length and thundering sound," words in full-bottomed wigs and court dress. He would have felt that Johnson was strangely feeble when he said that something "had not wit enough to keep it sweet," but he would have forgiven the great man when he corrected himself and said, "It has not vitality enough to preserve it from putre- faction." That is the sort of verbal thunderbolt Mr. Burns hurls at you when he has time to think. Yet, like Johnson, his first impulse is to express himself in brief, emphatic Saxon and homely imagery, of which he has an abundance. "Sir," speaking of two young politicians of cold exterior—"Sir, the only difference between them is that one is strawberry and the other vanilla—they're both ices." And of an acrid person who is reported to be suffering from stomach trouble —"What can you expect of a man who has drunk nothing but vinegar for forty years?" But when he has, so to speak, time to dress, he is a verbal aristocrat. His adjectives march in triplets, and his sentiments in antithesis, as though he belonged to the eighteenth century instead of the twentieth. He is more proud of his library of six thousand books than of his place in the Cabinet, and would rather be caught by the photographer while reading a book on the pavement outside a secondhand bookshop in Charing Cross Road than when coming from a *levée* in Court costume. Not that he has any objection to velvet coats, knee breeches, and shoe buckles. Privately, I think, he knows they suit him as well as the bowler hat and the reefer jacket that he wears on all other occasions as the sign of democracy.

His emotions are primal and are exhibited with entire candour. He has strong hates and strong

John Burns

affections, and expresses both with the frankness of a primitive nature. A noble sentiment well expressed delights him as a brightly coloured picture delights a child, and the sergeant who, when a gun carriage had overturned in some manœuvres on Salisbury Plain and Mr. Burns had helped to extricate the men, said, in reply to his inquiry as to whether anyone was hurt, "The men of the Royal Artillery are sometimes killed, but never hurt," captured his heart for ever. The truth is that he is a victim of phrases. If he may make the phrases he does not care who makes the Bills. And to be just to him, he has probably said more witty things than any man in politics.

It is not necessary, even if it were possible, to allocate the blame for the bitterness that has sprung up between him and the Labour party. At the root, I think, in spite of Tower Hill and Trafalgar Square, he was always something of an Individualist and a bureaucrat. But whatever the merits of the quarrel, he has certainly given knocks as hard as those he received. And at least no reminder of the past ever puts him to silence or to the blush. When someone at a meeting recalled his saying of other days, that no man was worth more than £500 a year, and contrasted that saying with his present salary, he answered with stentorian good humour, " Sir, I am a trade unionist. The trade union wage for Cabinet Ministers is £2000 a year. Would you have me a blackleg ? "

He has his foibles. He is himself the most interesting man he knows. He sees himself colossal, a figure touching the skies. He walks round himself, as it were, and he is filled with admiration at the spectacle. Wonderful! What a man! It is the egotism of the child, so frank, so irresistible, so essentially void of offence, so ready to laugh at itself. There is a story

—*ben trovato*, perhaps — that when Sir H. Campbell-Bannerman offered him a seat in the Cabinet he bowed himself out with the remark, "Well, Sir Henry, this is the most popular thing you have done." It is a story good enough to be true. It sums up so admirably the amiable weakness of this robust man.

Withal, what an asset he is to our national life! What a breeze he brings with him, what wholesome fresh air, what unconquerable buoyancy! I am told that he is less popular in Battersea than he was. Then so much the worse for Battersea. If it has ceased to follow him, it has ceased to follow an honest man and a great citizen. He has fallen away from grace in the eyes of the Labour Party, who find the accents of the Treasury Bench different from those of Tower Hill. So they are; so they must be. But, in spite of a certain stiffening, as it were, of the muscles of the mind, his heart beats true as ever to his first and only love—the common people. He chastises them; but he loves them, not with the aloofness of a superior person, but with the love of a comrade, who offers them a shining example. If he will only check the tendency to intellectual hardening which some of us observe, guard against the subtle advances of the official spirit, suspect the flatterer, and occasionally listen to old friends who will not flatter, he has a long career of service to the people before him.

But when all is said one cannot resist the conclusion that John Burns' true vocation is not that of a minister but of a challenger, and that public life has lost far more than it has gained by harnessing him to office. I would rather hear him in Hyde Park, his great voice booming across to the palaces of Park Lane, his huge fist shaking defiance at social wrong, than hear him trying to modulate his accents to the

John Burns

restraints of office from the Treasury bench. He was a more heroic figure when he burst, as Llewellyn Smith and Vaughan Nash have described, into the arena of the great Dock Strike than he is to-day, and it is better to think of him scaling the front of the Local Government Board office, determined to be heard by the authorities within, even though he had to be heard through the windows, than to think of him sitting inside and securing a K.C.B. for the official who tried to sweep him from the window-sill in the old rebellious days. He is the greatest voice and the biggest personality the people have produced in our time and he should have remained a free voice. As a statesman there are plenty to eclipse him, for he has little constructive genius and no gift for the manipulation of men. But as a citizen he has had no rival.

WILLIAM JENNINGS BRYAN

It was a wonderful apparition of vitality that burst in on me one morning at the Hotel Cecil, where I had called to breakfast with William Jennings Bryan. " Now, sir," he said with that air of plunging straight into business so characteristic of the American, " I find my resolution at the Inter-Parliamentary Conference is down for 9.30, and to save time I've had breakfast early, so that while you are breakfasting I can talk right along." And, seizing a chair, he sat down and " talked right along."

There is about him the primal energy and directness of nature. He is a Niagara of a man, a resistless torrent of inexhaustible force, thundering along in a sort of ebullient joy, mind and body in perfect equipoise. It is not the hurry and frenzy of the city that possesses him; but the free, untrammelled spirit of the West, with its spacious skies and primeval forests and illimitable prairies. He has the simplicity of a son of the plains. His mind moves in large curves, and sweeps along in royal unconsciousness of academic restraints and niceties. You do not remember the proprieties in his presence, any more than you would remember them in the presence of a hurricane. For he comes right down to the bed-rock of things, and his hammer rings out blows that seem to have the Universe for a sounding-board. As he talks, you understand that thrilling scene when the young unknown Nebraskan stamped the Democratic Convention in 1896 and swept all rivals out of the field with his " cross of gold " speech. It is a speech of

William Jennings Bryan

which he is probably not very proud to-day. It has passed into the lumber-room of history, and he knows that the reform of American currency will have to be achieved by methods other than the jejune scheme that brought him into prominence. But the incident revealed his enormous dynamic power even though it did not reveal an equivalent quality of statesmanship.

Before he has spoken his presence arrests you. You cannot come in sudden contact with him without a certain shock of expectation. He leaps out at you, as it were, from the drab canvas of humanity. The big, loose frame, the massive head, the bold sculpture of the face, the black, lustrous eyes, so direct and intense, the large governing nose, the wide, straight mouth, with lips tight pressed, and the firm, broad chin together convey an impression of decision and power which is irresistible. It is difficult to believe that a man can be so strong as Mr. Bryan looks. Together with this appearance of elemental power there is the sense of an elemental gentleness, a natural chivalry, a frank and human kindliness. He has the unaffected courtesy not of one who stoops to conquer, but of one who is unconscious of social or intellectual fences. He lives, as it were, on the broad, free plain of a common humanity.

His face is typically American. It is often said that the American type has not yet emerged from the welter of races out of which the ultimate American people are to be fashioned. But there is a dominant profile visible. It is the profile of M'Kinley and Bryan. It is the profile which suggests quite startlingly the characteristics of the aboriginal race of North America, and raises in perhaps the most piquant form the problem of the influence of climate on physique and character. Mr. Bernard Shaw gives so large a place to that influence that he seems to suggest that if only our dull English Broadbents could arrange to be born and to live in Ireland they would become as imaginative and bright-witted as himself. Certainly the tendency of the Americans to revert to the physical contours of the Red Man—a tendency which has been commented on by many observers, including Mr. Ford Madox Hueffer, whom I found after his visit to America deeply impressed with the phenomenon—is too well marked to be merely fanciful.

Mr. Bryan is typical, too, of the American in temperament and intellectual outlook. It is the temperament of youth, incident to a people in the making and to a light and stimulating air. The wine is new in the bottle. It lacks the mellowness of the

> . . . vintage that has been
> Cooled a long age in the deep delvèd earth.

It is exhilarating and expresses itself in a sanguine and dazzling optimism that goes out to meet great adventure with a challenging heart. There is a certain crudity in Mr. Bryan's mind. It seems the product not of centuries of civilisation, but of a civilisation that has just realised itself. The obvious has still the bloom of the dawn upon it, and that which the sophisticated mind takes for understood is subject to elaborate exposition. His intellect is bold rather than subtle, masculine rather than meticulous. His eye ranges over great horizons and sees the landscape in the large. His weapon is not the rapier, but the hammer of Thor. He is elemental and not " precious." If you talk to him of poetry you will find him indifferent to the heavy-laden incense of Keats, but quickly responsive to the austere note of Milton. For his mind is charged with the spirit of New England Puritanism, and if

William Jennings Bryan

ever a monument is erected to him it should be on Plymouth Rock.

For had Mr. Bryan not been a politician, he would have been the greatest revivalist of our time. His qualities as a statesman have yet to be proved, and may be very seriously doubted. But his qualities as a preacher are indisputable. He is, before all else, the hot gospeller of national righteousness. Even in appearance, with his expanse of white " front " and his black cravat, he suggests the Methodist divine. His appeal is always to the moral conscience. The name of the Almighty is as familiar on his lips as it was on the lips of Gladstone. And it is the highest tribute to his sincerity that in employing it he never gives you the sense of canting. The truth is that he lives in an atmosphere out of which our politics have passed. No one to-day in the House of Commons ever touches the spiritual note. When we say that oratory is dead we mean that faith, which is the soul of oratory, is dead. Oratory fell to earth when Gladstone and Bright ceased to wing it with spiritual passion, and to associate the thunders of Sinai with the ideals of politics.

Now the supreme fact about Mr. Bryan is that he mingles religion and politics in the same breath. They are not distinguishable from each other, but are fused into one theme. His talk is like the talk of Cromwell, so full is it of Biblical imagery and phraseology. Thus, speaking of the political awakening in America, he passes naturally to the moral and spiritual awakening as its basis. " Are you aware that the country has been going through a great revival of religion? Certainly it is true. Don't you know about the evangelistic movement, that most impressive movement towards a more personal realisation of the Gospel? It has taken possession of the Churches everywhere. It has quickened religion. It has brought in the men and organised them. And there is a new note in popular religion. While it is quickened on its personal side, it has come to a new understanding of the social significance of Christianity. Christ said—no, it was one of the Disciples, but the authority is pretty good still: ' He that saith he is in the light and hateth his brother is in darkness even until now.' "

" The time has come," he says, " when it is perceived that religion is a concern that has to do with the family, the city and the nation, with business and with politics, as well as with what is called the individual life. No man can individually be a religious man who commercially acts irreligiously or politically consents to irreligious measures. What we are witnessing is a revival of religion largely concerned with men and women as members of society."

All his political thinking springs out of this soil of moral ideas. " The wages of sin is death," he says, " to the nation as much as to the individual. In the case of a nation a century may elapse between the sowing of the wind and the reaping of the whirlwind, but the one follows the other." He stands by the historic view of America as the land of the ploughshare and not of the sword. Not that he is afraid of unsheathing the sword in a just cause. He himself raised a Nebraskan regiment in the Spanish-American war, and was himself its colonel. But aggression he hates. " What is this growth of militarism for? If it is due to a fear of labour troubles, why not deal with them through the Department of Justice rather than through the Department of War? If it is due to Imperialism, then Imperialism attacks the most vital Christian principle—namely, the propagation of good by example. What has Imperialism done in the Philippines? It has sought to propagate good by force. It has been a policy of philanthropy and five per cent. Sir, it can't be done. Philanthropy goes to the wall. The five per cent. blinds us to the real welfare of the Filipinos. The Bible plan of propagating good is by example. ' So live that others, seeing your good works, may glorify your Father.' "

So with the Tariff issue. It is the moral aspect of Free Trade on which he dwells. The open door is the gospel of Brotherhood. Build up tariff walls, and you build up national enmities and armies and navies to support them. Break down tariff walls, and you establish a common basis of peace between the nations. " Yes, I am a Tariff Reformer," he said to me—I had mentioned his visit to Glasgow, where he had heard Mr. Chamberlain open his fiscal campaign —" but a Tariff Reformer with us, you know, is a Free Trader. Protection is a stumbling block to progress and peace. It is a cruel injustice to the poor, for taxes upon consumption always bear heaviest upon the poor and lightest upon the rich. Under taxes on consumption, men contribute, not in proportion to property and income, but in proportion to what they eat, drink, wear, and use. Taxes on consumption are taxes upon our needs, and men's needs, being created by the Almighty, are much more nearly equal than their possessions. No, sir, to me the fact that Protection taxes our needs and Free Trade taxes our possessions, that the taxation of Protection is cunning and concealed and the taxation of Free Trade is open and direct, is final."

It is of Bright—Bright with a slight American accent—that you think as the broad stream of his talk flows on. " I sail from headland to headland," said Bright, " while Gladstone navigates every creek and inlet." And so it is with Bryan. His canvas bellies with the great wind. He does not tack and trim, but keeps to the well-charted highway and the open sea. It is this breadth of appeal, this large sculpture of his thought—the result of that moral purpose which gives its simple unity and coherence —that has made him one of the most powerful popular orators in the English-speaking world. It is true that he has twice failed to win the Presidency; but his failures were more dazzling than the triumphs of other men. There has been nothing in political annals to compare with those two great presidential campaigns. He went through the country like a whirlwind. Merely as a physical performance they stand alone. In the four months' electioneering in 1896 he travelled 18,000 miles and delivered 2100 speeches to an estimated total of 8,000,000 people. During the last few weeks he often spoke thirty-five times a day, and once forty-one times. His force never faltered and his passion never lost its hold. " I saw women in hysterics and men with tears in their eyes at his entrance," says an American journalist, describing the scene at a meeting at Indianapolis, where the great audience had sat in a temperature of 110 degrees waiting hour by hour for the candidate who had been held up by the train. " I timed the length of excitement. It was twenty minutes before Bryan could sit down." His power owes nothing to rhetorical trickery. His voice is rich, deep, and musical; but he does not use it with conscious display. He talks quite simply and naturally, and uses few gestures.

The physical resources which this Titanic campaigning indicates are a tribute to the stock from which he springs. " So far as I have been able to discover," he told me with a smile, " I embody the British Isles, for my ancestry is English, Irish, and Scotch."

William Jennings Bryan

The intensity of the feeling against him among the Republican and propertied classes can only be indicated by recalling the attitude of English society towards Sir H. Campbell-Bannerman at the time of the war. I had a sudden revelation of it at dinner one night when seated beside an American lady. At the mention of his name her serenity vanished, and she burst into a torrent of invective that left him a moral ruin. But, hateful as his democratic doctrines are to his opponents, no one ever challenges their sincerity or doubts his honesty. He has carried that honesty into business. He left the law for journalism, and owns a newspaper, *The Commoner*, at Lincoln, Nebraska, and in that paper he never allows any trust-made article to be advertised. That, nevertheless, he draws an income of £6000 a year from it is a pleasant evidence that it is possible to be at once honest and prosperous even in America.

And, indeed, whether he becomes President or not, the fact that a man of this type is one of the most popular figures in America is a reassuring feature in the dark sky of its future. All the elements of ruin and combustion are visible. A Constitution, rigid and inelastic and founded on unqualified individualism, has allowed the growth of a Trust system which holds the State in the hollow of its hand. The land of the free has become a land of economic serfs, its franchises exploited by financial highwaymen, its municipalities sinks of corruption, its necessaries shut out by a tyrannous Protective tariff built up by the Republican Party at the dictation of the plutocratic power that dominates it. Underneath is the volcanic fire of an insurgent people. If the disaster that threatens is to be escaped, it can only be by a new war of emancipation that will strike the fetters of private monopoly off the limbs of the democracy. It is the economic

Prophets, Priests, and Kings

liberation of a people that is the real problem of American politics. And as you look at the clear, resolute eye and the large, masterful face of Mr. Bryan, you feel that here is a man who will play a large part in that liberation. We may doubt whether he will carry it through, for his mental processes are too elementary for the practical engineering work of politics. There will need to be other more instructed, more acute, more scientific minds to plan the new social structure. But he will supply the moral fervour and the large purpose. He will not manipulate the storm, but he will give it impetus and direction. His task, in a word, is not that of statesmanship, but of revivalism, and it is as the field preacher of politics that he will do his best service to his country.

LEWIS HARCOURT

" WHAT I really think——," said Mr. Harcourt.

" What you *really* think," interrupted the other, laughing, " is known only to Mr. Lewis Harcourt and his Maker."

Mr. Harcourt smiled his inscrutable smile and proceeded. The thrust glanced off the impenetrable corslet. But it expressed what one feels about this dominating, masterful figure, that sits so tight in the saddle, wears ever an unruffled front, turns aside the smashing blow with a jest, seems never hurried, never worried, pursues his purpose with such stillness that he is forgotten—until the mine explodes and the match that fired it is seen in his hand.

The lightnings play about the path of Mr. Winston Churchill: Mr. Harcourt advances in the shadow, unobtrusively, unnoted, except by the few. Watch him casually, and he seems but a spectator of the game, amused and interested, but never caught in its central swirl—a man after Mr. George Russell's own heart, carrying with him the atmosphere of the eighteenth century, full of worldly, ironic wisdom, rich in stories of men and events, too fond of pulling the mechanism of the watch to pieces ever to become a wheel in its works.

That is the superficial view of Mr. Harcourt. Behind this easy, imperturbable exterior you find one of the most subtle, most far-seeing, most unswerving influences in politics. " It was the intrigues of young Harcourt that upset my apple-cart," Lord Rosebery is reported to have once said. The saying, if authentic, was not quite true. The man who upset Lord Rosebery's apple-cart was—Lord Rosebery. But those who know most of the intricate story of those troubled years when Sir Henry Campbell-Bannerman was holding aloft the old flag, surrounded by open enemies and cold friends, know how much of the ultimate triumph was due to the astuteness and passionless loyalty of Mr. Harcourt. I would rather have him at my back in a row than any man in politics.

Mr. Harcourt bides his time. He has the rare gift of immeasurable patience. Jacob toiled for Laban fourteen years; but Mr. Harcourt toiled for his father twenty. He gave up not only his youth but his maturity to that filial service. He took on himself the humblest secretarial tasks. He learned shorthand and typewriting to facilitate his father's work. He sought no place for himself. He drudged seventeen hours a day over his father's budgets; he grubbed among blue-books and dusty documents.

He was over forty before he sought a seat in Parliament. Even when he entered the House he was content to remain silent—to wait. He was, to the world, just " Lulu," Sir William's son, an amiable young man devoted to his father, the shadow of a great name. When he was given a place in the Ministry he had not uttered a word in Parliament, and there was a certain justice in the allusion to him as " an interesting experiment." The phrase tickled him. I have a letter from him signed " The Interesting Experiment."

He delivered his first Parliamentary speech as a Minister of the Crown, and he came into his kingdom at a stride. His long apprenticeship was over, and a new force of first-rate possibilities was added to the drama of politics. He emerged in a day from the obscurity of twenty years into the front rank of the conflict, equipped with every Parliamentary resource, knowing all the inner workings of the machine, familiar from his childhood with the great figures of the past, Gladstone, Disraeli, Salisbury, astute, serene, unfathomable, with the suavity of conscious power, and most dangerous when he was most suave. The glove was velvet, but the hand within was iron.

To-day Mr. Harcourt stands out as one of the three men in the Liberal Party to whom all things seem possible. Political life never furnished a more startling contrast in temperament and outlook than two of those three furnish—the one eager, restless, inquiring, passionate, modern as the morning's news-sheet, drinking life in great feverish draughts, as if he feared that every moment would snatch the goblet from his lips for ever, a mountain torrent in spate; the other calm and secure, cool and calculating, living as if he had all eternity to work in, as if he had the key to every problem and had tasted all that was in the cup of life. The orbit of the one incalculable: the orbit of the other known to the fraction of a second.

For Mr. Harcourt has his roots in the past. He treads in the established tradition of British statesmanship. To him the world is still divisible into Whigs and Tories, the old party lines still plainly mark the path before him. He will never lead a Social Revolution. He will never blaze out into any " raging, tearing propaganda." He will never desert the tabernacle, and if ever the Old Guard comes into action on the evening of some Waterloo, it will be Mr. Harcourt who will lead the van.

In a word, he is for the Party first and last, for Liberalism as he understands it and as his father understood it, for Liberalism as the instrument of sober, considered progress, upon familiar lines; yielding here a little and there a little to the fierce clamour of the new time with its new, strange voices; but keeping ever to the great trunk road, of which Walpole was the engineer in the eighteenth century and Gladstone in the nineteenth. How far a mind so rooted in the past, so remote from popular sympathies and the spirit of the modern democratic movement, so governed by a conception of society organically unchanging, can control the lightnings that flash in the political sky of the twentieth century and bring them into the service of the cause to which he is devoted is one of the most interesting problems of the future. It is the problem of Liberalism itself—the problem of how far the principles of Liberalism which have worked out the civil and religious freedom of the people can be successfully applied to securing their economic freedom, and their liberation from the serfdom of circumstance and the wrongs of social injustice.

Few men have appealed less to the gallery than Mr. Harcourt. He does not scan far horizons. He does not declare any vision of a promised land. He has no passionate fervour for humanity, and is too honest to pretend to any. He is a practical politician, with no dithyrambs. He loves the intricacies of the campaign more than the visionary gleam, the actual more than the potential, present facts more than future fancies. He is the man without a dream.

But he is the type of man who brings the dreams of others to pass—the builder who translates the imagination of the architect into terms of wood and stone. Other men will prophesy; he will perform. Other men will create the atmosphere of change; he will give it form and shape. He is the man who " puts things through." There has been no more striking feat of supple capacity combined with unyielding purpose than his conduct of the Small Holdings Act last Session. His smile is more potent than the speeches of other men. He has you unhorsed with a phrase. And when you think to catch him napping, you find that he has all his battalions within earshot, ready to descend on you like an avalanche. He is the organiser of victory, the general who will not lose a gun. If his possibilities are not realised it will be because in his secret heart he distrusts the eager movement of the time and conceives his function to be that of a check upon its enthusiasms rather than an inspiration, and because he has too much of the spirit of the *grand seigneur* to be entirely at home in the heat and dust of these democratic days. To the general he will always be a little caviare. "The general" is not responsive to persiflage and elaborate irony.

Mr. Harcourt has the manners and the mental habitudes of the *ancien régime*. He would not pass for a *parvenu*. You would not associate his origins with dry goods. His philosophy is that of Walpole, and it is of that statesman more than any other that he reminds you. There is about him nothing of the hurry of the Twentieth Century, and no suspicion of its feverish intellectual unrest. The riddles of the universe do not disturb him. He is the man of leisure and of taste, who is very pleased with the world and entirely at home in it, and who has the security and ease that come from generations of spacious life. If he drops into poetry you expect it to be Horatian, and when he tells a story it has the flavour of the great world. He suggests ancestors, knights in armour, bishops in lawn sleeves, stalwart Eighteenth-Century squires striding over ploughed lands with a gun and drinking their three bottles at night in Georgian mansions, masterful men all, lords of many acres, politely familiar with the classics, their walls hung with Lely's leering ladies and Kneller's unimaginative wigs.

He is at once curiously like and unlike his father. He has Sir William's great height—he stands six foot two or so—but he is as lean as Cassius, while his father's girth was Falstaffian. Sir William was a famous trencherman, with the constitution of a Norse hero; his son is delicate and fastidious, and when he comes into the room he looks for the draughts. He has much of his father's wit, but none of his father's irascibility. He smiles urbanely and darkly where his father thundered. He has the Olympian manner of Sir William, but it is more restrained, and men never joke about his Plantagenet descent, though to his father's Royal pedigree he adds another kinship with royalty through his mother, a Clarendon. The toast of " Sir William Harcourt and the rest of the Royal Family " is never adapted to his case. But he is not indifferent to the other branch of the family, and is a close friend of the King, whom he entertains at Nuneham in regal state. For he has great wealth through his wife, the daughter of the late Mr. W. H. Burns, of New York. The heavy, untuned voice— like the late Duke of Devonshire's, the voice of an authentic aristocracy, broken, I suppose, in the " view halloo " of generations of fox-hunting forebears—is not adapted to rhetoric; but his speeches are of the same vintage as Sir William's, and when he rises the House knows that it is going to have some innocent merriment. Sometimes his merriment is out of touch with the modern sentiment, as in the case of his speeches on the woman suffrage question which would have done very well, no doubt, in his own Eighteenth Century, but ring a little unpleasantly in ours.

There is a certain incongruity between a man of

such powers and his office. It is like Hackenschmidt wheeling a perambulator. But he wheels it astonishingly well, and seems to enjoy the task. He has raised the office of First Commissioner of Works to a level that it had never reached before. He has shown in it the same managing spirit that he revealed at the Home Counties Liberal Federation—for the triumph around London in 1906 was largely his—and which is restoring the ancient glories of the Nuneham seat which came to him in some embarrassment and decay. He has saved the time of the House by simplifying the divisions; he has reorganised the catering as adroitly as though he had spent his youth at Spiers and Pond's instead of Eton; he has rearranged the dining-rooms and won the heart of everybody by his thoughtful stewardship. He has inaugurated a great scheme for the development of the public galleries, and has worked wonders in the Royal parks, raising wages, cheapening refreshments, giving facilities for games. I know of no pleasanter fact about him than his consideration for the children. He has some charming children of his own, and perhaps that is why he remembers other people's little girls and boys who have no Nuneham Park to play in. His happy idea of making some of the animals in the Zoo visible from the outside where the children play in Regent's Park is an illustration of this engaging side of his character and administration.

When he resigns the perambulator, Parliament will discover behind this exterior of polite persiflage one of the ablest executive brains in politics, a capacious mind moving without haste and without deviation to deeply considered ends, subtle, adroit, resourceful—*omnia capax imperii*, but most capable of all in ruling men whom he knows through and through, while he himself remains always something of a mystery. For he has none of the self-revelation of Mr. Churchill, who throws all his cards on the table with the careless frankness of Fox, and turns out his mind with the joy of a boy turning out his pockets. Mr. Harcourt has his battalions masked.

"What I really think," he says.

"What you *really* think!" you reply.

AUGUSTINE BIRRELL, K.C.

IF a vote were taken in the House of Commons on the question of the most popular member, it is certain that Mr. Augustine Birrell's name would be in the first half-dozen. For Mr. Birrell is an impostor who has been found out. He affects to be a very gruff and menacing person. He looks fiercely at you from below his corrugated brows. He raps out an answer like a schoolmaster cracking an unruly pupil across the knuckles with a ruler. He will have you understand, sir, that he is not to be trifled with. You are to know, sir, that he is a very hard and ruthless taskmaster— not at all the person to stand any nonsense, sir. Do you not flinch before this fierce eye, sir? do you not tremble at the roll of this terrible voice?

You do nothing of the sort, for you have discovered long since that all this stage thunder is deplorable make-believe. The eyes that try to look so fierce are really twinkling with good-humour behind the spectacles, and the mouth that is closed with such firmness gives itself away by curving up at the corners into an avuncular benevolence. You suspect that his hand is feeling in the avuncular pocket for half a crown. He is, indeed, " the whitewashed uncle " of the " Golden Age," who comes up on the horizon like a black cloud and vanishes in an auriferous shower. Even the little boys in Battersea Park found him out, for has he not told us that when he was wandering there, excogitating his speech on the Education Bill, all the youngsters pursued him with the refrain, " Please, sir, will you tell me the right time? " That

fact is a certificate. When a little boy asks you for
" the right time, please, sir," you are entitled to regard
yourself as an amiable figure. It is a mark of public
confidence and esteem. It is a tribute to you not
only as a man of property and of leisure, but as a man
of that easy, companionable exterior, that placid
frame of mind that invites the casual intrusion. You
have room and to spare in your capacious nature for
the little amenities of life. You may be thinking in
continents, but there are lollipops in your pocket. I
can imagine no more conclusive epitaph than this:
" The children loved him, and asked him for the right
time."

There is an idea that Mr. Birrell is a cynic—that,
like Walpole, he believes every man has his price and
that humanity in the lump is a very bad lot. But his
cynicism, too, is a masquerade. It is a cynicism not
of Swift, but of Thackeray, of whom he is reminiscent
both in temperament and appearance. His heart is so
tender that he pretends he hasn't got one. " Man
delights me not, nor woman neither," he seems to
say. " Look what a rogue you are, sir, and see what
a merciless, inhuman fellow I am. I am an ogre, sir,
and you are another—we're all ogres." And then,
down in his comfortable study in Elm Park Road,
you run the reality to earth and discover in him a
man full of the milk of human kindness, sensitive to
a fault, endowed with a large and spacious tolerance,
bearing the burden of office with a sympathy and an
anxious solicitude that bring to mind John Redmond's axiom that only a man of the toughest fibre
and indurated heart can fill the Irish Office under
present conditions, and that Mr. Birrell has far too
much feeling for the job.

Mr. Birrell, indeed, has not the temperament which
is adapted to politics. Parliament is no place for the

man of feeling. It demands either a rare moral elevation that is unconscious of the whips and scorns of
office, or a hard integument that is impervious to
them. The big motives move in the atmosphere of
an attorney's office, and he is the most successful who
has the fewest scruples. Your principles must hang
about you, in Falstaff's phrase, "lightly, like an old
lady's loose gown," and you must be able to tack and
turn with the veering wind. You must have, in fact,
the barristerial frame of mind, emotionally detached
from the cause it advocates, cool, agile, and sincerely
cynical—cynical, that is, in fact and not in form.
If your conscience is a little seared, so much the better,
for politics is a compromise with conscience, and a
seared conscience gives least trouble. All this means
that the lawyer and the business man are most at
home in the atmosphere of politics.

Now Mr. Birrell is not a lawyer. It is true that he
has lived in chambers, is a King's Counsel, and has
earned his bread by the law. But no man I know has
less of the lawyer temperament—less of the mental
outlook of so typical a lawyer as, let us say, Sir
Edward Carson. You cannot imagine Mr. Birrell
treating a client with the cold detachment of an
algebraical problem. He regards him less as an
intellectual exercise than as a human emotion. It is
not enough to think for him: he must feel with him,
or against him, as the case may be. His mind is never
engaged alone; his heart must be engaged too. Intellect and feeling are not in watertight compartments,
as they ought to be in every well-equipped lawyer;
they are one and indivisible.

This is a serious handicap for the politician. It
prevents him making out the best possible case for a
thing in which he does not believe. Here we have
the cause of the singular variations in Mr. Birrell's

Parliamentary manner. When he brought in the
Irish Councils Bill—a legacy from his predecessor in
the Irish Office—he brought it in in the accents of
defeat. The key was minor, the terms apologetic.
When at the close Mr. Balfour rose and said, " The
right hon. gentleman has brought in a Bill which the
House does not believe in, and which, I venture to
say, the right hon. gentleman does not believe in
himself," you felt that he spoke the truth and held the
winning hand. How different when Mr. Birrell brought
in his Universities Bill! Here he believed in his client
whole-heartedly, and his speech had an elevation and a
conviction that carried the House as one man. If I
were a client with an honest case I would rather
have him as my advocate than any man I know; but
as *advocatus diaboli* he should be given the widest
berth. He would throw up his brief and leave the
Devil in the lurch.

His candour is a fatal bar to the fulfilment of the
promise which he gave in Opposition. He has no
concealments, none of that atmosphere of impenetrable mystery which all artful leaders cultivate, and
his valour is greater than his discretion, which is a
serious defect in a leader. He does not suffer fools
gladly, or at all. If he tires of a job he says so, and
his patience with bores and with peddling opposition
is soon exhausted. " God takes his text and preaches
pat-i-ence," says Herbert, but Mr. Birrell does not
listen to the sermon. He is sometimes more than a
little impatient with his own political friends. " You
may as well tear up the Bill," he says hotly to a
committee worrying him to concede something he
won't concede, and he foreshadows a new measure
with the honest if impolitic announcement that two
of his legislative attempts have been defeated, and
that if the third fails he will take his quietus.

Augustine Birrell, K.C.

It is this blunt frankness with himself and with the world that handicaps him as a statesman, and makes him so dear to the House. He is always himself—never filling a part or playing for safety. He is what in Lancashire they would call "jannock." Dissimulation vanishes at his breezy presence, and his gay veracity and unequivocal good faith win all hearts even though they may lose votes. He clears up the spirits and restores the humanities of debate. He is like an oasis in the desert of arid talk, bubbling with fresh waters and rich with

> Verdurous glooms and winding mossy ways.

He has indeed the most individual note that is heard in Parliament—a certain mingling of mellow wit and mellow wisdom that is unique. He brings with him the atmosphere of the library, and moves, as it were, under the arch of a great sky. His dispatch-box may contain the draft of a Bill, but you suspect that *Lavengro*, a thin-paper, leather-covered, dog's-eared volume, is in his pocket. Or perhaps it is the *Religio Medici* or the *Apologia*, for his sympathies have no limits within the limits of noble literature and honest feeling. He loves to hear "the wind on the heath, brother"; but he loves, too, the cool, cloistral calm of Newman. He is true to the tradition of Free Churchmanship, which he derives both from his father, the Rev. Charles M. Birrell, a distinguished Baptist minister of Liverpool, and from his mother, a daughter of the Rev. Dr. Grey, one of the Disruption fathers; but he cares little for creeds either in religion or politics. "Liberalism is not a creed, but a frame of mind" he says somewhere, and he turns from the conflicts of the sects with unconcealed wrath. In all things he cares more for the spirit than the letter—

> For forms of faith let graceless zealots fight,
> He can't be wrong whose life is in the right.

Prophets, Priests, and Kings

He would be the last man to scrape an acquaintance with on the ground of community of creed: the first to greet you on the ground of human sympathy.

Mr. Birrell, in fact, is not primarily a politician or a lawyer, but a literary man of strong humanist sympathies. It was as a literary man that he swam into our ken. The freshness and sanity of *Obiter Dicta* made him a marked man. We came to look to him for a certain generous wine, " with beaded bubbles winking at the brim "—a wine compounded of all the great vintages of the past, but with a bouquet all its own. His wit has a distinction that is unmistakable. It is at once biting and genial. It is like the caricature of " F. C. G." in its breadth and humanity. It does not wither you. It buffets you with great thwacking blows; but without malice. He thumps you as though he loved you, with a jolly humour that makes you the sharer rather than the victim of his fun. The Birrellisms that he has scattered in his path are unlike any other blossoms of wit. You know them as you know the demure pleasantries of Holmes or the archaic solemnities of Lamb. " The House of Lords represent nobody but themselves, and they enjoy the full confidence of their constituents." Or, " a pension of five shillings a week is not much encouragement to longevity." Or of Mr. " Tim " Healey, " he loves everybody except his neighbour." His humour leaps out with a kind of lambent playfulness that makes you feel happy because it involves pain to none. " Are you going to punish people," he asked in a libel action before Mr. Justice Darling, " simply for having a lively fancy? " " There wouldn't be many to punish," interposed Mr. Justice Darling, the licensed jester of the Bench. " I don't know," said Mr. Birrell, with that heavy gravity with which he loves to envelop his fun,

Augustine Birrell, K.C.

—" I don't know that many judicial vacancies would be created, my lord." It is the summer lightning of a gracious sky—luminous but kindly.

There is in him a touch of chivalry that borders on Quixotism, a generous and uncalculating spirit that makes him the leader of forlorn hopes. Who but he would have surrendered the security of West Fife in the midst of the khaki election to go out and fight North-East Manchester? It seemed like an act of political *felo-de-se*. It meant years of exclusion from Parliament, and possibly the wreck of his whole career. This disinterestedness, so rare in politics, was revealed in his acceptance of the Irish Secretary-ship. He had just borne the brunt of the battle at the Education Office, and was entitled to a period of pause and to any office that he chose to ask for. I am revealing no secret in saying that other men, more discreet, declined the most thankless task the Ministry has to offer. Mr. Birrell took it, and for the second time in succession became the centre of all the lightnings of the political sky, charged with a Bill which was not his conception and faced with the problem of cattle-driving. It is the highest tribute to his good sense and to his mingled firmness and reasonableness that he got through that ugly diffi-culty without disaster. It might have meant coer-cion, with all its calamitous consequences. It is that dread hanging over the Irish Secretary that must make the office a nightmare. For no Ministry and no Minister is safe from it. Convictions may be strong, but external rule must rest ultimately upon coercion. You cannot get rid of the danger until you have got rid of the system. Mr. Birrell knows that. " There is only one remedy for Ireland," he says, and as he says it you recall Lincoln's axiom that " God never made one people good enough to govern another people "—not even though the governing people were so virtuous as the English and the governed so imperfect as the Irish.

It is curious to recall that there was a time when Mr. Birrell was regarded as a possible leader of the Liberal party. That possibility soon disappeared when he was seen in office. He has none of the masterful grip of the House which Mr. Asquith possesses and none of the swiftness and subtlety of Mr. Lloyd George or Mr. Balfour. He wears harness uneasily, is apt to be brusque and impatient, to blurt out what is in his mind with a " take-it-or-leave-it " air, and to give the impression that he will see you hanged before he will do this, that or the other. With all his delightful humour, in short, he has little *suaviter in modo* and little skill in the management of men and situations.

The wear and tear of office have left their mark more visibly on him than on any other member of the Ministry. It is the price which the literary temperament has to pay for entering into the sphere of affairs. A literary man in office is like a fish out of water. His temperament is too nervous and apprehensive for the rough task of politics. He may create the atmosphere of politics, but it is the "rude mechanic fellows," to use Cromwell's phrase, the men of action, the men who can handle facts rather than ideas, and who are governed by mind rather than spirit, who are necessary for statesmanship. It is a significant fact that no essentially literary man has ever made a first-rate position in practical politics, and the *succès d'estime* of Mr. Birrell and Lord Morley does not surprise by its modesty, but by its relative magnitude. It is like a defiance of a natural law. And however boldly Mr. Birrell writes his name on the Statute Book, the real place to find his authentic signature

Augustine Birrell, K.C.

will always be on the flyleaf of a merry book. " Would you return to the bar if the Government went out of office? " he was once asked. " When we are kicked out of office," he is said to have replied, " I shall retire with my modest savings to —— and really read Boswell." It is an enviable ambition. We may wish him a long evening for its fulfilment.

RUDYARD KIPLING

Mr. Rudyard Kipling is the first Englishman to be awarded the Nobel Prize for Literature. He is the first Englishman to be crowned in the Court of Literary Europe. He is chosen as our representative man of letters, while George Meredith, Thomas Hardy, and Algernon Charles Swinburne are still amongst us. The goldsmiths are passed by and the literary blacksmith is exalted. We do not know the grounds of the decision; but we do know that Mr. Kipling is not our King. " Where O'Flaherty sits is the head of the table." Where George Meredith sits is the throne of English literature.

Twenty years ago Mr. Kipling went up in the sky like a rocket—a rocket out of the magic East, scattering its many-coloured jewels in the bowl of night. Never was there such a dazzling spectacle. The firmament with all its stars was a mere background of blackness for its sudden splendour. To-day we see that the firmament with its stars is still there. What of the rocket?

It was a portent. It proclaimed the beginning of a decade of delirium, which was to culminate in a great catastrophe, twenty thousand British dead on the South African veldt and the saturnalia of Mafeking night in London. The rocket that rose in the East completed its arc in the Transvaal. Mr. Kipling, in a word, was the poet of the great reaction. " This voice sang us free," says Mr. Watson of Wordsworth. It may be said of Mr. Kipling that " this voice sang us captive." Through all the amazing crescendo of the 'nineties, with its fever of speculation, its Barney Barnatos and Whitaker Wrights, its swagger and its

Rudyard Kipling.

violence, its raids and its music-hall frenzies, the bard of the banjo marched ahead of the throng, shouting his songs of the barrack-room, telling his tales of the camp-fire and the jungle, proclaiming the worship of the great god Jingo. What did they know of England, those pitiful, mean-souled Little Englanders, prating of justice, slobbering over natives, canting about the " righteousness that exalteth a nation "? Righteousness! Had we not the mailed fist, and was not the God of battles with us?—

For the Lord our God most High
He hath made the deep as dry,
He hath smote for us a pathway to the ends of all the Earth.

Was not this fair earth ours by purchase and right of race? Had we not bought it from Jehovah by blood and sacrifice?—

We have strawed our best to the weed's unrest,
    To the shark and the sheering gull.
If blood be the price of admiralty,
    Lord God, we ha' paid in full.

And should we not do as we would with our own? The Indian in India, the Boer in the Transvaal, the Irishman in Ireland—what were they but food for our Imperial hopper? " Padgett, M.P., was a liar," a wretched emissary of Exeter Hall, prowling around the quarters of gentlemen and cackling about the grievances of Indians. What did he know of India? What were the natives that they should have grievances? And the Irish, what were they but traitors— traitors against the Chosen People of the God of blood and iron of his inflamed vision, that God

Beneath Whose awful Hand we hold
Dominion over palm and pine.

And Labour? What was the insurgence of Labour but the insolent murmurings of the Walking Delegate? For the Chosen People were few. They did not include the miserable rabble who toiled and who only became interesting to the god-like mind when they took the shilling and entered " the lordliest life on earth." The Chosen People, in a word, had Mr. Cecil Rhodes at one end of the scale and the " raw recruity " at the other. And the Empire was an armed camp, governing by drum-head court-martial, its deity a strange heathen god of violence and vengeance.

The war came, and Mr. Kipling turned contemptuously to the " little street-bred people," and commanded them to " Pay, pay, pay." It was their paltry share in the glorious enterprise of conquest and Empire. And when peace followed, and down at Rottingdean Lady Burne-Jones, the aunt of the poet, pointed the moral by hanging out the legend from Naboth's vineyard, " Hast thou killed, and also taken possession," and the people, with the dregs of the war-fever in them, came about and demonstrated violently, there emerged from the house a small dark man in spectacles with words of soothing and peace. It was Mr. Rudyard Kipling face to face with the passions that he had done so much to kindle.

It is all like a bad dream, the tale of those years— a bad dream, with the strum of the banjo sounding through it a sort of mirthless, demoniac laugh— the laugh heard at its most terrible in the " Gentlemen Rankers ":

> We're poor little lambs who've lost our way,
> Baa! Baa! Baa!
> We're little black sheep who've gone astray,
> Baa-aa-a!
> Gentlemen rankers out on the spree,
> Damned from here to Eternity,
> God ha' mercy on such as we,
> Baa! Yah! Bah!

What was the secret of the hypnotism he exercised? It was partly the magic of an appeal perfectly attuned

to the temper of the time. Israel had waxed fat,
and had turned to the worship of the golden calf.
It was the emergence of the baser passions, the lust
of power without a purpose, of wealth without
industry. The gold of South Africa had set up a
fever in the blood. It was as though the nation had
left the temples of its ancient worship to fall down
before the Baal of the Stock Exchange. And in its
haste to grow rich it turned passionately upon the
stupid little pastoral people that stood insolently in
its path, and

> Drunk with sight of power, we loosed
> Wild tongues that had not Thee in awe.

In that momentary flash of the " Recessional," Mr.
Kipling pierced to the heart of the disease, and
delivered his own merciless sentence.

And partly it was due to the astonishing intensity
of his vision. Coleridge said of Kean that to see him
act was like reading Shakespeare by flashes of lightning. Mr. Kipling sees life by flashes of lightning,
and sets it down in phrases that strike like lightning.
It is a world filled with sudden and sinister shapes—
not men, but the baleful caricatures of men; not
women, but Mænad sisters, with wild and bloodshot
eyes and fearful dishevelled locks; with boys that
drink and smoke and swear like dragoons; animals
that talk and machinery that reasons like a Yellow
journalist. It is all a disordered, frenzied motion,
soulless and cruel—a world seen in a nightmare, with
all the intensity and literalness of a nightmare and all
its essential untruth. It is

> Fantastic mockery, such as lurks
> In some wild poet when he works
> Without a conscience or an aim.

There is the essential fact. Mr. Kipling is a pre-
cocious boy with a camera. He has the gift of vision,

but not the gift of thought. He sees the detail with
astonishing truth, but he cannot co-ordinate the parts.
He gives the impression of encyclopædic knowledge,
for everything he sees is photographed on his retina
and everything he hears is written down in his brain.
There is nothing he does not seem to know, from the
habits of Akela the wolf in the jungle or the seal in
the Behring Straits to the building of a bridge and
the mechanism of a liner; from the ways of Fuzzy-
Wuzzy in the desert to the ways of the harlot in Whitechapel. All lands are an open book to him; the Seven
Seas as familiar as the Serpentine. He uses the dialect of M'Andrew or Mulvaney as readily as the jargon
of the East, and is as much at home in the Ratcliff
highway as on the road to Mandalay. He is like the
Encyclopædia Britannica, fused with imagination at
white heat. And as the *Encyclopædia* is to literature
so is he to life. He knows everything except human
nature. He knows all about life; but he does not
know life, because he does not know the heart of man.

And to the intense vision of the boy he joins the
passions of the boy. I am told by one who was with
him when he came from India to England to school
that he remembers him chiefly by the pranks he used
to play at the expense of a mild Hindoo, kneeling on
board at his devotions. It was the instinctive dislike
of the boy of the thing outside the range of his experience. Mr. Kipling has never outgrown that outlook.
It is the outlook of the unschooled mind, vivid and
virile, confident but crude, subject to fierce antipathies
and lacking that faculty of sympathy that is the
highest attribute of humanity. He dislikes everything he does not understand, everything which does
not conform to that material standard which sub-
stitutes Mayfair for Sinai and speaks its prophecies
through the mouth of the machine-gun.

Rudyard Kipling

A further cause of the unrivalled sway he exercised over the mind of the public was his fervid patriotism. He sang of England with a defiance that sounded a challenge to the world and sent the blood singing through the veins. It was said of General Kleber that merely to look at him made men feel brave. To read Kipling made men feel martial and aggressive. We went out like the children of Hamelin town to the sudden rattle of a drum. But the England of his hot passion was not the little England that we know, the England of Shakespeare and Milton, the England of a high and chivalrous past, that freed the slave, stretched out its hand to the oppressed and taught the world the meaning of liberty. "What do they know of England who only England know," he cried scornfully as he marched on singing his fierce songs of an England that bestrode the world like a Colossus, treading the little peoples of the earth into the dust beneath its iron heel. It was an appeal to the patriotism not of a people proud of its splendid services to humanity, proud of having been ever "foremost in the files of time," but of a people filled only with the pride of material conquest. It was not the soul of England that he loved and sang, but the might of England, the thunder of its battleships and the tread of its armies across the plains.

Mr. Kipling, in short, was not the prophet of a philosophy or of an ideal, but of a mood. The world of his imagination is a world without a meaning or a purpose, for it is divorced from all moral judgments and values. His gospel of violence leads nowhere except to more violence. The lesser breeds are trodden in the dust, but the Chosen People are touched to no fine issues by their victory. They have enslaved their foes without ennobling themselves. Justice and liberty, mercy and tolerance—all that gives humanity vision and nobleness is sacrificed to an idol whose nostrils breathe fire and smoke and whose eyes blaze with vengeance.

From all this it is doubtful if he is of the Immortals. With all his wonderful gifts, his swift phrase, his imaginative power, his intellectual energy, he is temporary as the moment's passion, transient as the moment's hate. For his vision is of the lightning, fantastically real; not of the sun, sovereign and serene. Hence his astonishing influence while the mood to which he appealed was in the ascendant, and his subsidence when that mood had passed. He knows much of hate, but he knows little of love, and in literature, as in the angel's recording book, it is Ben Adhem's name, the name of him who loved his fellow-men, that leads all the rest. He knows much of the street, but nothing of the stars. "And indeed," wrote Tennyson, "what matters it what a man knows or does if he keep not a reverential looking upward? He is only the subtlest beast of the field." A reverential looking upward! Where in all that literature of passion and horror, of the humour of the death's head, and the terrible gaiety of despair, of a world "without a conscience or an aim," do we find the recognition that man has a soul as well as faculties, a moral law as well as the law of the jungle? Once only, and in all the little ironies of literature, there is none more significant than that Mr. Kipling will probably be best remembered by that flash of a nobler inspiration when he turned and rent himself and the gospel that he preached:

> For heathen heart that puts his trust
>   In reeking tube and iron shard—
> All valiant dust that builds on dust
>   And, guarding, calls not Thee to guard—
> For frantic boast and foolish word,
> Thy mercy on Thy People, Lord.

Prophets, Priests and Kings

GILBERT K. CHESTERTON

WALKING down Fleet Street some day you may meet a form whose vastness blots out the heavens. Great waves of hair surge from under the soft, wide-brimmed hat. A cloak that might be a legacy from Porthos floats about his colossal frame. He pauses in the midst of the pavement to read the book in his hand, and a cascade of laughter descending from the head notes to the middle voice gushes out on the listening air. He looks up, adjusts his pince-nez, observes that he is not in a cab, remembers that he ought to be in a cab, turns and hails a cab. The vehicle sinks down under the unusual burden and rolls heavily away. It carries Gilbert Keith Chesterton.

Mr. Chesterton is the most conspicuous figure in the landscape of literary London. He is like a visitor out of some fairy tale, a legend in the flesh, a survival of the childhood of the world. Most of us are the creatures of our time, thinking its thoughts, wearing its clothes, rejoicing in its chains. If we try to escape from the temporal tyranny, it is through the gate of revolt that we go. Some take to asceticism or to some fantastic foppery of the moment. Some invent Utopias, lunch on nuts and proteid at Eustace Miles', and flaunt red ties defiantly in the face of men and angels. The world is bond, but they are free. But in all this they are still the children of our time, fleeting and self-conscious. Mr. Chesterton's extravagances have none of this quality. He is not a rebel. He is a wayfarer from the ages, stopping at the inn of life, warming himself at the fire and making the rafters ring with his jolly laughter.

Time and place are accidents: he is elemental and primitive. He is not of our time, but of all times. One imagines him drinking deep draughts from the horn of Skrymir, or exchanging jests with Falstaff at the Boar's Head in Eastcheap, or joining in the intellectual revels at the Mermaid Tavern, or meeting Johnson foot to foot and dealing blow for mighty blow. With Rabelais he rioted, and Don Quixote and Sancho were his " vera brithers." One seems to see him coming down from the twilight of fable, through the centuries, calling wherever there is good company, and welcome wherever he calls, for he brings no cult of the time or pedantry of the schools with him.

He has the freshness and directness of the child's vision. In a very real sense indeed he has never left the golden age—never come out into the light of common day, where the tone is grey and things have lost their imagery. He lives in a world of romance, peopled with giants and gay with the light laughter of fairies. The visible universe is full of magic and mystery. The trees are giants waving their arms in the air. The great globe is a vast caravanserai carrying us all on a magnificent adventure through space. He moves in an atmosphere of enchantment, and may stumble upon a romance at the next street corner. Beauty in distress may call to him from some hollow secrecy; some tyrannous giant may straddle like Apollyon across the path as he turns into Carmelite Street. It is well that he has his swordstick with him, for one never knows what may turn up in this incredible world. Memory goeth not back to a time when a sword was not his constant companion. It used to be a wooden sword, with which went a wooden

helmet glowing with the pigments of Apollo. Those
were the days when the horn of Roland echoed again
through Roncesvalles, and Lancelot pricked forth to
the joust, and

> Ever the scaly shape of monstrous sin
> At last lay vanquished, fold on writhing fold.

Ah, *le bon temps où j'étais — jeune*. But he still
carries with him the glamour of the morning; his
cheek still blanches at Charlemagne's "What a marching life is mine!" I burst in on him one afternoon
and found him engaged in a furious attack on a row
of fat books, around which his sword flashed like the
sword of Sergeant Troy around the figure of Bath-
sheba Everdene. His eye blazed, his cheek paled,
and beads of perspiration—no uncommon thing—
stood out on his brow. It was a terrific combat, and
it was fortunate that the foe were not, as in the leading
case of Don Quixote, disguised in wine-skins, for that
would have involved lamentable bloodshed. As it
was, the books wore an aspect of insolent calm. One
could almost see the contemptuous curl upon the lip,
the haughty assurance of victory. I own it was
hard to bear.

Adventure is an affair of the soul, not of circumstance. Thoreau, by his pond at Walden, or paddling
up the Concord, had more adventures than Stanley
had on the Congo, more adventures than Stanley
could have. That was why he refused to come to
Europe. He knew he could see as many wonders
from his own backyard as he could though he
sought for them in the islands of the farthest seas.
"Why, who makes much of miracles?" says
Whitman.

> As to me, I know of nothing else but miracles . . .
> To me every hour of the light and dark is a miracle.

Prophets, Priests, and Kings

Miracles and adventures are the stuff of Mr. Chesterton's everyday life. He goes out on to the Sussex downs with his coloured chalks—in the cavernous mysteries of his pockets there is always a box of pastels, though " the mark of the mint," in his own phrase, may be unaccountably absent—and discovers he has no white chalk with which to complete his picture. His foot stumbles against a mound, and lo! he is standing on a mountain of chalk, and he shouts with joy at the miracle, for the world has never lost its freshness and wonder to him. It is as though he discovers it anew each day, and stands exultant at the revelation.

It is a splendid pageant that passes unceasingly before him—

> New and yet old
> As the foundations of the heavens and earth.

Familiarity has not robbed it of its magic. He sees it as the child sees its first rainbow or the lightning flashing from the thunder-cloud. Most of us, before we reach maturity, find life stale and unprofitable—" a twice-told tale vexing the dull ears of a drowsy man." We are like the *blasé* policeman I met when I was waiting for a 'bus at Finchley one Bank Holiday. " A lot of people abroad to-day? " I said interrogatively. " Yes," he said, " thahsands." " Where do most of them go this way? " " Oh, to Barnet. Though what they see in Barnet I can't make out. I never see nothin' in Barnet." " Perhaps they like to see the green fields and hear the birds," I said. " Well, perhaps," he replied, in the tone of one who tolerated follies which he was too enlightened to share. " There'll be more at the Exhibition, I suppose? " I said, hoping to turn his mind to the contemplation of a more cheerful subject. " The Exhibition! Well,

Gilbert K. Chesterton

I was down there on duty the day it was opened, and I never see such a poor show. Oh yes, the gardens; they're all right, but you can see gardens anywhere." Despairingly I mentioned Hampstead as a merry place on Bank Holiday. " Well, I never see nothin' in 'Ampstead myself. I dunno what the people go for. And there's the Garden City there, and crowds and crowds a-going to look at it. Well, what is there in it? That's what I asts. What-is-there-in-it? I never see nothin' in it."

The world of culture shares the policeman's physical ennui in a spiritual sense. It sees " nothing in it." We succeed in deadening the fresh intensity of the impression, and burying the miracle under the dust of the common day—veiling it under names and formulas. " This green, flowery, rock-built earth, the trees, the mountains, rivers, many-sounding seas; —that great deep sea of azure that swims overhead; the winds sweeping through it; the black cloud fashioning itself together, now pouring out fire, now hail and rain; what *is* it? Ay, what? At bottom, we do not yet know; we can never know at all. It is not by our superior insight that we escape the difficulty; it is by our superior levity, our inattention, our *want* of insight. It is by *not* thinking that we cease to wonder at it. . . . This world, after all our science and sciences, is still a miracle; wonderful, inscrutable, *magical* and more, to whomsoever will *think* of it." It is this elemental faculty of wonder, of which Carlyle speaks, that distinguishes Mr. Chesterton from his contemporaries, and gives him kinship at once with the seers and the children. He is anathema to the erudite and the exact; but he sees life in the large, with the eyes of the first man on the day of creation. As he says, in inscribing a book of Caldecott's pictures to a little friend of mine—

335

Prophets, Priests, and Kings

This is the sort of book we like
  (For you and I are very small),
With pictures stuck in anyhow,
  And hardly any words at all.

.   .   .   .

You will not understand a word
  Of all the words, including mine;
Never you trouble; you can see,
  And all directness is divine—

Stand up and keep your childishness:
  Read all the pedants' screeds and strictures;
But don't believe in anything
  That can't be told in coloured pictures.

Life to him is a book of coloured pictures that he
sees without external comment or exegesis. He sees
it, as it were, at first hand, and shouts out his vision
at the top of his voice. Hence the audacity that is
so trying to the formalist who is governed by custom
and authority. Hence the rain of paradoxes that
he showers down. It is often suggested that these
paradoxes are a conscious trick to attract attention—
that Mr. Chesterton stands on his head, as it were,
to gather a crowd. I can conceive him standing on
his head in Fleet Street in sheer joy at the sight of
St. Paul's, but not in vanity, or with a view to a
collection. The truth is that his paradox is his own
comment on the coloured picture.

There are some men who hoard life as a miser
hoards his gold—map it out with frugal care and vast
prescience, spend to-day in taking thought for to-
morrow. Mr. Chesterton spends life like a prodigal.
Economy has no place in his spacious vocabulary.
" Economy," he might say, with Anthony Hope's
Mr. Carter, " is going without something you do want
in case you should some day want something which
you probably won't want." Mr. Chesterton lives the
unconsidered, untrammelled life. He simply rambles
along without a thought of where he is going. If he

Gilbert K. Chesterton

likes the look of a road he turns down it, careless of
where it may lead to. " He is announced to lecture
at Bradford to-night," said a speaker, explaining his
absence from a dinner. " Probably he will turn up
at Edinburgh." He will wear no harness, learn no
lessons, observe no rules. He is himself, Chesterton
—not consciously or rebelliously, but unconsciously,
like a natural element. St. Paul's School never had
a more brilliant nor a less sedulous scholar. He did
not win prizes, but he read more books, drew more
pictures, wrote more poetry than any boy that ever
played at going to school. His house was littered
with books, filled with verses and grotesque drawings.
All attempts to break him into routine failed. He
tried the Slade School, and once even sat on a stool
in an office. Think of it! G. K. C. in front of a
ledger, adding up figures with romantic results—
figures that turned into knights in armour, broke into
song, and, added together, produced paradoxes unknown to arithmetic! He saw the absurdity of it all.
" A man must follow his vocation," he said with
Falstaff, and his vocation is to have none.

And so he rambles along, engaged in an endless
disputation, punctuated with gusts of Rabelaisian
laughter, and leaving behind a litter of fragments.
You may track him by the blotting-pads he decorates
with his riotous fancies, and may come up with him
in the midst of a group of children, for whom he is
drawing hilarious pictures, or to whom he is revealing
the wonders of his toy theatre, the chief child of his
fancy and invention, or whom he is instructing in the
darkly mysterious game of " Guyping," which will
fill the day with laughter. " Well," said the aunt to
the little boy who had been to tea with Mr. Chesterton,
—" well, Frank, I suppose you have had a very in-
structive afternoon?" " I don't know what that

means," said Frank, "but, oh!" with enthusiasm,
"you should see Mr. Chesterton catch buns with his
mouth." If you cannot find him, and Fleet Street
looks lonely and forsaken, then be sure he has been
spirited away to some solitary place by his wife, the
keeper of his business conscience, to finish a book
for which some publisher is angrily clamouring. For
"No clamour, no book," is his maxim.

Mr. Chesterton's natural foil in these days is Mr.
Bernard Shaw. Mr. Shaw is the type of revolt. The
flesh we eat, the wine we drink, the clothes we wear,
the laws we obey, the religion we affect—all are an
abomination to him. He would raze the whole fabric
to the ground, and build it anew upon an ordered and
symmetrical plan. Mr. Chesterton has none of this
impatience with the external garment of society. He
enjoys disorder and loves the haphazard. With
Rossetti he might say, "What is it to me whether the
earth goes round the sun or the sun round the earth?"
It is not the human intellect that interests him,
but the human heart and the great comedy of life.
He opposes ancient sympathies to new antipathies,
hates modernism and science in all their aspects,
and tends more and more to find refuge in miracles
and mediævalism. He is capable of believing anything that the reason repudiates, and can stoop on
occasion to rather puerile juggling with phrases in
order to carry his point. Thus, when someone says,
"You cannot put the clock back," meaning that you
cannot put events back, he answers with triumphant
futility, "The reply is simply this: you can put the
clock back." Johnson, with all his love of verbal
victory, never got so low as this.

No man, indeed, was ever more careless of his
reputation. He is indifferent whether from his
abundant mine he shovels out diamonds or dirt.

Gilbert K. Chesterton

You may take it or leave it, as you like. He cares
not, and bears no malice. It is all a blithe improvisation, done in sheer ebullience of spirit and having no
relation to conscious literature. He is like a child
shouting with glee at the sight of the flowers and the
sunshine, and chalking on every vacant hoarding he
passes with a jolly rapture of invention and no
thought beyond.

But there is one thing, and one only, about which
he is serious, and that is his own seriousness. You
may laugh with him and at him and about him.
When, at a certain dinner, one of the speakers said
that his chivalry was so splendid that he had been
known to rise in a tramcar and " offer his seat to three
ladies," it was his laugh that sounded high above all
the rest. But if you would wound him, do not laugh
at his specific gravity: doubt his spiritual gravity.
Doubt his passion for justice and liberty and patriotism—most of all, his patriotism. For he is, above all,
the lover of Little England, and the foe of the
Imperialist, whose love of country is " not what a
mystic means by the love of God, but what a child
might mean by the love of jam." " My country,
right or wrong! " he cries. " Why, it is a thing no
patriot could say. It is like saying, ' My mother,
drunk or sober.' No doubt, if a decent man's mother
took to drink, he would share her troubles to the last;
but to talk as if he would be in a state of gay indifference as to whether his mother took to drink or
not is certainly not the language of men who know
the great mystery. . . . We fall back upon gross and
frivolous things for our patriotism. . . . Our school-
boys are left to live and die in the infantile type of
patriotism which they learnt from a box of tin
soldiers. . . . We have made our public schools the
strongest wall against a whisper of the honour of

England. . . . What have we done and where have we wandered, we that have produced sages who could have spoken with Socrates, and poets who could walk with Dante, that we should talk as if we had never done anything more intelligent than found colonies and kick niggers? We are the children of light, and it is we that sit in darkness. If we are judged, it will not be for the merely intellectual transgression of failing to appreciate other nations, but for the supreme spiritual transgression of failing to appreciate ourselves."

But sincere though he is, he loves the argument for its own sake. He is indifferent to the text. You may tap any subject you like: he will find it a theme on which to hang all the mystery of time and eternity. For the ordinary material cares of life he has no taste, almost no consciousness. He never knows the time of a train, has only a hazy notion of where he will dine, and the doings of to-morrow are as profound a mystery as the contents of his pocket. He dwells outside these things in the realm of ideas. Johnson said that when he and Savage walked one night round St. James' Square for want of a lodging, they were not at all depressed by their situation, but, in high spirits and brimful of patriotism, traversed the square for several hours, inveighed against the ministry, and " resolved that they would *stand by their country*." That is Mr. Chesterton's way. But he would not walk round St. James' Square. He would, in Johnson's circumstances, ride round and round in a cab—even if he had to borrow the fare off the cabman. He is free from the tyranny of things. Though he lived in a tub he would be rich beyond the dreams of avarice, for he would still have the universe for his intellectual inheritance.

I sometimes think that one moonlight night, when

G·K·Chesterton.

he is tired of Fleet Street, he will scale the walls of the
Tower and clothe himself in a suit of giant mail, with
shield and sword to match. He will come forth with
vizor up and mount the battle-steed that champs its
bit outside. And the clatter of his hoofs will ring
through the quiet of the city night as he thunders
through St. Paul's Churchyard and down Ludgate
Hill and out on to the Great North Road. And then
once more will be heard the cry of " St. George for
Merry England! " and there will be the clash of swords
in the greenwood and brave deeds done on the King's
highway.

H. C.

THE
TEMPLE PRESS
LETCHWORTH
ENGLAND

THE WAYFARERS' LIBRARY

"The Wayfarers' Library" embraces all that is healthy, clean and good in the lighter field of modern literature, ranging from works of pure romance to the best collective essays of the day. Fcap. 8vo. Cloth, with Bookmark. Frontispiece in colours. 1/- net.

VOLUMES NOW READY

The Story of the Regiments

L. COPE CORNFORD
and F. W. WALKER
The Black Watch

F. W. WALKER
The Seaforth Highlanders

Romance and Adventure

A. E. W. MASON
Running Water

H. G. WELLS
The Wheels of Chance
The Wonderful Visit

H. de VERE STACPOOLE
The Blue Lagoon
The Pools of Silence

ARNOLD BENNETT
The Grand Babylon Hotel
The City of Pleasure

PERCEVAL GIBBON
The Adventures of Miss Gregory

JOSEPH CONRAD
'Twixt Land and Sea

GILBERT SHELDON
Bubble Fortune

MAURICE HEWLETT
The Fool Errant

GUY BOOTHBY
A Lost Endeavour

ROBERT LOUIS STEVENSON
St. Ives

HAROLD BINDLOSS
The Mistress of Bonaventure

S. R. CROCKETT
The Lilac Sunbonnet
The Raiders

C. E. LAWRENCE
Pilgrimage

MARMADUKE PICKTHALL
The Valley of the Kings

AGNES & EGERTON CASTLE
The Pride of Jennico

H. B. MARRIOTT WATSON
Once upon a Time
The Privateers

Social and Domestic Fiction

Mrs. SIDGWICK
The Professor's Legacy

THOMAS HARDY
Under the Greenwood Tree

H. A. VACHELL
The Pinch of Prosperity

BESANT & RICE
Chaplain of the Fleet

ISRAEL ZANGWILL
Children of the Ghetto
Grandchildren of the Ghetto

RICHARD WHITEING
No. 5 John Street

HUGH WALPOLE
The Wooden Horse

H. B. MARRIOTT WATSON
Rosalind in Arden

PETT RIDGE
The Wickhamses

Mrs. BELLOC LOWNDES
The Heart of Penelope

Author of Elizabeth and her German Garden
Princess Priscilla's Fortnight

Mrs. de la PASTURE
The Lonely Lady of Grosvenor Sq.

FLORENCE CONVERSE
The Children of Light

EDWARD C. BOOTH
The Cliff End

THE WAYFARERS' LIBRARY

VOLUMES NOW READY—*continued*

Social and Domestic Fiction (*cont.*)

CHARLES DICKENS
A Christmas Carol
The Cricket on the Hearth

HORACE A. VACHELL
The Face of Clay
Her Son

J. J. BELL
Dancing Days

GEORGE GISSING
Demos

JOHN OLIVER HOBBES
The Serious Wooing

Historical Fiction

STANLEY WEYMAN
Shrewsbury
The Abbess of Vlaye
The Castle Inn
Chippinge

MARY BRADFORD WHITING
The Plough of Shame

HENRYK SIENKIEWICZ
Quo Vadis?

DAVID M. BEDDOE
The Lost Mameluke

ALPHONSE DAUDET
Kings in Exile

SIR GILBERT PARKER
A Ladder of Swords

L. COPE CORNFORD
The Master Beggars of Belgium

BERNARD CAPES
A Jay of Italy

S. R. CROCKETT
The Black Douglas

STANDISH O'GRADY
In the Wake of King James

Humour

Sir A. T. QUILLER-COUCH
Troy Town
The Delectable Duchy

CHARLES LAMB
Essays of Elia

CHARLES LEE
The Widow Woman

MARK TWAIN
Innocents Abroad and
Jumping Frog

FRANK R. STOCKTON
Rudder Grange

BARRY PAIN
De Omnibus

F. ANSTEY
Baboo Jabberjee

Belles Lettres, History, etc.

LETTERS FROM DOROTHY OSBORNE TO SIR WM. TEMPLE

G. K. CHESTERTON
The Defendant

Rt. Hon. G. W. E. RUSSELL
Selected Essays

CLEMENT SHORTER
The Brontës and their Circle

HILAIRE BELLOC
The Historic Thames

AUSTIN DOBSON
Eighteenth Century Studies

A. G. GARDINER
Prophets, Priests, and Kings
The War Lords

HOLBROOK JACKSON
Southward Ho! and
Other Essays

J. MILNE
The Epistles of Atkins

HERBERT PAUL
Queen Anne

J. A. SPENDER
The Comments of Bagshot

Miss BETHAM-EDWARDS
Under the German Ban
in Alsace and Lorraine

W. L. COURTNEY
Rosemary's Letter Book

Travel and the Open Air, etc.

RICHARD JEFFERIES
The Open Air

W. CLARK RUSSELL
Round the Galley Fire

GEORGE GOODCHILD
The Lore of the Wanderer
(An Open-Air Anthology)

J. M. DENT & SONS LTD., BEDFORD ST., W.C.